SOUL ON THE COUCH

Spirituality, Religion, and Morality in
Contemporary Psychoanalysis

RELATIONAL PERSPECTIVES BOOK SERIES

STEPHEN A. MITCHELL AND LEWIS ARON
Series Editors

SOUL ON THE COUCH

Spirituality, Religion, and Morality in Contemporary Psychoanalysis

edited by

CHARLES SPEZZANO

GERALD J. GARGIULO

THE ANALYTIC PRESS

1997   Hillsdale, NJ   London

Published by
The Analytic Press, Inc.
 Editorial Offices:
 101 West Street
 Hillsdale, NJ 07642

Library of Congress Cataloging-in-Publication Data

Soul on the couch : spirituality, religion, and morality in
 contemporary psychoanalysis / edited by Charles
 Spezzano, Gerald J. Gargiulo.
 p. cm. — (Relational perspective book series ; v. 7)
 Includes bibliographical references and index.
 ISBN 0-88163-181-7
 1. Psychoanalysis and religion. I. Spezzano, Charles.
 II. Gargiulo, Gerald J. III. Series.
BF 175.4.R44S68   1997
291.1'75—dc21   97-16523
                                                       CIP

Printed in the United States of America
10 9 8 7 6 5 4 3 2 1

Contents

To my family
for infusing my life with spirit
C.S.

For
Julia
Paul and Connie
Robert
Nicole and Eric
for the gift of life they are
G.J.G.

Contributors

Joseph Bobrow, Ph.D. is an advanced candidate at the Psychoanalytic Institute of Northern California and an independent Zen master at the Harbor Sangha, San Francisco.

Kevin Fauteux, Ph.D. is director of a clinic in San Francisco and author of two books and numerous articles on psychology.

Stephen Friedlander, Ph.D. is director of studies, Institute for Psychoanalytic Education and Training, New York, and past president, International Federation for Psychoanalytic Education.

Gerald J. Gargiulo, M.A. (ed.) is president, International Federation for Psychoanalytic Education; past president, Training Institute, National Psychological Association for Psychoanalysis, and in private practice in Greenwich, CT and East Hampton, NY.

Joel Greifinger, M.A. teaches in the Social Studies Department at Harvard University and is in private practice in Cambridge, MA.

James W. Jones, Ph.D. is a faculty member in the Department of Religion at Rutgers University and author of *Contemporary Psychoanalysis and Religion* and *Religion and Psychology in Transition*.

Steven H. Knoblauch, Ph.D. is a supervisor at Adelphi University's Derner Institute of Advanced Psychological Studies and at Yeshiva University's Ferkauf Graduate School.

Daniel J. Rothenberg, Ph.D. is director and associate professor at The Psychological Counseling and Adult Development Center, Graduate School and University Center, City University of New York, and associate editor of *Contemporary Psychoanalysis*.

Jeffrey P. Rubin, Ph.D. is on the faculties of the Postgraduate Center for Mental Health and the Object Relations Institute in New York City and author of *Psychotherapy and Buddhism* and the forthcoming *Psychoanalysis on the Couch*.

Randall Lehmann Sorenson, Ph.D. is an associate professor at Rosemead School of Psychology and Training and a supervising analyst at the Institute of Contemporary Psychoanalysis in Los Angeles.

Charles Spezzano, Ph.D. (ed.) is a training and supervising analyst at the Psychoanalytic Institute of Northern California and author of *Affect in Psychoanalysis* (TAP, 1993).

Foreword

JAMES W. JONES

I've heard it said that writing a foreword to a collection of essays is a little like borrowing someone's watch so you can tell him the time. The chapters in this book stand on their own and do not require additional comment to make their content or value apparent to readers. One useful and nonredundant task, however, is to describe the contexts in which this book was created and in which it is likely to be read.

First, there is the cultural context of the contemporary dialogue of psychoanalysis and spirituality. Here we find ambiguity. On one hand, we have experienced an obvious secularization of our culture at the institutional level. On the other hand, there has been perhaps a slight increase in the number of people who report that they believe in God or some spiritual force, who pray or engage in some spiritual practice, who are willing to report a religious or mystical experience. The renewed interest on the part of clinicians in religious and spiritual issues does not take place in a cultural vacuum but is part of a larger cultural movement.

One context, then, in which this discussion of morality, spirituality, and psychoanalysis takes place is the ambiguous relationship between religion and modern American culture; certain public and institutional structures have been weakening for decades. Beneath this surface, however, there is a continuing, perhaps increasing, kaleidoscope of spiritual vitality of which the growing interest in religion on the part of psychotherapists and psychoanalysts is both an example and a carrier.

To help explain this spiritual vitality, I would like to map onto these sociological data about growing spread of religious interest and experimentation, data about the relationship among religion, well-being, and emotional and physical health. Such psychological research into the function of religion in health and sickness is the second context to which I want to direct our attention. The mental and physical benefits of having a sense of meaning and purpose in one's life have been widely documented. As a purveyor of meaning, purpose, and coherence, religion has a direct and documentably positive effect on mental and physical health even when one controls for such factors as health status, economic class, and social support.

Such metaphysical constructs as hope and meaning and purpose, whether religious or not, turn out, therefore, to be critical for mental and physical health and for psychological resilience and coping. It is not surprising, then, that even when confidence in institutional religion wanes, the drive for meaning and purpose and value does not disappear. And psychoanalysts and psychotherapists who become interested in religious issues are not just living out some idiosyncratic fantasy or even just following a cultural fad but are, rather, recovering a major, perhaps necessary, source of human wholeness.

Third, the twentieth century has witnessed a transformation in our epistemological models that has profound implications both for psychoanalysis and for the relationship between religion and science. A careful analysis of the actual conduct of science reveals that our popular theories about the rationality of science are misleading. Instead of the usual empiricist model of reason as a set of universal rules, scientific rationality (and by extension reason in general) involves what Richard Bernstein (1983) calls "imagination, interpretation, the weighing of alternatives, and application of criteria that are essentially open" (p. 56). A more contemporary and nuanced view of science challenges any strict dichotomy between natural science and all other fields, including psychoanalysis and religion.

The twentieth century's recognition of the contextual, mediated, and metaphoric nature of human understanding sensitizes us to the limits inherent in any discipline. Empirical science is only one lens through which reality is to be viewed. Science does not claim that science is the only way to see the world. Indispensably useful in some contexts, empiricism is impotent in others.

If we want to understand why a billiard ball goes into the corner pocket, there's nothing like Newtonian mechanics. If we want to understand why a child touches a hot stove only once, there's nothing like conditioning theories. But if we want to address the questions of meaning and value and purpose, so essential for human well-being, experimental method will be of little use. If we want to know why Einstein was attracted to mathematical physics, a good psychobiographical account will surely help us. If we want to know if the theory of general relativity is complete, an account of Einstein's childhood will be pretty irrelevant. Likewise, if we want to know why Martin Luther's or Krishnamurti's religious experiences took the forms they did, psychohistorical accounts like those provided by Erikson or Kakar are very useful. But if we want to know if there is a purpose in life or if forgiveness triumphs over death, the psychoanalysis of religious experience is no substitute for religious experience.

To argue, as Freud did, that religion is inherently irrational is to presuppose a unitary definition of rationality which cannot be supported even from within the empirical sciences. The rationality needed to solve a problem in mechanics is rather different from that employed in constructing multidimensional geometries, and is different still from the skills needed to interpret the results of an experiment in high energy physics. As Stephen Toulmin, one of the most vigorous philosophers of science in the twentieth century, wrote in 1964:

> It is only if we suppose that religious arguments pretend to . . . [compete] with science on its own ground that we can be justified in attempting to apply to them the logical criteria appropriate for scientific explanations; and only if we do this that we have any grounds for concluding that all utterances about the nature of God are nonsensical or that religion is an illusion. Provided that we remember that religion has other functions than that of competing with science and ethics on their own grounds, we shall understand that to reject all religious arguments for this reason is to make a serious logical blunder [p. 212].

Another context in which a contemporary analyst's interest in religion takes place is, then, in a transformed understanding of the place and nature of empirical science. Obviously there are many from both sides who have a stake in the conflict between religion and science. Freud focused only on the most infantile aspects of religion which he then easily rejected in the name of science and progress. But both religion and rationality are more complex and multidimensional than Freud and other early analysts allowed for.

The discussion between religion and psychoanalysis involves, therefore, multiple contexts: The cultural context of spiritual discovery and vitality in the midst of institutional decay; the empirical demonstration of the importance of religious constructs like meaning and purpose and value for mental and physical well-being in the midst of a culture whose official ideology denies their import; and a transformation in our understanding of science that brings with it an increased sensitivity to the limits of any single frame of reference. In these contexts, an interest on the part of psychoanalysts, both the writers of these essays and their readers, in religious and spiritual issues makes sense and contains the possibility of a further contribution to the welfare of our patients and a deepening and broadening of the psychoanalytic understanding of human nature and its potentials and possibilities.

REFERENCES

Bernstein, R. (1983), *Beyond Objectivism and Relativism*. Philadelphia: University of Pennsylvania Press.
Toulmin, S. (1964), *The Place of Reason in Ethics*. Cambridge: Cambridge University Press.

Introduction

GERALD J. GARGIULO

CHARLES SPEZZANO

This is a book about mystery, awe, and meaning. What God and the unconscious have in common is their paradoxical combining of meaning and unknowability. The unconscious is that which creates meaning in the unfolding event we call a human life. God is that which gives meaning to the unfolding event we call human history.

As prime meaning-givers, God and the unconscious have been natural competitors for first place in our thinking and talking about ourselves. Ever since Freud put religion on the couch in "The Future of an Illusion," there has been an uneasy peace, with occasional skirmishes, between these two great disciplines of subjectivity. Freud, in his bold manner, found projection, fear, and denial to be the wellspring of religion's domination over man. So convinced was he of having uncovered its power that he was unable to look beyond religion's possible abuses to its potential role in human subjectivity.

Freud gave analysts a way to ignore the conflict with God by treating the human quest for meaning as neurotic and by emphasizing (although not exclusively) the unconscious as container of knowable repressed ideas. As psychoanalysis evolved, one or another aspect of unconscious mental content or activity was treated as that which makes me who I am. From instincts and fantasies to ego defenses and object-relational representations, analysts have, by and large, understood our ultimate meanings as, at least in principle, knowable enough to obviate any interest in an extrapersonal source of meaning. This was, arguably, the psychoanalytic equivalent of those 20th-century movements in philosophy to construct a self-contained ethics that could refer to nothing but its own logic or lack of it for its truth value.

In much the same way that psychoanalysis could treat ideas about God, religion, spirituality, or morality that appeared anywhere in human consciousness as defenses against anxiety or as unconsciously created narratives of childhood experiences, those giving primacy to the soul over the unconscious could treat psychoanalysis as mechanistic and reductionistic. With the work of Frazer's *Golden Bough* and the numerous and profound works of Mircea Eliade, as well as of Joseph Campbell, the myth-meaning function of religious doctrine became clarified; and religion's creedal formulas could be seen in a broader context than blind denial of death and existential limitations. That is, their functions as organizing experiences necessary to negotiate the inevitably turbulent experiences of life came into focus. As this awareness grew, psychoanalysis itself became, not so much the neutral, rational science of the mind, but rather an equal contender in the field of organizing models of *personal* meaning.

"Religion," Alfred North Whitehead (1926) wrote, "is what the individual does with his own solitariness" (p. 16)—likewise for psychoanalysis. One presents a myth from without, the other from within: myth understood as an organizing model to create order out of the chaotic givenness of human existence. But to speak of religion, of dogma, even of ritual, is only half the story. What Freud did not address was the whole area of spirituality. That is, what is spirituality? Is it tied to creedal beliefs? Is it essential to understanding human existence? Or is it tangential? Such perennial questions need no final answers; they are neither possible nor desirable.

This book was conceived as an opportunity to explore the possibility that discourses about the soul and the discourses of the couch could inform, and not simply argue with or ignore one another. The essays we have brought together address such questions in ways that avoid the respective dangers, we hope, of either reductionism or of salvation—settling instead for reflective inquiry.

REFERENCE

Whitehead, A. N. (1926), *Religion in the Making*. New York: Macmillan.

— 1 —

Inner Mind/Outer Mind and the Quest for the "I"

Spirituality Revisited

GERALD J. GARGIULO

In this essay I suggest that some of the fundamental concerns of traditional Western spirituality can be understood as addressing not only
the search for the "hidden God," but the need to experience, as well as
to delimit, the autonomous "I." Psychoanalysis, it can be argued, stands in
the tradition of Western spirituality in its inquiry into personal meaning
and in its efforts to achieve reconciliation.[1] Although analysis does not
hold the promise of salvation in a distant heaven, it does offer a more present, if less comprehensive, form of salvation, one that psychoanalysts
have been slow to talk about since it entails a redefinition of mind, culture,
and the notion of the "I."

Long before psychoanalysis spoke of the need for an object, or of object
constancy, Meister Eckhart, the 13th- and 14th-century theologian mystic,
spoke of internality as externality (Fox, 1980, p. 2), meaning that individuals are not separate monads, figuratively speaking, but are interconnected
by our very nature to all that is. His idea was that to know oneself is to
know the world, and to know the world is to know oneself. Speaking in
the Christian religious symbols of his day, Eckhart went on to indicate
that the self was destined to incarnate God. He taught that the Christian
belief of God's incarnation in Jesus was not meant as a singular event to be
worshipped, but rather as an exemplar event to learn from—an educa-
tional event, so to speak. What this "learning" might mean will be the
subject of this chapter. Eckhart's theology, in the tradition of what is categorized as negative theology, was one of a radical immanence; that is, he

---

[1]To understand the past (an essential task of psychoanalysis) is ultimately to forgive the
past; more specifically, in Erik Erikson's (1964) thoughts, maturation is evidenced by a
capacity to will the inevitable that has happened to us.

eschewed a God over against man, a God who is spoken of as utterly transcendent. He was impatient with any "dogmatic" that attempted to capture the "holy" awe of life within human language. Thus he could write, in the 13th century, "God, rid me of God" (Fox, 1980, p. 217). That there is a bridge between Eckhart's theology and Buddhist thought is, as Suzuki (1957, p. 221) has observed, rather clear. Today, reflecting Western categories, we might speak of the fact that all life is to be valued, a manifestation, in Alfred North Whitehead's thought (in Jordan, 1968), of an overriding creative life principle. Further, to speak of our individual capacity to be alive, to be the breath of life, as it were, is to speak of man's soul. And, as Bruno Bettelheim (1983) has reminded us, Freud himself had no difficulty in speaking of man's soul.

Actually, psychoanalysis, in its commitment to resolving projection(s) and in its desire to help people live in the present, free of the troubling past and the elusive future, would have little difficulty in embracing many of Eckhart's thoughts. Admittedly his optimism about finding the "living God" within us and the world would have to be read on more than a linear, fundamentalist level. Historically, following the work of the 20th-century theologian and scriptural scholar Rudolph Bultmann (1971), we would have to "demythologize" this concept in order, paradoxically, to find a truer (i.e., latent) meaning. But this is not as foreign as it might at first appear, since any translator is, ultimately, a demythologizer, and psychoanalysts are translators—midwives of meaning. It is also in this sense that I spoke of them as heirs to Western spiritual traditions. That is, at their best they are Virgilian guides to wandering Dantes, ferreting out what is true from what is no longer true, what is real from what is no longer real, and what is realizable from what is no longer so. They are physicians, not of the body, but of culture and mind, of word and symbol. Although such psychoanalytic interpretative readings of man's meanings and values are clearly culture-bound and intellect-limited, they reflect both scientific and spiritual pursuits. They are scientific in limiting the range of inquiry, with an openness to alternate viewpoints and formulations; they are spiritual in the desire to know the truth of a given life beyond the recurrent distortions and reactions that cloud such knowing.

In order to explore what Eckhart's thoughts entail when he speaks of imitating God rather than worshipping him, we have to understand the "problem" of the autonomous "I." That is, we have to rethink some of our basic concepts about the psyche.

One such reconceptualization entails broadening our understanding of the concept of mind. In Winnicott's (1949) seminal article on mind he writes "*I do not think that mind really exists as an entity*" (p. 243) but that it is *no more than a special case of the functioning of psyche-soma* (p. 244). While he describes in this essay how mind can be pathologically split off, his generic thoughts about mind can, I believe, be applied to his notions of culture and transitional space. And in doing so we are able to speak, I believe, of mind as a special function of psyche/soma/culture. For example, when we speak of culture we mean, among other information conduits, the experience of language. Language which, paradoxically, both forms us and which we, collectively, create. Winnicott provides the foundation for our conceptualizing the cultural dimensions of mind when he elaborates on the transitional space of childhood as the seedbed of culture. In writing of the child's developmental stages of the me-not me experiences, with the early mother-other-environment, Winnicott grounds man's capacity to play with, and therefore to both find and create, the world. Such is the birthplace of culture. Mind, then, is clearly an achievement, it is not a given; consciousness is a prerequisite for the experience of mind, but it is not simply coequal. Consequently, we can say that to speak of culture is to speak of mind, and to speak of culture is necessarily to speak of a gestalt; there is no culture without different people, and implicit in that, no notion of self except within a particular social context. If mind comes to be in the works of our hands, so also does our sense of self. In our culture, our "I" experience reflects a collective presumption.

Just as Winnicott could write, now rather obviously, that there is no such thing as a baby (without a mothering environment), so we can say that the self does not exist in itself. The "I" is a cultural-imaginative construct. It is a way in which our culture attempts to organize experience into meaningful patterns. Lewis Thomas (1974), struggling with similar thoughts, uses the image of looking down on a giant ant hill as an analogue of human cultural activity. The self, seen from enough distance, is understandable more as a process within a context than as autonomously individuated. Such a perspective is not easily accepted, particularly in Western political and social experience, named as we are as separate "I's." What our culture conveys and what psychoanalysis has augmented is that self-experience and interiority are synonymous. Thus, interiority being experienced as radically distinctive, it is no wonder that Western culture gave birth to Descartes—no wonder that "I think therefore I am." We have been taught to experience ourselves more as individual, separate human beings than as structurally interrelated and interdependent members of humanity. Obviously, I am arguing for a more relational, structurally interdependent understanding of the "I" self than has been operative in traditional psychoanalytic drive theory, or for that matter, in political economic theory.

One of the factors that complicates our rethinking the experience of "I" and of "mind" is the fact that psychoanalysis, particularly in America, has spoken of the integration and the resolution of neurotic conflicts in terms of achieving an adequate level of "separation-individuation." With few exceptions, most notably in the philosophical work *The Self in Transformation* by Herbert Fingarette (1963), as well as *Love's Body* by

Norman O. Brown (1966), psychoanalytic theory has unreflectedly presumed that an "individuated" autonomous "I" was not merely an intellectual possibility but a therapeutic ideal. Psychoanalytic clinical practice followed this belief, not only in its everyday therapeutic goals, but most notably in accenting, and consequently aggravating, the "postulated" difference(s) between patient and analyst. Had we listened more, perhaps, to Sandor Ferenczi (Dupont, 1988), when he spoke of the actual as well as the therapeutically necessary interdependence of analyst and patient, we might have taken a different route.

Today those demarcations are lessened, and with good reasons. For if the goal of psychoanalysis is to be able to love and to work, we are immediately in the arena of "the other." Despite all of Freud's mapping of the inner terrain, his model(s) of mental agencies, his postulating an arcane unconscious and the ego's hidden defenses, when he speaks of the goal of analysis he is relational and communal. In the case of "love," the other is experienced as more desired than the self, as its fulfillment. Actually, were one not capable of loving, neither the world nor oneself would have emotional reality. In such a scenario, one would merely exist, one would not be alive. This is certainly the thrust of Winnicott's (1960) thought when he observes that therapy can go on for many years under the false assumption that the patient is alive. In the stability of love, the individual has an experience that Winnicott characterizes as "an-ongoing-in-being"—an essential prerequisite for being alive. "Work," for its part, enables us to interact with the environmental world on many levels. Work supplies an essential "process" identity because it mediates a community's recognition of personal competence. Love and work are made possible only in community. The overemphasis on intrapsychic phenomena, as if there is a separate self, independent of the self's self-revelation, has been misleading and dangerous in its consequences, as has the exaggerated notion of personal autonomy. And this is true without our discussing how we are culturally molded, from our very beginnings, by language—the exact opposite of any solipsistic notion of individuality.

Psychoanalysts name and give voice to the meanings of a self, their own and their patients', and in doing so, they situate an individual within a particular cultural framework. The analytic place mirrors the family, just as the family mirrors society, in its defining functions for the individual. Twentieth-century philosophy has helped us to understand that language forms consciousness, just as consciousness forms language. We are formed by the language that is spoken to us—a language that we had no power in creating. We repeatedly have to be called by a name; we repeatedly have to be told we are an "I" for us to be able to organize our experience in these terms. And how we are called by and within our culture commits us to what we are allowed to hear about ourselves and about our world. Nor do we have a choice. This process is neither good nor bad—it is simply the way we pass on our cultural patterning. But a society, in all its various components, does have an obligation to examine the contact lenses, as it were, that it gives its members so that their vision may become more expansive, not less so. The fact that our particular cultural conditioning makes individuals prone to be experienced as if they are individual products, that is, as essentially unrelated to each other, should not be lost sight of, particularly since such consequences serve a capitalistic economic system rather well. (In most spiritual traditions, by way of contrast, a life of poverty is not a repudiation of work or a masochistic disdain of matter, but a desire not to be stuck in "thing" consciousness.)

Psychoanalysis looks for the hidden in the obvious, for an alternate meaning behind the manifest meaning. From such a perspective, one would have expected psychoanalysis to be a radical critique, following Fenichel and some of the early analysts, of society's identifying processes. Why this did not occur has been discussed by Russell Jacoby (1983) in *The Repression of Psychoanalysis* and need not detain us here; but the question of whether psychoanalysis should address the cultural product of the "I" should concern us, even in a preliminary way.

One of the difficulties in the task of correcting the distortions of the overemphasis on the autonomous "I" is related to Freud's theoretical conceptualizations of the early vicissitudes of narcissism. As a point of reference and reflection, Freud speaks of the individual child as possessing both primary and secondary narcissism. Primary narcissism, as a postulate for the life force, holding together and fostering growth, is understandable. Secondary narcissism, as the capacity of a young infant to withdraw "libido" from the other and invest it in the self, is more than misleading. It is misleading because there is no "self" except in context of another. Freud assumes what he is trying to prove, namely that the self is "self-contained," as if there is a separate operational "I" directing the flow of libidinal investment(s). But libidinal investments are always a context experience, that is, child-mothering-environment. The child can *imaginatively pretend* that he/she has withdrawn interest from the world, but this results in what Winnicott refers to as "split off intellect," that is, mind thought of as located in a thing we call the brain. Without an adequate parental environment supporting the young infant, he or she starts on the road of splitting from that environment with the concurrent *illusion* of being a separate entity—an "I" unto him/herself.

It is at this important point of discussion that Winnicott's and many of the English object-relational theorists' observations are particularly applicable. The mothering person is defined by his/her caring for the child's developing physical needs and concurrent language-social-emotional needs. And if that individual mix-up of mutual needs and services goes well enough, both the caretaker and cared-for have an experience of being alive in their bodies, without experiencing themselves as locked in their heads. Within a positive environmental framework, the cultural transmission of the self as an "I" can be experienced as primarily relational and interdependent, not as separate and autonomous. One of the indications that a relational and interdependent self is present is a person's capacity to experience cross-identification—that ability to put ourselves in another's shoes. Is such a capacity what Winnicott (1963) has in mind when he reflects that were we able to raise children with good enough environmental provision, there would be no need to teach them morality—they would have a natural ethics? We are, to repeat, only an "I" in context. Without this context, our drives cease to be human drives and become merely physical sensations. To love and to work, as Freud knew, means infinitely more than negotiation of physical sensations. In this sense, we can note that instincts do not have vicissitudes, people do.

Another difficulty in the path of analysts fully appreciating the import of an interdependent and totally relational "I" is the traditional model of the unconscious. With Freud's introduction of the structural model, the unconscious went, so to speak, from being a noun to being an adjective; it was, however, still thought of as "located" in a person—individually. Although this is an exceptionally complex topic, I will offer a few thoughts in line with the general thesis of this essay. We can postulate, as has been done by many thinkers outside the mainstream of analytic theory, that *the unconscious* is only created, and therefore revealed, by and through interpretations. It has no existence in itself and should not be spoken of as if it has. It is essentially an interpretative experience and not an ontological one. Furthermore, inasmuch as mind is a communal experience, none of its complexity can be split off from that communality. Basically, meaning is as culture-bound as is the autonomous "I." Both are imaginative cultural constructs. The reading of any text, and here I include both dreams and symptoms, depends on the cultural framework of the reader. An analyst's interpretative reading of an unconscious component is primarily one among many possible interpretations. Actually analyst, patient, and culture join together to create the "mind" out of which come particular interpretations. Human thoughts and actions are complex because they are capable of alternate meanings; put differently, the human is an animal capable of generating and understanding metaphor(s). Because we can think metaphorically, interpretations are potentially endless.

Now we can return to Eckhart's thought that internality is externality, and that spirituality is not necessarily searching for a God we cannot know, but can be equally a capacity to find, unobtrusively in the present, whatever is holy in life. Although Eckhart would postulate a theistic God as *the* source of that which is holy, such is not necessary in order to understand a spiritual quest. Human life, Winnicott reminds us, entails more than the resolution of neurotic conflict; it is the capacity to find life interesting and worthwhile by experiencing ourselves as connected with the world, not isolated in our own thinking, creative in our interactions, not simply reactive to our environment. Consequently, "internality as externality" means, I believe, that the "I" is better understood as a (necessary?) individuated referent point within communal experience. Communal (cultural) experiences and individual experiences are inextricably related, so much so that *mind* does not exist as a locatable thing, primarily because it is a process that occurs between people, between self and other—as other and as world. Such an approach does no violence to our *personal* psyche-soma experiences of memory and imagination. It does help us understand, however, that mind resides in all the cultural bridges we have built: language, art, philosophy, religion, and psychoanalysis, to name a few. *Meaning*, which is integral to our appreciation of mind, is, as Marcia Cavell (1988) has noted, inextricably communal. To all appearances the Earth is stable, just as to all appearances we are autonomous "I's." Both are false. We walk on bridges; our very coming to be is a bridge experience. And so when Winnicott says that the first thing a patient should be able to do is play, he is talking about getting someone off an illusory island and on to a bridge, getting someone out of the house of mirrors of the "anxious ego" (mind and "I" as *pathological isolates*) and into the marketplace of life.

Fingarette (1963), as mentioned above, made analysts aware that their task is not so much the resolution of neurotic conflict in itself as it is the overcoming of the anxious ego, which then makes possible a sensible living in the *now* of time and the *here* of place. To experience our interdependence, familial and cultural, is not only realistic, it resolves the illusion that one has an "I" that is definable *in itself*. Within such a framework, psychoanalysis re-presents a spiritual tradition that has among its operational goals an individual's capacity for communal civility (i.e., cross-identification) rather than schizoid isolation; unencumbered personal presence rather than neurotic repetition; love that sees the other as other, not as mirror or mother; and, finally, work that is done competently but not necessarily self-consciously. Cross-identification does not entail obliterating the differences of the *here* and *now* of one's existence. Rather it develops as one is able to recognize the relativity of the autonomous "I"; such recognition fosters a willingness to entertain differences in time, place, and cultural identity. To recognize our commonality with others, by resolving the narcissism(s) of the anxious ego, is, as we have mentioned, a hoped-for outcome of the analytic process. Desire, which is integral to our understanding of the "I," can be understood, as I have noted elsewhere (Gargiulo, 1989), as transference desire (self-preoccupation) or relationship desire. I can barely touch on this enormously complex topic, except to note that psychoanalysis in naming desire, both manifest and latent, provides for its partial integration. *Partial* because desire, similar to the "I," is not a solitary experience; it is created and augmented by the culture, familial and social, in which one lives. T. S. Eliot (1943), in "Little Gidding," spoke to such issues:

> This is the use of memory:
> For liberation—not less of love but expanding
> Of love beyond desire, and so liberation
> From the future as well as the past.

Psychoanalysis offers the possibility for a spirituality that is humanly possible rather than religiously necessary. It offers a liberation, as Eliot alludes, that is more an ongoing task than an accomplishment. A liberation that, by experiencing the interconnection of self and other, of past, present, and of necessity future, provides the possibility for the nonconflictual *now*. Is that the (Western) experience of *I am who am*? Is that the experience of the holy?

Augustine (1943), long before Freud, advocated that we should "love, and what you will—do." That is, find yourself as a self, with, through, and in others—not in yourself. In Eckhart's thought, to know the self is to know the other. This has nothing to do with masochistic functioning, which is simply another manifestation of getting caught in the anxious ego.

That psychoanalysis reminds human beings of the normative role of love is particularly well stated in Jonathan Lear's *Love and Its Place in Nature*. As we are listened to, we know that we have a voice; as we are cared for, we know that we can love the world. Thus we can see the profundity of Winnicott's simple prayer to be "alive when I die"—a prayer that life not *un-soul* him. In view of Winnicott's wish, we can also ask, "For what will it profit a man if he gains the whole world and forfeits his life?" Such a biblical question is one with which most psychoanalysts, heirs as they are to an old tradition, could agree.

REFERENCES

Augustine, Saint (1943), *Confessions of Saint Augustine*. New York: Sheed & Ward.
Bettelheim, B. (1983), *Freud and Man's Soul*. New York: Random House.
Brown, N. O. (1966), *Love's Body*. New York: Random House.
Bultmann, R. (1971), *The Gospel of John*, trans. G. R. Beasley-Murray. Oxford: Oxford University Press.
Cavell, M. (1988), Solipsism and community. *Psychoanal. & Contemp. Thought*, 11:587–613.
Dupont, J., ed. (1988), *The Clinical Diaries of Sandor Ferenczi*. Cambridge, MA: Harvard University Press.
Eliot, T. S. (1943), *Four Quartets*. New York: Harcourt Brace.
Erikson, E. (1964), *Insight and Responsibility*. New York: Norton.

Fingarette, H. (1963), *The Self in Transformation*. New York: Harper & Row.

Fox, M. (1980), *Meister Eckhart's Creation Spirituality in New Translation*. New York: Image.

Gargiulo, G. A. (1989), Authority: The self and psychoanalytic experience. *Psychoanal. Rev.*, 76:149–161.

Jacoby, R. (1983), *The Repression of Psychoanalysis*. New York: Basic Books.

Jordan, M. (1968), *New Shapes of Reality*. London: Allen & Unwin.

Suzuki, D. (1957), Mysticism: Christian and Buddhist. In: *Meister Eckhart, Mystic and Philosopher*, by R. Schurmann. Bloomington: Indiana State University Press, 1978.

Thomas, L. (1974), *The Lives of a Cell*. New York: Bantam.

Winnicott, D. W. (1949), Mind and its relation to the psyche-soma. In: *Collected Papers*. New York: Basic Books, 1958, pp. 243–254.

—— (1960), Ego distortion in terms of true and false self. In: *The Maturational Processes and the Facilitating Environment*. New York: International Universities Press, 1965, pp. 140–153.

—— (1963), Morals and education. In: *The Maturational Processes and the Facilitating Environment*. New York: International Universities Press, 1965, pp. 93–105.

— 2 —

Self-Reparation in Religious
Experience and Creativity

KEVIN FAUTEUX

In this essay I examine the psychological regression that takes place in religious experience. Some readers will take offense at the suggestion that religious experience is a return to primitive psychological processes. Others will say it is obvious. Their differing views can be traced back in this century to the debate between the French philosopher Romain Rolland and Sigmund Freud. Rolland agreed with Freud that religion is an expression of childish needs, but he challenged Freud to consider "oceanic" experiences, in which a person felt selflessly united with God or Nirvana, yet this did not "in any way harm critical faculties" (quoted in Fisher, 1976, p. 21). Freud responded that a dissolution of ego boundaries and merger with another *can* be reparative, as in therapeutic transference, but that oceanic experience—which induces "feelings of an indissoluble bond, of being one with the external world as a whole"—is a regressive flight from reality and pathological return to maternal unity (Freud, 1930, p. 39).

A reader of the following analysis of religious experience who expects allegiance either to Freud or to Rolland will be disappointed. Instead of taking sides, I suggest that religious experience is neither an unconscious undertow that drags people deeper into its grasp, nor an idealized state free from the relentless pull of underlying needs. The experience *is* regressive, as discussed in the first section, when Nirvana and communion with God are analyzed as a loss of ego boundaries and a restoration of maternal unity. But as examined in the second section, the dismantling of self and return to unconscious processes that takes place in religious experience can be as reparative as the regression that takes place in experiences such as creativity and therapy. A final section offers a new stage of religious experience, comparable to that of elaboration in creativity (i.e., the expression of that which inspires), in order to expand the definition of a healthy religious experience to include acting on that which was experienced.

11

REGRESSION

Psychological development normally proceeds from less complex states to more complex states. Its earliest and least complex structure, as understood by Freudian drive theory, is dominated by primary processes, such as wish fulfillment and instinctual immediacy, that gradually give way to the development of more complex psychological functions, such as tolerating frustration and thinking logically. The progressive development of these ego strengths is reversed when, due to any number of intrapsychic or environmental factors, the demands placed upon them make a person feel anxious, and he or she returns to less complex psychological structures: where once again choices are simple, anxiety is overcome with wishes, and instincts are not frustrated. Freud (1933) states, "The libido will finally be compelled to resort to regression, to seek satisfaction in one of the organizations it had already surmounted or in one of the objects it had relinquished earlier" (p. 368).

Religious experience, as we shall see, represents this reversal of ego development and restoration of primitive psychological processes. It does so, in general, by way of its three stages; beginning with purgation of self.[1] A variety of spiritual disciplines—e.g., obedience, celibacy, and sensory deprivation—are employed to purge or "die to" a prideful and possessive self. Underhill (1911) writes: "All the mystics agree that the stripping of personal initiative, the I . . . is an imperative condition of the attainment of the unitive life" (p. 508). Buddhism's Four Noble Truths, for example, emphasizes the role of ego in causing suffering and, hence, the need to rid the ego (annatta). Christians similarly learn to conquer the prideful and possessive self in order to experience God. "If anyone would come after me, he must deny his very self" (Luke 9:23).

Although purgative acts might reflect a sincere wish to renounce self-centeredness, they also can be motivated by the unconscious (as well as conscious) wish to escape the responsibilities of adulthood. Renunciation of volition and assertiveness, for example, frees the person of egocentricity but also relieves him or her of the anxiety of making choices and of acting on those choices. It induces even greater relief when, in the form of surrendering self to God, earlier modes of functioning are restored (e.g., passivity to and dependence on parents) that gratify needs without involving stressful autonomy or assertiveness. Freud (1933) calls this "a regressive revival of the forces which protect his infancy" (p. 164).

---

[1]Purgation of self and experience of God or Nirvana distinguishes the religious experience that is considered in these pages from a religious belief in which God is not directly apprehended. "Enclose me not in cages of matter or mind; through heavenly vastness my soul does soar, unfenced by the walls of heart or deed, by walls of ethics or logic; I thirst for truth, not concepts of truth" (Kuk, 1951, p. 79).

"Monks have neither free will nor free body, but must receive all they need from the abbot" (Rule of St. Benedict).

Surrendering autonomy and control regressively rends the fabric of the self. An internal psychological frame grew out of, and had been relatively successful in resisting the regressive pull back to, primitive instinctual processes. In the absence of this autonomous structure (via self-abnegation) instincts are restored to the archaic state that existed prior to ego control (Rapaport, 1958, p. 18). Their unfettered and rapturous resurgence into consciousness is equated with divine illumination (second stage of religious experience).

The illuminative surge of unconscious processes shifts attention away from reality and toward primitive mental processes. It is manifested in several aspects of religious experience: euphoric transcendence of time (restoration of the timeless unconscious state—Freud, 1920, p. 168); ineffability (return to preverbal cognition—"The Tao that can be spoken/Is not the Tao," Lao Tzu); surrender of secondary functions and restoration of primitive primary processes that exist prior to rational rules and that allow for the coexistence of contradictory thoughts ("what is the sound of one hand clapping?")[2]; magical thinking—"You know when I sit and when I rise, You perceive my thoughts from afar (Psalm 139:2); passionate surrender to God that ecstatically releases sexual urges without having directly to act on them—"He (the angel in Saint Theresa of Avila's vision) held in his hand a long golden dart," which by "plunging" it into her heart "wounded" her and set her aflame with divine love (Underhill, 1911, p. 392); and on a more dramatic level, supernatural visions.[3]

Finally, surrender of self and ascendance of unbounded primary processes dissolves the dualistic mentality of inner and outer, knower and known. Underhill (1911) states that "The aim of every mystic is union with God" (p. 96). Unity is the third and final goal of religious experience. It also completes the backward movement from the development of a separate and conscious system of the mind to an undifferentiated and unconscious mental organization. For when ego functions and psychological boundaries that normally define a separate sense of self are dismantled (dying to self), an underlying "wish for reunion with the 'love object' " is awakened (Mahler, 1975, p. 77). Surrender of self and submersion of a single drop of water into the ocean (Upanishad

---

[2]"The governing rule of logic carries no weight in the unconscious; it might be called the Realm of the Illogical" (Freud, 1940, p. 168).

[3]Visions manifest the reversal of mental processes based on perception and cognition back to those based on wish-fulfilling fantasy and hallucinations, with the latter being projected onto an external screen where, regardless of whether the percept is based in reality or on the intensity of drives that create need-gratifying images, they are taken literally and redefine what is real.

metaphor for unitize consciousness) fulfills the unconscious longing to undo separateness and to return to the earliest oceanic state—represented in communion with God or Nirvana[4]—out from which the self originally was differentiated.

For the Christian, regression to primitive maternal unity takes place when psychological boundaries that separate self from God are dissolved and the individual merges into divine communion. "If therefore I am changed into God and He makes me one with Himself, then, by the living God, there is no distinction between us" (Meister Eckhart). The individual feels herself to be an intimate and inseparable part of God, and God to be the innermost part of herself: a symbiotic organism within an organism. "No longer I but Christ who lives within me (Gal. 2:20).

Nirvana—which literally means extinction, as in the extinguishing of self—dedifferentiates the boundaries that distinguish separateness and restores the anxiety-free state of selflessness. "By the destruction of desires, there is complete disinterest and cessation, Nirvana" (Udana Kidaay, 33, of the Buddhist Sutras). Islam's "fan-f'allah" expresses a similar extinguishing of self, though into Allah, and Hinduism creates a womblike environment in which individuality is suppressed and the person regressively merges into an archaic selfless Unity.

> As the bees, my son, make honey by collecting the juices of distant trees, and reduce the juice into one form, and as these juices have no discrimination, so that they might say, I am the juice of this tree or that, in the same manner, my son, all these creatures, when they have become merged in the True, know not that they are merged in the True [Mahdyamakakarida, 10; quoted in Nakamura, 1964, p. 68].

If this unity that offers refuge from autonomy could be compared to a jigsaw puzzle, its completed picture would not be organized according to the coming together of unique pieces. Rather than uniting jagged pieces with other pieces in ways that do not deny their uniqueness, it would throw all the pieces together, ignoring whether they properly fit. And the way it would throw them together would be through using self-denying spiritual disciplines, such as obedience, that bend unique edges of people's autonomy so as to fit them into a seamless whole, or through acts of celibacy that round out angles of sexuality in order to make the individual less personal and less distinct from others, until finally he or she merges back, egolessly and perfectly, into the "oceanic feelings of complete fusion and oneness with mother" (Mahler, 1968, p. 66).

---

[4]Margaret Mahler concluded that the symbiotic state that occupied so much of her research was the same as that referred to by Freud and Rolland when they "discussed in their dialogue the sense of boundlessness of the oceanic feeling" (1975, p. 44).

ADAPTIVE REGRESSION

Although a psychological analysis of self-denial and "oceanic" unity offers insights into the regressive nature of religious experience, it does not consider what can take place in this experience beyond a defensive escape from the demands of reality. It relegates the regressive encounter of God-Nirvana to a final psychological resting place, a no-return realm of infantile fixation and anxiety-free fantasy. Such a description does not take into account the experience of those for whom a divine encounter *does* create archaic feelings of security, of selfless, nondifferentiated unity, but for whom that experience does *not* result in fixated selflessness or utopia. It instead results in a unitive state that leads to repairing the unconscious conflicts that motivated the experience, and to resuming psychological development from the point at which it first derailed. Erikson (1958) wrote that "One basic form of heroic asceticism, one way of liberating man from his existential delimitations, is to retrace the steps of the development of the I, to forego even object relations in the most primitive sense, to step down and back to the borderline where the I emerged from its matrix" (p. 119).

Purgation of self and return to primitive psychological processes *is* regressive, but, rather than pathological, the loss of self can be the adaptive dismantling of the "false" self we have become, while the return to archaic processes can be the regenerative recovery of the "true self" repressed beneath that false self. The true self is the earliest openness and instinctual freedom of the infant, awaiting the benevolent guidance of parents to direct its development. The false self unfolds when the infant learns that instincts are to be feared and repressed rather than creatively expressed. Rogers (1964) writes that "The infant learns a basic distrust for his own experiences as a guide to his behavior. He learns from others a large number of conceived values, and adopts them as his own, even though he may be distancing himself from what he is experiencing" (p. 162).

The false self[5] is built upon a shell of a self, not on an integrated core identity. It forms upon an autonomy and logic and other secondary ego functions that are critically necessary to "transform freely mobile energy into bound energy," and thereby to expand the area of control in which a person feels confident (Freud, 1937, p. 217). But an overemphasis on control and assertiveness causes those functions to bind that energy too

---

[5]R. D. Laing (1967) called the false self the "egoic self" (p. 70), while Jung (1953) gave it the more familiar label "persona" and suggested it was "designed on one hand to make a definite impression upon others, and on the other hand to conceal the true nature of the individual" (p. 190).

tightly and to extend control too rigidly. They sacrifice the spontaneity of primary processes and forfeit the freedom of greater openness.

As the child grows, he or she learns to relate to the world out of this shell, "the false self gradually becomes a care-taker self" (Winnicott, 1965, p. 281). The false self's defensive superficiality is reinforced in an adult world that encourages conformity rather than creativity. By rewarding people for external signs of success, such as power and possessions, and by punishing them—or at least withholding rewards—for more intro-spective or substantive pursuits, the inner desires and frustrations of the true self are further silenced. As a result, people learn to identify them-selves by an external image of what they do (and do in conformity to what is expected of them to do). "Society does its best to turn us into everything other than what we are" (E. E. Cummings).

Christians call this false self the sinful self, the prideful and materialis-tic self that alienates the person from God. Like Winnicott, the Trappist monk Thomas Merton (1969) called it a "mask and fabrication" that hides the true self (p. 70). Buddhism and Hinduism describe the false self as *maya*, as that which is compulsively driven to seek gratification instead of truth, and which in the process separates the person from one's true self. In the words of René Daumal,

> The Modern Man believes himself adult, a finished product, with nothing to do for the rest of his life but alternately earn and spend material things (money, vital forces, skills), without those exchanges having the slightest effect on the thing called "I." The Hindu regards himself as something still to be formed, a false vision to be corrected, a composite of substances to be transmuted, a multitude to be unified [quoted in Shattuck, 1963, p. 152].

When society's emphasis on external strengths (agency) causes those strengths to become synonymous with identity and to preclude the development of the true self (communion), the former need to be dimin-ished if not expunged. Bakan (1966) states, "In order to integrate the agency and communion features within himself, it was necessary for the agentic to be reduced and allow the repression of communion to be over-come" (p. 204). A return to the true self takes place by confronting, and overcoming, the false self that keeps the true self repressed. Such is the adaptive task of the purgative stage of religious experience. It is also the first stage of creativity.

CREATIVITY AND ADAPTIVE
EGO REGRESSION

Creative processes begin with a disciplined effort to rid the false self in order to recover the true self. The psychoanalyst Ernst Kris (1952) called it "regression in the service of the ego" (p. 60). Like Freud, Kris noticed artistic experiences often involve a regressive diminution of ego functioning, followed by a return to more primitive areas of the psyche. Whereas Freud (1928) abandoned the possibility of understanding how this could be healthy—"Before the problem of the creative artist analysis must, alas, lay down its arms" (p. 177)—Kris examined what took place in creativity to make it healthy. Unlike Freud, he found in the artist's "dip" into the unconscious a potentially creative recovery of untapped inner resources, rather than the pathology of a weakened ego or a defense against repressed unconscious processes. As Proust wrote (Shattuck, 1963), "I had to recapture from the shadow that which I had felt, to reconvert it into its psychic equivalent. But the way to do it, the only way I could see, what was it but to create a work of art" (p. 149).

Kris's suggestion that art involves an inspirational stage that is both a regression to, and a progressive recovery of, unconscious processes, can be useful to understanding a similar dynamic in religious experience. To make such a comparison we will divide the inspirational stage of creativity into a preparatory stage and the inspirational stage proper. The earliest stage expresses the period of ego regression, a regression, however, that can be an adaptive dismantling of the false self. Normal day-to-day processes and the ego functions that support them are, in spite of apparent strengths, found by the artist to be too rigid, dry, stereotyped, or limiting. She seeks another way to look at life besides that of a superficial vision, another means of expressing what she perceives beside reasonable representations. She wants to recapture the wonderment and openness of primary processes, the unimpeded responsiveness to stimuli lost in the development of bounded ego functions. To do this, she first purposively suspends stereotypical perceptions, frees herself of linear thinking, and eliminates habitual ways in which the brain takes in and processes stimuli. Gordon (1961) writes that "to make the familiar strange is to distort, invert or transpose the everyday ways of looking and responding which render the world a secure and familiar place" (p. 35).

The creative person sets upon a particular discipline—dance, music, art—that helps free her from a constricted perception of life. This is the preparatory stage of inspiration. Its rigorous discipline forms a resistance to laziness (i.e., living according to preconceived notions rather than innovative thinking) and refocuses attention away from external pursuits and toward inner processes. Only then, after developing new skills—such as the pianist learning to concentrate—is she adequately free of external distractions. And only then is she technically prepared—as the pianist becomes skilled in musical scales—to relax control or to "let go" of herself and to be inspired (to be discussed next). The choreographer-dancer

Martha Graham suggested the artist must "destroy himself if he is to be creative" (quoted in Morgan, 1941, p. 142).[6]

When the self that religious experience purges is a self that excels exclusively at agentic ego control, and does so in part to defend against repressed communion feelings, then the diminishment of self can be a similar dismantling of the false self. Like the initial stages of creativity, dismantling the defensive self requires disciplined work. Compare the teachings of various spiritual traditions—from the Rule of Saint Benedict to Buddha's Eight-Fold Path—that expect discipline and sustained effort, with that of the preparatory stage of creativity. The latter is expressed by Caudwell (1951): "In order that he should be able to give expression to the inspiration that visits him he must work constantly, keeping himself in readiness, preparing his faculties, sharpening his vision and his understanding" (p. 64).

Religious experience begins with similar disciplined preparation. Meditation, scriptural readings, chanting, and yoga are like the scales a musician must learn or the choreography a dancer must practice. The religious person, like the artist, surrenders herself to a discipline—to the practices of a particular tradition or to a spiritual teacher—that helps her develop the skills to overcome the false self.[7]

Silence, therefore, as well as celibacy, sensory deprivation, and the other purgative practices that were examined earlier as being ego regressive, can be the disciplined skills that dismantle ego functioning in order to become free of the false self. A vow of silence can restore a primitive preverbal state, but it also can cultivate a greater openness to hearing others' wisdom, or to being receptive to the inner inspirational "voice" that was not heard because a faulty way of listening was learned in conformance to what the world taught was supposed to be heard.[8] Hegel (1984) said the task in teaching philosophy was to help students realize they "must first die to sight and hearing, must be torn away from concrete representations, must be withdrawn into the night of the soul and so learn to see on this new level" (p. 280).

So, too, the Zen student's struggle with "What is the sound of one hand clapping?" dismantles the neatly ordered rational thought processes that

---

[6]Maslow labeled the experience "voluntary surrender," while artist-psychoanalyst Milner called it "creative surrender" and Ehrenzweig "heroic self-surrender of the creative mind" (Maslow, 1958, p. 80; Milner, 1955; Ehrenzweig, 1967, p. 121).

[7]"No matter what the subject may be, there is only one course for the beginner; he must at first accept a discipline imposed from without" (Stravinsky, 1962, p. 20).

[8]Silence can also be the confrontation of talking as a defensive habit against having to be alone with one's inner self. "The silent spaces terrify me" (Pascal). A similar fear takes place in art, referred to as "horrum vacuui," whereby the artist meticulously fills in every space of her painting.

inhibit more intuitive ways of thinking. In a similar way, Coleridge (1907) suggested secondary imagination in poetry needed to be "dissolved, diffused and dissipated" in order to recreate "the living power" of primary imagination (p. 144).

RESISTANCE

The vow of obedience to a religious superior is one of the more prominent examples of a regressive loss of self that can be a disciplined dismantling of the false self. Obedience to a religious superior or to a Zen *roshi* can help overcome the unconscious resistance of the false self to experiencing the true self. It puts a person outside his limited and egocentric self in order to learn from the other just how limited and egocentric is his false self. "Blind obedience" wrote Simone de Beauvoir (1979), "is the only chance for radical transformation to a human being" (p. 324). Obedience to an other or Other might abandon adult ego functions, such as personal volition, but it also abandons what Buddhism calls "dittha": the prejudicial perspective of the false self. Hence, the sacrifice of ego strengths, such as independent decision making and personal opinion, is necessary because they arise out of an egocentric self and create an image of the world that is based less on what the world is, and more on the illusion created by what the false self wants or has learned the world to be: exaggerated by the conscious and especially unconscious needs projected onto the world.

> People through finding something beautiful
> Think something else unbeautiful,
> Through finding one man fit
> find other men unfit.
> (Lao Tzu)

The problem, however, of purging the ego is that the ego consciously resists its own demise. It does so even more tenaciously on an unconscious level. The ego is formed in infancy—in part, although to a great part—not only to express an emerging separate identity but to repress and to defend against the possible return of the true self and its various communion longings. It develops an autonomy and assertiveness, for example, that were instrumental in initiating individuality, but that unconsciously guarded against the expression of underlying attachment feelings. Sartre (1957) wrote, "The essential role of the ego is to mask from consciousness its very spontaneity" (p. 100). Freud (1937) called it "splitting of the ego in the process of defense" (p. 224).

Purgation of the ego and of its resistance to the true self, therefore, is an extremely difficult task. It is a particularly difficult task to be undertaken on one's own. An individual authentically might wish it, and even follow a prescribed course of action to achieve it, but the tenacity with which the unconscious aspects of the ego resist being dismantled and recovering inner processes prevents the desired purgation of self. That is where surrendering his will to a teacher enters—a teacher who has gone through the experience herself and who is learned in the ways in which the ego can sincerely seek change while also resisting change.[9]

A similar resistance is found in therapy. Freud (1933) first noticed it in patients who voluntarily came to therapy. "Only think of it! The patient who is suffering so much from his symptoms, who is ready to undertake so many sacrifices," also resists therapy (p. 287). One of the critical tasks in therapy is to recognize and interpret this resistance, for in the resistance is the clue to the fears the person resists. Various disciplines are applied to help the person confront the false self and its resistances. Regular and dependable hours, free association, and the comfort and anonymity of the couch help to overcome the tenacity of the self's opposition to opening up. Freud (1933) believed that "If we can induce him to take our view of it [resistance] and to reckon with its existence, that already counts as a great success" (p. 286).

When spiritual mentors say the above, in reference to a disciple surrendering self-will and accepting their view, our psychological warning lights go on. Psychology has been rightly suspicious of those who, in the name of becoming free of egocentricity and of submitting themselves to a "higher" consciousness, instead experience the tragedy of Jonestown or the mind-altering practices of those whose promise of salvation is a thinly disguised form of inducing psychological bondage. However, without diminishing the dangers of dependency, people who voluntarily[10] seek help from a spiritual teacher soon discover that the false self they want to rid resists its demise. But they eventually can come face to face with it in their resistance to—and in their teacher's interpretation of their resistance to—"letting go" of themselves. "What we need to do" Merton (1969) wrote "is bring the director into contact with our real self, as best we can, and not fear to let him see what is false in our false self. Now this right way implies a relaxed, humble attitude in which we let go of ourselves, and renounce our unconscious efforts to maintain a facade" (p. 24).

---

[9]The composer Stravinsky (1962) said the same takes place in creative experience. "No matter what the subject may be, there is only one course for the beginner; he must at first accept a discipline imposed from without" (p. 20).

[10]The surrender or purgation of self that is addressed in these pages is voluntary. The voluntary aspect of a person's surrendering resistance to a teacher (or to a therapist) is what distinguishes it from the experience in which a person's surrendering resistance is due to coercion or brainwashing (see Lifton, 1963). Kris (1952) similarly suggested that voluntary surrender of self in creativity is a salient factor in making the experience a regression in the service of the ego.

Spiritual disciplines might be more ascetical than the subtle sensory deprivation of a therapist's couch or ego-relaxing free association, but they similarly help a person to break free from the false self and to gain greater access to the inner psychological processes. Freud himself (1917a) acknowledged the similarities:

> Certain practices of the mystics may succeed in unsettling the normal relations between the different regions of the mind, so that, for example, the perceptual systems become able to grasp relations in the deeper layer of the ego and in the id which would otherwise be inaccessible to it . . . we must admit that the therapeutic efforts of psychoanalyses have chosen much the same method of approach [p. 11].

ILLUMINATION

Purgation of secondary ego functioning dismantles secondary ego functioning and restores the unconscious primary processes against which the false self was a defense. The return to these primary processes is regressive because, as discussed, it is a return to an archaic realm based on wish fulfillment and unbounded energy. But just as secondary functions are not as healthy as they appear (and instead can be defensive) so, too, primary processes are not as undesirable and primitive as originally learned in the drive to form secondary functions. Just the opposite. Primary processes might originally represent wish fulfillment and immediate drive gratification, but are also expressions of the spontaneity and lack of inhibition that make a child receptive to new experiences. Schachtel (1959) wrote, "The drive to seek out and to explore the new is the strongest in childhood of animals and men, in the period of exploratory play" (p. 184).

The child's instinctual freedom and openness to experience gradually faded, as discussed earlier, and was relegated to an unconscious realm of unfulfilled longings, as he or she learned the exclusive importance of autonomy and control. In the case of the artist, his or her experience represents a piercing of this false self and the recovery of primary processes. Once free of the filters through which he or she learned to perceive reality, the creative person refocuses perception according to an inner inspirational gaze: a less controllable realm of unfettered energy, through which life is perceived more intuitively, spontaneously, directly, imaginatively, and uninhibitedly. Hence the artistic renunciation of the normative might be "a going backward, but a going back to look for something which could have real value for adult life if only it could be reached" (Milner, quoted in Fuller, 1980, p. 234).

Ernst Kris (1952) labeled the irruption of primary processes into consciousness the inspirational stage of creativity (p. 61). Previously repressed instincts and tightly bound primary processes are let loose.

They make the artist feel moved, as if overtaken by an unknown force or
hit by a sudden flash of insight: the "ah-ha" experience. They inspire her
with a novel perspective that comes from within, rather than one that had
been made lifeless or colorless due to the routine of external perceptions.[11]
In the words of Yeats,

> God guard me from those thoughts men think
> In the mind alone,
> He that sings a lasting song
> Thinks in marrow bone.
>
> ("Preface to King of the
> Great Clock Tower")

Inspiration that arises in religious experience is called "illumination."
The sudden flash of insight to the artist is to the religious person being
grasped by God or having truth unveiled. By cracking the crust of the false
self that had kept hidden beneath it the true self and its vital openness to
experience, the religious person "dies" to the old and becomes receptive
to the new.[12]

> If the doors of perception were cleansed, everything would appear to man as
> it is, infinite. For man has closed himself up, til he sees all things through the
> narrow dinks of his cavern (W. Blake, 1975, p. 5).

> A death blow is a life blow to some
> Who, till they died, did not alive become,
> Who, had they lived, had died, but when
> They died, vitality begun.
> (Emily Dickinson, quoted in Phillips, 1977, p. 43)

Once the "doors of perception" are cleansed, the inner psychological
processes that were kept in the dark are illuminated. Whereas instinctual
freedom once was repressed, there now exists an experience of God that

---

[11]Milner (1950) wrote of how she intentionally forfeited linear styles of painting in order to
expose herself to this less ordered and more open inner psychological realm.

[12]Jesus' familiar exhortation that heaven was available only to those who "become like little children" warned adults that their authority and control often inhibited unbridled experiences, an exhortation similar to Jung's (1970) suggestion that early repressed drives and
affect are a potential source of wisdom to the adult and "Can only be found if the conscious
mind will suffer itself to be led back to the "children's land," there to receive guidance from
the unconscious as before" (p. 337). From a different perspective, Freud (1917b) recognized
that loss of ego control and resulting greater "flexibility of repression" can be therapeutically
reparative, whereas Hartmann (1964) wrote the ego needs at times "to be able to abandon
itself to the id" (p. 177).

represents the ecstatic reactivation of this instinctual freedom. Whereas ego functioning had based its perceptions and interpretations on the accumulation of previously stored input (automatization), there now exists a direct experience of God that represents the illuminative restoration of primary processes immediacy.

"Dharmakya," for example, is the Buddhist state of a person who, having "emptied himself," has pierced normative perception and has experienced life directly. The koan, mentioned earlier, similarly helps to dismantle ineffective logical reasoning and restore intuitive primary processes. Christians who "die to self" subsequently are inspired by the Holy Spirit, whereas yoga aims to overcome rational cognitive processes (*vighana*) in order to reactivate *prana* (an energy that seems to be the stuff of primary processes). Hence, although this intuitive apprehension often involves the previously discussed regressive absorption of self—for example, a loss of self into a primitive sense of timelessness—such an experience can evoke the immediacy of unconscious processes that can be as creative, for example, as the artist's descent into the primary process timelessness of her inspirational absorption (Neumann, 1959, p. 150). Consider these lines from Blake's "Auguries of the Innocence."

> To see the world in a grain of sand
> And heaven in a wild flower,
> Hold infinity in the palm of your hand,
> And eternity in one hour.

UNITY AND REPARATION

The religious individual, like the artist, becomes comfortable with, and learns to trust, this illuminated unconscious realm. She does not try, as she did before, to dominate it, to turn its craziness into logic or its chaos into control. She experiences what the poet Keats called "negative capability": the capacity to risk "being in uncertainties, mysteries, and doubts without any irritable reaching after fact and reason" (quoted in Bion, 1973, p. 115). Comfort with this inner unconscious realm marks the return of the "true self." Unified experience, for the mystic or artist, is the feeling of oneness, of connection or belonging to the instinctual spontaneity and imagination of this previously unacknowledged self. The religious individual experiences this unity in the form of communion with God or Nirvana. The artist experiences it in the dismantling of dualistic distinctions between seer and seen, beauty perceived and perceiver of beauty.[13] Milner (1950) recalls,

---

[13]Underhill (1919) suggested the mystic's experience of the oneness of "seer and seen" is "the essential action of the artist" (p. 26).

"There occurred, at least sometimes, a fusion into a never-before known wholeness; not only were the object and oneself no longer felt to be separate but neither were thoughts and sensations and feelings and actions" (p. 142).

What, however, makes the artist or religious person comfortable with the unconscious processes with which he now feels united, when previously these unconscious processes were deemed dangerous and hence repressed? So, too, how is it that the ecstatic recovery of primary processes, in the form of directly experiencing God or of artistic inspiration, is not simply a divinely sanctioned indulgence in wish-fulfilling fantasy or an exhilarating release of sexual tension? The answer is in the experience of unity. For here is where the person not only recovers repressed primitive processes but then has the opportunity to resolve the original conflicts that forfeited their healthy development.

The artist is able to feel comfortable with reactivated hidden conflicts or needs because she experiences them in a secure place. The psychoanalyst and art critic Ehrenzweig (1967) called it a type of "'womb' in which repressed and dedifferentiated images are safely contained, melted down, and reshaped for re-entry into consciousness" (p. 121). This womblike experience is the "incubation" stage of creativity. The *Oxford Dictionary* describes incubation as the "practice of sleeping in a temple or sacred place for oracular purposes." It is the "fallow period" that occurs after the person gives up the struggle to solve a problem and allows that problem to gestate in the unconscious until a creative solution is found therein (Rhodes, 1961, p. 308).

The artist then finds in his art work—his canvas, acting, music, and so forth—another type of safe environment, an "aesthetic illusion," in which to express these processes incubating in his unconscious. Aesthetic illusion is the sense of unity that exists between the artist and her work. This bond turns art into a safe environment for expressing the unconscious feelings that otherwise would not be able to be expressed. Instead of acting directly on hostile impulses or being overwhelmed by the repressed trauma that arises in the inspirational dip into the unconscious, the artist is able to "play" with and work it out. She accomplishes this by bringing it safely to life on her canvas. By displacing repressed feelings or drives on a canvas where they do not cause destruction, and where they simultaneously are experienced as "out there" but also as an extension or a part of herself (aesthetic illusion), the artist safely is able to lift hidden feelings and impulses out of her unconscious. Yeats conveys this extension:

> O swaying music
> O brightening glance,
> Who can tell
> The dancer from the dance.

The experience of communion with God can be a similar aesthetic illusion. Communion with God begins when the mystic, like the artist and inspiration, ceases trying to make the experience happen and instead waits for God to take over.[14] "In this state of contemplation which the soul enters when it forsakes meditation for the state of the proficient, it is God who is now working in the soul" (Saint John of the Cross). God working in the soul is the mystic having given up trying to create God in his own image and instead letting God gestate in the unconscious. Repressed desires and fears safely incubate in this secure environment until the individual feels comfortable with them.

The length of Time a person waits in this incubational unconscious before he or she becomes comfortable enough in it to be inspired or illuminated varies from person to person. For the unconscious to reveal its "truths," to illuminate its or God's mysteries, certain depths that are relative to each individual have to be plumbed. They are relative to the tenacity with which a person resists illuminating those depths. Coleridge's "Kubla Khan," for instance, came to him in a short reverie, whereas many of Yeats's inspirations came to him in a "flash." Nietzche's *Thus Spake Zarathustra*, on the other hand, took 18 months of gestation. Waiting for divine illumination similarly can be of a relatively short duration, as the three days Saint Paul waited after being blinded in his Damascus encounter, or can require a "long" time, as signified by the use of the number 40 to describe Jesus' days in the desert or Moses' sojourn in the wilderness.

THERAPEUTIC TRANSFERENCE

Therapy can instill a transference state that is a similarly safe experience for an individual to recover and to repair unresolved conflicts and needs. Transference begins in a therapeutic relationship that establishes the "holding environment"—the authority and benevolence of the therapist, for example, as well as regular and dependable hours—wherein a person feels sufficiently secure to relax defensive ego control (Winnicott, 1965, p. 248). Diminution of ego rids the clear boundaries between the individual and therapist, and subsequently restores—in the form of unconscious libidinal attachment and trust in the therapist—fantasized images of the trustworthy and libidinally bonded parent (positive transference). The reactivated feelings of acceptance, of a therapist who will not judge and, especially, will not abandon the person for expressing previously resisted

---

[14]The experience of passively waiting might be a defense against aggression, as described, but in it is where Kris found the roots of inspiration, and James suggested that the illumination "Often comes about not by doing, but by simply relaxing and throwing the burden down" (Kris, 1952, p. 317; James, 1961, p. 389).

impulses or secret feelings,[15] makes her or him feel safe enough to express and eventually resolve the conflicts that were left unresolved in significant relationships from the past.[16]

Heinz Kohut (1984) suggested that transference can take place in areas outside of therapy.

> When we feel uplifted by our admiration for a great cultural ideal, for example, the old uplifting experience of being picked up by our strong and admired mother and having been allowed to merge with her greatness, calmness and security may be said to form the unconscious undertones of the joy we are experiencing as adults [p. 49].

Religious experience can be one of these transference relationships that rids normative ego boundaries and reparatively restores archaic feelings. As stated previously, spiritual disciplines might be more ascetical than the subtle sensory deprivation of a therapist's couch or ego-relaxing free association, but they similarly help a person voluntarily break free from the false self and gain greater access to inner psychological processes.

Purgation of ego and merger into a nondual relationship with God was earlier described as a regressive return to symbiosis. Symbiosis, however, can be restored in the form of oceanic experiences—as it can in therapeutic transference—*not* in order to escape intrapsychic conflicts. It can reactivate unconscious feelings of libidinal attachment (positive transference) so as, first, to reassemble a secure symbiotic environment. Kernberg (1970) suggested that experiences of this sort "reactivate past internal object relations as a source of internal support in times of crisis, loss of external support, or of loneliness" (p. 270).

The experience of unity with an omnipotently loving God or a sense of perfectly blissful Nirvana restores the idealized internal object that makes the person feel what it was like in infancy to be unconditionally loved and unfailingly contented. She once again feels affirmed, as she did when her parents loved her for no other reason then that she existed. She does not have to prove herself to God to receive God's love, nor does she have to prove her worth to feel worthy of God's presence. Hence, for the first time since childhood, the individual does not anxiously feel she always has to be independent and constantly in control in order to subdue the abandon-

---

[15]Expression of these unresolved conflicts and forbidden impulses is "negative transference."

[16]Freud's (1905) original thought that transference hindered therapy (since it regressively resisted dealing directly with issues) was changed when he realized projecting onto the therapist the authority and trust given to parents in childhood made transference—and the analysis of the person's resistance to it—"the most powerful ally" in the therapeutic recovery of unconscious conflicts (p. 117).

ment anxiety first experienced in the loss of symbiotic paradise. She instead is able to reclaim basic trust in the openness, libidinal bonding, and other expressions of communion and primary processes that once were the foundation of her self and that now, in religious experience, have an opportunity to be so once again.

Furthermore, the person can feel so loved and secure in the experience of God that even when frustrations and conflicts arise, as they inevitably do (negative transference[17]), she continues to trust in the perfect God as she did in the maternal image that God represents. Without this aesthetic illusion of communion the person would feel starkly alone with these fears and forbidden impulses. But she no longer experiences them on her own when she safely experiences previously feared feelings and instincts as belonging to the experience of unity. In this encounter of a God who, like a therapist, is experienced as not supporting her any less for expressing once feared and forbidden feelings, the person learns a more tolerable way of managing that which before she could not mange[18]—("optimal frustration" Winnicott, 1965, p. 238). Hence in religious experience the return to archaic unconscious processes might have regressively "frozen" fears, which was Winnicott's (1955) way of describing how regressive experiences temporarily help a person escape anxiety, but also allow for the possible reparation of the underlying conflicts and hidden needs that unconsciously motivated the regression.

> Along with this goes an unconscious assumption (which can become a conscious one) that opportunities will occur at a later date for a renewed experience in which the failure situation will be able to be unfrozen and re-experienced, with the individual in a regressed state, in an environment that is making adequate adaptation possible [p. 18].

MARTIN LUTHER

An example of how religious experience reactivates basic trust in communion feelings that lead to reparation of unconscious conflicts was

---

[17]The same negative transference that elicits repressed feelings of being abandon or of hating the therapist is encountered in the religious individual's dreaded "dark night" experience.

[18]Because the person does not aim those potentially destructive or bewildering feelings directly at herself, and instead expresses them at the God with whom communion makes her experience those feelings as not being entirely her own, she, like the artist, can "play" with and express them in the safety of her divine "aesthetic illusion." In this way she learns more about these repressed feelings and is able to test them—to see in her relationship with God if they are acceptable or manageable—without having to act directly on what could be their overwhelming intensity.

presented by Erikson (1958) in his study of Martin Luther. Luther was a man of vast intelligence and resolve, qualities Erikson suggests came from an early relationship with his father. He had developed a strong personal identity—even a rigid, retentive identity—in response to the pressure of his father (and of society) to disidentify himself from his mother and to become independent and in control. As a result, Luther became assertive but failed to integrate the early basic trust he experienced in feelings of openness and communion with his mother. He was logical and competitive, but he could not express feelings of spontaneity and receptivity, even in his relationship with God. " 'I did not know the Christ child any more,' (non novi puellum) Luther said later, in characterizing the sadness of his youth: he had lost his childhood" (Erikson, 1958, p. 119).

Luther's "death" to the world and seclusion in the monastery was a retreat into a womblike existence, but it was also the purgation of a rigid self and the formation of a deeply trusting and reparative relationship with his mentor. In that secure environment he felt comfortable surrendering the rigid control and detachment that defined his identity. Jung (1970) described the experience of surrendering control and forging a formative relationship in therapy: "It almost seems as though these patients had only been waiting to find a trustworthy person in order to give up and collapse" (p. 110). Through the trustworthy relationship with his mentor, Luther was able not only to abandon his defensive ego and "morbid conscience" (Erikson, 1958, p. 119), but was also subsequently able to open himself to a loving God who represented the reactivation of the communion feelings he sacrificed in becoming overidentified with defensive autonomy and control. In the restored basic trust of that experience he was able to confront the defensive qualities of his overidentification with the agentic qualities of his father, so as to repair the loss of basic trust in communion feelings. Erikson (1958) states "I have implied that the original faith which Luther tried to restore goes back to the basic trust of early infancy inspired by Luther's mother and then threatened by Luther's father (p. 265).

CONCLUSION

Although religious experience regressively dissolves a person's autonomy and reactivates one's psychological past, it can do so, not to flee the present, but to make the psychological past more meaningful to the present. Like therapy or creativity, religious experience can be a detour toward maturation of self via a temporary retreat from reality and a return to early unconscious structures. It thereby allows for the opportunity to repair unresolved conflicts and to redirect the development of a personal identity away from its fixated past and toward a new maturity. Erikson (1963) asks:

> Must we call it regression if man thus seeks again the earliest encounters of his trustful past in his efforts to reach a hoped-for eternal future? Or do religions partake of man's ability, even as he regresses, to recover creatively? At their creative best, religions retrace our earliest inner experiences, giving tangible form to vague evils and reaching back to the earliest individual sources of trust: at the same time, they keep alive the common symbols of integrity distilled by generations. If this is partial regression, it is a regression which, in retracing firmly established pathways, returns to the present amplified and clarified [p. 264].

Beyond Unity

Religious experience has been examined in this work according to the traditional image of its beginning with self-purgation and reaching its goal in a unified state. I suggest here, however, that Oneness or Communion with God is not the final stage of religious experience. At least it is not the final stage if the experience is psychologically healthy. It *is* the final stage when a person avoids the challenges of the next stage by remaining attached to the unity state, an attachment difficult to resist because of various inducements found in the unity encounter. In the remaining pages I examine the inducements that forfeit the fullness of a final stage of religious experience, and why this final stage manifests a degree of psychological health not present in the traditional goal of unity.

To accomplish this task, I suggest we expand our earlier examination of creative processes. A final stage of creativity, we will see, is characterized by the artist's "emergence" out of early inspirational stages, and by what he or she then does with what was inspirational. What the individual does, or fails to do, will be the lens through which what transpired in the unity experience—whether creative or religious—will be seen to be psychologically defensive or healthy.

Erikson (1964) states that "We all relive earlier and earliest stages of our existence in dreams, in artistic experience, and in religious experience, only to emerge refreshed and invigorated" (p. 69). An artistic submersion into inspirational unconscious processes begins as a retreat from the distractions or stereotypical perceptions of the world. This retreat, if creative, will return the artist—armed with new perceptions and insights—more fully and richly whence she escaped. "Man can find no better retreat from the world than art," wrote Goethe, "and man can find no stronger link with the world than art" (quoted in Stierlin, 1976, p. 56). Kris (1952) labeled the experience of emerging out of the unconscious, and "giving color" to that which it inspired, "creative elaboration" (p. 60).

Elaboration[19] is the final stage of creativity. It is the act of expressing, of communicating to others and giving shape to what inspired the artist. The intense feelings and archaic images that arise from the artist's dip into the unconscious are inspirational, but are not in themselves creative. Art is not the reactivation of these unbounded sensations nor its derivative flash of insight; art, writes Collingwood (1950), is "the experience of expressing one's emotions" (p. 275). Abel (1957) describes this process.

> When the artist has something to report from the nether world . . . When he has received from the depths a creative conception, or at least feels a stirring of a creative impulse . . . Then he must reverse his orientation and, so to speak, return to earth. There, using tools and material, he must seek to embody his conception in objective form [p. 331].

Elaboration is as critical in making religious experience healthy as it is in turning inspiration into creativity. Just as it defends against the artist's temptation to equate the intensity of inspiration with creativity, so too it guards against the religious individual associating euphoria and divine visions with the final stage of religious experience. The mystic, like the artist, resists returning from her "other-worldly" experience. She is afraid the "world" and its superficiality or sinfulness will disturb its tranquillity or desecrate its purity. To depart the euphoria is to experience a type of separation anxiety, a fear of forfeiting paradise and being exposed to the limitations and vagaries of life outside the unity state.

The devil's offer to Jesus of glory and power, for example, represents the projection of Jesus' inner temptation to cling to the magical omnipotence of his desert experience (Luke 4:1–4). So too, Buddha's temptation[20] to remain permanently pacified beneath the bodhi tree represents his reluctance to emerge out of the euphoric and into the mundane. Joseph Campbell (1950) said the same of the hero's experience.

> The first problem of the returning hero is to accept as real, after an experience of the soul-satisfying vision of fulfillment, the passing joys and sorrows, banalities and noisy obscenities of life. Why re-enter such a world? Why attempt to make plausible, or even interesting, to men and women consumed

---

[19]Other psychologists refer to the elaboration stage differently. Kubie (1961), for example, called it the intelligo phase of creativity that emerges out of the preconscious cogito, whereas Mckellar (1957) described it as autistic "A" thinking that lies beneath reality oriented "R" thinking.

[20]This temptation was, like that of Jesus, represented in the devil, or *mara*, who suggested Buddha should stay beneath the bodhi tree because it would be a waste of time to teach his experience to those who would not understand it.

with passion, the experience of transcendental bliss? As dreams that were momentous by night may seem simply silly in the light of day, so the poet and the prophet can discover themselves playing the idiot before a jury of sober eyes. The easy thing is to commit the whole community to the devil and retire again into the heavenly rock-dwelling, close the door, and make it fast [1950, p. 218].

Jesus, however, did not succumb to the temptation to cling to the desert experience, Buddha did not remain permanently pacified beneath the bodhi tree, and Moses did not stay transfixed in the burning intensity of his mountaintop encounter. Like the artist, their retreat from the world and descent into inspirational unconscious processes was temporary.[21] "Grant me a break from myself," Robert Frost (1963) declaimed, "but let me come back." Their retreat was a time of ridding themselves of self-centered thinking and of wrestling with demons. In the end, rather than confusing their experience with spiritual fulfillment, they emerged from the desert and came down from the mountain.

If a person confuses the experience in the desert or under the bodhi tree with the fullness of religious experience, then the experience, which might once have brought the person into direct contact with God, becomes, as the Trappist monk Thomas Merton wrote, "a retreat into the realm of images and analogies which no longer serve for a mature spiritual life" (1969, p. 77). Such a pseudo-enlightening experience represents the inauthenticity, or at least the premature closure, of the experience. As Saint Theresa suggested, "If anyone told me that after reaching this state of union he had enjoyed continued rest and joy, I should say that he had not reached it at all" (quoted in Duerlinger, 1984, p. 68).

The final stage of religious experience, however, is more than emergence (or failure to emerge) out of unity. Return to the world involves the mystic's, like the artist's, expression or communication of what was inspirational. Hence Jesus not only left the desert but elaborated on what he experienced in his gospel message. Buddha emerged from beneath the bodhi tree and expressed his experience through the dharma, whereas Moses came down from the mountain and expressed the intensity of his experience through the Ten Commandments.

---

[21]Kris (1952) suggested inspiration in art is temporary (p. 253). The artist's dip into repressed primary processes is what inspires her, but it is of a relatively short or limited duration. William James preceded Kris's psychological inquiry into the temporary state of inspiration when he suggested one of the four salient qualities of mystical experience was its transitory nature (1961, p. 375). More recently, Maslow (1971) expressed the same idea when he described peak experience as "transitory self-actualization." "If this is going into another world, then there is always a coming back to the ordinary world" (pp. 48, 159).

Joseph Campbell (1950) similarly said that the hero, after his adventures and conquests,

> still must return with his life-transmuting trophy. The hero shall now begin the labor of bringing the runes of wisdom, the Golden Fleece, or his sleeping princess back into the kingdom of humanity, where the boon may redound to the renewing of the community, the nation, the planet, or the ten thousand worlds [p. 193].

Recovered Primary Processes Lead to
Psychosis as Well as to Illumination

The task of elaborating religious experience seems simple: What began as a loss of self and a subsequent submersion into unity is reversed and leads back to reality when the individual begins to express what she experienced. Something has to take place, however, that makes the person do something creative with what she experienced. Otherwise, the unconscious processes recovered in that experience can only seduce the person to stay attached to her regressed realm of paradisiacal pleasures. More dramatically, they can overwhelm the person with the fury of the unconscious forces they unleash.

This work has presented the illuminative recovery of unconscious processes as potentially transformative, because a person cannot achieve greater psychological fullness until he awakens the repressed fears and unfulfilled longings that thwarted growth. As Jung (1953) states, "He gives way to the regressive longing and deliberately exposes himself to the dangers of being devoured by the monster of the maternal abyss" (p. 180). A person, however, might find the maternal abyss too seductive or voracious, and it *does* devour him. That is, when the ego that once maintained control over unconscious drives is surrendered or "died to," the primary processes and instincts that were frozen in their orally voracious state ascend to consciousness, and they ascend with such unneutralized force that the person experiences them as beyond control.[22] He feels flooded with insufferable emotions and overwhelmed by

---

[22]Early aggression is an uninhibited drive that is experienced with raw intensity because it has not yet been "neutralized" (Hartmann, 1955). In their primitive state, aggressive drives seek goal gratification independent of libidinal drives. While libido seeks only bonding, without respect for individuality or assertiveness, aggression attempts to overcome deprivation through a similar single-mindedness, regardless of libidinal cravings for closeness. Only later in development is the child able to synthesize aggression and libido: "the fusion of both instinctual drives" (Hartmann, 1964, p. 19). Before this, however, unintegrated aggression is experienced as rage: "An id in which individual instincts have made themselves independent, pursue their aims regardless of the person as a whole and henceforth obey the laws only of the primitive psychology that rules in the depths of the id." (Freud, 1926, p. 203)

insatiable appetites. A nonexistent or passive ego makes him feel controlled by thoughts, instead of in control of them, and dominated by impulses, instead of having them under his authority.

Ernst Kris (1952), for instance, observed that inspiration in the creative process makes available unconscious primary processes, which—because they are unneutralized and unrelenting—can result in the "the psychotic condition in which the ego is overwhelmed by the primary processes" (p. 60). Like Jesus' parable of the man who feverishly swept his house clean only to have its emptiness inhabited by demons (Luke 11:24), the religious individual can "sweep" herself clean of her ego, can become celibate to be free of lust and obedient in order to lose willfulness, only to find that instead of the expected enlightenment, she experiences a frightening resurgence of demonic impulses. She is overwhelmed by the swirling whirlpool of drives and conflicts that she feels powerless to manage. That is why Jung (1969), in apparent contradiction of his openness to numerous approaches to experiencing the unconscious, warned Westerners against utilizing Eastern meditation practices: they "abolish the normative checks imposed by the conscious mind and thus give unlimited scope to the play of the unconscious 'dominants'" (p. 520). Maslow (1967) similarly warned about the type of experience he labeled the "Jonah syndrome," whereby the individual is exposed to an inner "fear of being torn apart, of losing control, of being shattered and disintegrated, even of being killed by the experience" (p. 163). R. D. Laing (1967) even more graphically described this recovered unconscious state with the image of "body half-dead, genitals dissociated from heart, heart severed from head" (p. 55).

Why is one person *not* overwhelmed by an experience that reactivates a bewildering realm of feelings and, instead, experiences a creative breakthrough, whereas another's seemingly same descent into unconscious processes leads to being overwhelmed by them? Both have had experiences that exposed them to the dark caves of the inner self and forced them to do battle with the dragons of the unconscious (as Jung was earlier quoted in reference to the hero); but while one was devoured by the dragon of maternal abyss, as Jung (1953) went on to say, the hero mastered it (p. 180). Mastering the experience—whether religious or creative—rather than being overwhelmed by it, comes about by doing something with it. That is, the person elaborates or acts on her experience. In art, the inspirational recovery of primary processes is the energy that fuels the creative process, but that energy requires the artist's particular aesthetic discipline in order, first, to prevent its raw instinctual intensity from being overwhelming, and second, to turn untamed instinctual energy into socially meaningful and creative expressions.

In regard to the first, Melanie Klein (1937) suggested that the artist's unbounded primitive impulses—especially aggression—are safely channeled into the "container" of aesthetic form. A particular work of art provides the tangible structure within which intolerable or chaotically unmanageable primary processes can be expressed without having to act directly on them. By displacing repressed feelings or drives onto a canvas, where they do not cause destruction and where they are experienced simultaneously as "out there" and as an extension or a part of herself (aesthetic illusion), the artist safely is able to lift hidden feelings and impulses out of her unconscious.[23] "Playing" with these unbounded primary processes, through the discipline of her particular art form, allows the artist eventually to gain control over—rather than feel controlled by—these intense and sometimes chaotic inner processes. As Freud (1911) states, "The artist finds the way back to reality from his world of fantasy by making use of special gifts to mold his fantasies into truths of a new kind which are valued by men as precious reflections of reality (p. 223).

Kris (1952) made control the salient factor in creativity. "Inspiration—in which the ego controls the primary processes and puts it into service—needs to be contrasted with the opposite, the psychotic condition in which the ego is overwhelmed by the primary process" (p. 60) The psychotic does not feel in control of tapped unconscious processes and so is frightened, even paralyzed, by the inner feelings and conflicts that reveal her to herself. The psychologist Wild (1965) performed several experimental studies that compared how creativity in art students made them feel about themselves with how creativity in schizophrenics made them feel (p. 169). He concluded that a major difference between the two was that art students were excited about what their art had to tell them about themselves, whereas schizophrenics were fearful of the introspective nature of their art. The psychotic might have been enchanted by what she experienced in the inspirational stage of creativity, especially by the heightened awareness, but, lacking the control of nonpsychotic art students, she was not able to manage what was experienced. She could only remain hyperexcited by the experience or tremble in fear; she could not make the revealing experience an integral part of her identity. The artist, on the other hand, was able to organize—through her disciplined art work—what was experienced within her unconscious into a self-identity, and thereby felt inspired by the variety of drives and needs she experienced.

More than control, however, artists' expressions of unconscious processes also give shape to their hitherto unformed nature.[24] If the exhilarating freedom of inspirational and unconstrained primary processes is

---

[23]So too those who observe her art might experience a similar evocation within themselves of the forbidden impulses or conflicts that are expressed in that work. The experience is most notable in theater, where a safe environment is created in which people can experience—without punishment or guilt—the resurgence of their own hidden impulses in response to observing the same being acted out on the stage.

[24]Neumann (1989) called it the "gestaltwerdung": "That is, the turning into form of what until then had been just formless energy" (p. 41).

to become more than a mere cathartic explosion of emotions or release from tension, the artist must consciously use her creative discipline to direct their development. She has to work with the unconscious processes that irrupt into consciousness; she has to struggle for the right word or the most descriptive color. By doing so, she provides necessary direction and shape to the unconscious primary processes that inspire creativity, but which are also directionless and boundless. "The great work of art," wrote Gombrich (1963), "is marked by an intensity of impulse, matched and dominated by an even greater intensity of discipline" (p. 22). Or as the philosopher Dewey (1910) succinctly said, "Unconsciousness gives spontaneity and freshness; consciousness, conviction and control" (p. 217).

Just as the potter's wheel gives shape to the artist's inspiration, so too the gospel, dharma, or Ten Commandments give shape and structure to religious experience. Jesus' sermon on the mount, for example, was a type of "container," similar to the artist's, that gave mature direction to primitive primary processes restored in his experience of God. Through it he was able to work out, to gain control over, and to develop, the unbounded sensations and unconventional ideas[25] elicited in the desert of his unconscious. The concrete ways in which his message taught others to love, for instance, and in which he himself loved others, shaped and reshaped the experience of feeling unreservedly loved by God. It became the way he worked at these various feelings and thoughts until he, like the artist, "got it right." An archaic image of libidinal bonding thereby was able to be transformed into mature expressions of intimacy,[26] just as aggressive feelings once projected onto a devil were able to be realistically expressed in angry feelings and messages of justice.

Furthermore, the individual's concrete expression of a religious or artistic experience makes that which inspired her accessible to others. That is,

---

[25]Jesus' gospel was a way of wrestling (as the artist does on her canvas) with what must have been not only its innovative but, to some extent, perplexing contents. His words and ministry crystalized and clarified—for himself as well as for others—the sometimes incomprehensible images and sensations experienced in the desert. As Coleridge (1895) wrote about the effect of the poet's words to master inspirational processes and, thereby, to become the "Gods of love which tame the chaos" (p. 96), so too Jesus' gospel was his way of finding the words to communicate, and thereby to tame or develop, the often chaotic unconscious processes that arose in the illuminative experience of God.

[26]The failure to give structure to recovered unconscious processes, on the other hand, causes their surge into consciousness to be at best a cathartic explosion of emotions and at worst an act of self-destruction. The mythological figure Icarus represents the individual whose experience of unconstrained primary processes—symbolized in his ability to fly—did not lead to doing something creative with that freedom and instead lead to those processes dominating him till they destroyed him. Intoxicated by the freedom to fly (i.e., having ecstatically lost his limited self to unbounded primary processes) Icarus forgot to place constraints around his wishes—as his father Daedalus warned—and kept flying higher until the sun melted his wings and he plunged to his death.

it is communicated. By partaking in common cultural forms such as language and symbols to share their experience, artists, as well as people like Jesus and Buddha, are able to keep an intensely personal experience from becoming solipistically relevant only to themselves while incomprehensible to others. As Arieti (1976) writes, "It must be something that sooner or later, ordinary thinking will understand, accept and appreciate, otherwise the result would be bizarre, not creative" (p. 121).

Because the psychotic's experience of unconscious processes, on the other hand, does not have the structure through which to act on or make sense of it, it has no relevance to those outside his experience and remains meaningful only to his private, idiosyncratic inner world. LaBarre (1970) described the prophet's success in being a prophet: "The more he expressed a real social need, the more he succeeded; but the more he expressed a mere narcissistic wish, the more he failed." For example, "Moses and Aaron handled snakes, and so did George Went Hensley. But Moses and Aaron also embodied larger social and ethical ends; the Southern snake handlers, absorbed in strictly personal sins, were a poor second in this feature" (p. 613).

The Gospel and dharma that communicate religious experience provide a type of cartography for others. They are maps that, by describing personal experience, reveal to others a potential direction to follow in discovering their own experience. But they are only maps. Like the artist's canvas, they represent the expression of one's experience and are not meant to interpret that experience for others. What Jung (1966) said of the artist is true of the religious individual. "He has done his utmost by giving it form, and must leave the interpretation to others and to the future" (p. 107).

Finally, the communication of what took place in the desert or in the imagination is more than an automatic expression of what was passively received in that experience. It is a conscious acting on or doing something with it. In the words of Martin Buber, "He has stepped out of the glowing darkness of chaos into the cool light of creation. But he does not possess it yet; he must first draw it truly out, he must make it into a a reality for himself, he must find his own world by seeing, hearing, touching and shaping it" (quoted in Johnston, 1986, p. 163).

George Bernard Shaw is said to have written that genius is ten percent inspiration and ninety percent work. Hence, more than spouting words or automatically splashing onto canvas whatever comes to mind,[27] the creative artist refines and polishes what inspires her as if it was a rare gem from her unconscious. In this way, the artist transforms a passive recep-

---

[27]The painter Pollock labeled art that is automatically and uncritically expressed an "accident" of the unconscious or a mere "illustration" of what was revealed. "The method of painting is the natural growth out of a need. I want to express my feelings rather then illustrate them" (quoted in Read, 1967, p. 45).

tion to inspirational processes into an active encounter with them: "participating in 'what the voice' has done" (Kris, 1952, p. 61).

Mozart, for example, worked feverishly to put into particular notes and chords the complete symphonies that spontaneously reverberated in his imagination, and the poet's product—which might appear smooth and effortless—often is accomplished only after she struggles to find the "mot juste," the one exact word, the right balance and fluid rhythm that best express her idea. In the words of Coleridge (1895), "Idly talk they who speak of poets as mere indulgers of fancy, imagination, superstitions, etc. They are the bridlers by delight, the purifiers" (p. 96).

In the end, creativity not only takes from life that which is inspirational, but through its active elaboration gives back to life something new. That is, creativity is innovative. It is bringing out of the inspirational unconscious and applying to life a new insight that enhances life. Thus we see in Picasso's paintings not only the keen observation of an image that was given to him from nature but a giving back to nature of his effort to do something creative with it. An equally perceptive artist, Van Gogh, said "L'art c'est l'homme ajouté à la nature"—Art is man added to nature (1959, p. 189).

Religious experience also actively adds to life. Its earlier passive nature—the infused contemplation that necessitated a "hands off" attitude in order not to get in its way, but instead to let it gestate and come forth on its own—comes to an end, however, when, as in creative processes, the individual acts on his experience. What was encountered as a sense of "I have had an experience" is changed into "I do something with the experience."

The psychotic, on the other hand, does not have to do anything with what was incubating in his unconscious for it to be brought to life. Simply because he does not act on what was uncovered in the descent into the unconscious does not keep him from thinking that his experience directly affects the world. Kris (1952) examined this type of thinking in his study of the difference between the way in which healthy artists perceive the effect of their work and the perception of psychotic artists (p. 62). He suggested a psychotic artist believes that what she expresses on her canvas actually changes people (just as the experience changed her). Rather than substituting magic for aesthetics, the healthy artist knows her painting does not directly change people. She instead recognizes that her work might influence people, or inspire them, but does not magically manipulate them (as in voodoo practices). So, too, healthy religious people might believe that praying in a monastery can indirectly influence others, but they do not believe it directly changes their lives. To believe that sitting on a mountain or praying in a monastery, without having to do anything with that experience, will directly affect others, is, like the psychotic's experience, a magical attempt to twist reality (usually to fit a self-fulfilling image). "Art has deteriorated from communication to sorcery" (p. 61).

Unlike the psychotic, Jesus, for example, not only expressed the love he experienced from God but acted on it through concrete works of intimacy and caring. As Kris (1952) said of the artist, his acting on what inspired him "repeats actively what had been passively experienced" (p. 91). So too, Buddha emerged out of a tranquil Nirvana and worked diligently at the dharma of "right action" and "right living"[28] whereas Hindus combat *tama*, or spiritual laziness, through *raja*: the "will power" to act on what was passively experienced.

An effortless and undisciplined expression of illuminative unconscious processes, on the other hand, merely takes what was experienced and, in art, splashes it onto a canvas, and in religious experience, expects feelings such as love or communion to be cathartically expressed without work or frustration. Thus Hamlet declares, "My words fly up, my thoughts remain below,/ Words without thoughts never to heaven go." When the bliss or security of unitive experience is not acted on, and instead is confused with a final product, the person becomes passively and permanently fixated in the third stage of religious experience. She prefers the instant gratification of paradise and the effortless expression of wishes to having to work on what has been experienced. Neumann (1968) called experiences of this type "urobic mysticism." It's similar to what the poet Auden (1962) said of art that is wonderful in its "primary imagination" but lacks the "secondary imagination" to express it: "its beauty soon becomes banal, its rhythms mechanical." Or as Confucius said:

> If you have the wisdom to pursue the truth
> But not the manhood to keep it,
> You will find it
> But lose it

The manner in which a person learns (or fails to learn) to act on what was inspirational determines the nature of her religious experience. That is, whether she does something constructive to develop what she experienced determines if that which is ecstatically recovered forms maturely or defensively. It determines if the experience results in fleeting inspiration or enduring wisdom, temporary insight into life or living that insight. "A

---

[28]Somerset Maugham said the same when he wrote in his *Writers Notebook* that the value of art is not in beauty alone "but in right action. . . . Art, unless it leads to right action, is no more than the opium of an intelligentsia" (quoted in Schneider, 1950, p. 303). And Descartes wrote: "For it is not enough to have a good mind: one must use it well. The greatest goods are capable of the greatest vices as well as the greatest virtues; and those who walk slowly can, if they follow the right path, go much further than those who run rapidly in the wrong direction."

beautiful thought or word which is not followed by a corresponding action, is like a bright hued flower that will bear no fruit" (Buddha). Or as Jesus more succinctly stated, "By their fruits you shall know them."

In conclusion, the active elaboration of religious experience changes life rather than reacts to life. Jesus and Buddha and others like them did not use their religious experience to make life more manageable or more easily adaptable, but to offer new meaning to, and transformative perspectives on, reality. They took what illuminated them and, by expressing it and applying its diverse insights, they offered something novel. As Van Gogh was earlier quoted concerning the artist, they added to and shaped life. In the stroke of a brush or the teaching of love they recreated reality.

REFERENCES

Abel, W. (1957), *The Collective Dream in Art*. Cambridge, MA: Harvard University Press.

Arieti, S. (1976), *Creativity: The Magic Synthesis*. New York: Basic Books.

Auden, W. H. (1962), Making, knowing and judging. In: *The Dyer's Hand*. London: Faber.

Bakan, D. (1966), *The Duality of Human Existence*. Chicago, IL: Rand McNally.

Beauvoir, S. de (1979), *The Second Sex*. New York: Vintage.

Bion, W. (1973), Attention and integration. *Internat. J. Psychiat.*, 54:110–121.

Blake, W. (1975), *The Marriage of Heaven and Hell*. New York: Oxford University Press.

Campbell, J. (1948), Schizophrenia: The inward journal. In: *Consciousness*, ed. D. Coleman. New York: Harper & Row.

——— (1950), *The Hero with a Thousand Faces*. Princeton, NJ: Princeton University Press.

Caudwell, H. (1951), *The Creative Impulse in Writing and Painting*. London: Macmillan.

Coleridge, S. T. (1895), *Anima Poetae*, ed. E. H. Hartley. London: Heinemann.

——— (1907), *Biographic Literia, Vol. 1*. Oxford: Oxford University Press.

Collingwood, R. (1950), *The Principles of Art*. Oxford: Oxford University Press.

Dewey, J. (1910), *How We Think*. Boston, MA: D.C. Heath.

——— (1934), *A Common Faith*. New Haven, CT: Yale University Press.

Duerlinger, J. (1984), *Ultimate Reality and Spiritual Discipline*. New York: Paragon House.

Ehrenzweig, A. (1967), *The Hidden Order of Art*. Berkeley, CA: University of California Press.

Erikson, E. (1958), *Young Man Luther*. New York: Norton.

——— (1963), *Childhood and Society*. New York: Norton.

——— (1964), *Insight and Responsibility*. New York: Norton.

Fisher, D. (1976), Sigmund Freud and Romain Rolland. *American Imago*, 33:1–59.

Freud, S. (1905), Fragments of an analysis of a case of hysteria. *Standard Edition*, 7:3–122. London: Hogarth Press, 1958.

——— (1911), Formulations on the two principles of mental functioning. *Standard Edition*, 12:218–226. London: Hogarth Press, 1958.

—— (1917a), A difficulty in the path of psycho-analysis. *Standard Edition*, 17:135–144. London: Hogarth Press, 1955.

—— (1917b), Introductory lectures on psycho-analysis, Part III. *Standard Edition*, 16:243–463. London: Hogarth Press, 1963.

—— (1920), A general introduction to psychoanalysis. *Standard Edition*, 18:235–254. London: Hogarth Press, 1955.

—— (1926), The question of lay analysis. *Standard Edition*, 20:183–258. London: Hogarth Press, 1959.

—— (1928), Dostoevsky and parricide. *Standard Edition*, 21:177–196. London: Hogarth Press, 1961.

—— (1930), Civilization and its discontents. *Standard Edition*, 21:64–145. London: Hogarth Press, 1961.

—— (1933), New introductory lectures on psychoanalysis. *Standard Edition*, 22:5–182, London: Hogarth Press, 1964.

—— (1937), Analysis terminable and interminable. *Standard Edition*, 23:216–253. London: Hogarth Press, 1964.

—— (1940), An outline of psycho-analysis. *Standard Edition*, 23:144–207. London: Hogarth Press, 1964.

Frost, R. (1963), *Selected Poems of Robert Frost*. New York: Holt.

Fuller, P. (1980), *Art and Psychoanalysis*. London: Writers Publishing.

Gombrich, E. (1963), *Meditation on a Hobby Horse and Other Essays on the Theory of Art*. London: Phaidon Press.

Gordon, W. (1961), *Synetics: The Development of Creative Capacity*. New York: Collier.

Hartmann, H. (1955), Notes on the theory of aggression. *The Psychoanalytic Study of the Child*, 1:11–30. Madison, CT: International Universities Press.

—— (1964), *Essays on Ego Psychology*. New York: International Universities Press.

Hegel, G. (1984), *The Letters*. Bloomington, IN: Indiana University Press.

James, W. (1961), *The Varieties of Religious Experience*. New York: Macmillan.

Johnston, C. (1986), *The Creative Imperative*. Berkeley, CA: Celestial Books.

Jung, C. G. (1953), Two essays on analytic psychology. In: *The Collected Works of C. G. Jung, Vol. 7*. Princeton, NJ: Princeton University Press.

—— (1966), *The Spirit in Men, Art and Literature*. Princeton, NJ: Bollingen Foundation.

—— (1969), Psychological commentary on the Tibetan book of the dead. In: *The Collected Works of C. G. Jung, Vol. 2*. Princeton, NJ: Princeton University Press.

—— (1970), *Psychological Reflections*. Princeton, NJ: Princeton University Press.

Kernberg, O. (1970), *Borderline Conditions and Pathological Narcissism*. New York: Aronson.

Klein, M. (1937), *Love, Hate and Reparation*. London: Hogarth Press.

Kohut, H. (1984), *How Does Analysis Cure?* ed. A. Goldberg & P. Stepansky. Chicago, IL: University of Chicago Press.

Kris, E. (1952), *Psychoanalytic Exploration in Art*. New York: International Universities Press.

Kuk, A. I. (1951), *Lights of Holiness*. Jerusalem: Rav Kuk Institute.

LaBarre, W. (1970), *The Ghost Dance*. New York: Dell.

Laing, R. D. (1967), *The Politics of Experience*. New York: Ballantine Books.

Lifton, R. (1963), *Thought Reform and the Psychology of Totalism*. New York: Norton.

Mahler, M. (1968), *On Human Symbiosis and the Vicissitudes of Individuation*. New York: International Universities Press.

——— (1975), *The Psychological Birth of the Human Infant*. New York: Basic Books.

Maslow, A. (1958), Emotional blocks to creativity. *J. Indiv. Psychol.*, 14:51–56.

——— (1967), The creative attitude. In: *Explorations in Creativity*, ed. R. Mooney. New York: Harper & Row.

——— (1971), *The Further Reaches of Human Nature*. New York: Viking Press.

McKellar, P. (1957), *Imagination and Thinking*. New York: Basic Books.

Merton, T. (1969), *Contemplative Prayer*. New York: Imago.

Milner, M. (1950), *On Not Being Able to Paint*. London: Heinemann.

——— (1955), The role of illusion in symbol formation. In: *New Directions in Psychoanalysis*, ed. M. Kleine. London: Tavistock.

Morgan, B. (1941), *Martha Graham*. New York: Pearce.

Nakamura, H. (1964), *Ways of Thinking of Eastern People*. Honolulu, HI: University of Hawaii Press.

Neumann, E. (1959), *Art and the Creative Unconscious*. Princeton, NJ: Princeton University Press.

——— (1968), Mystical man. In: *The Mystic Vision*, ed. J. Campbell. Princeton, NJ: Princeton University Press.

——— (1989), *The Place of Creation*. Princeton, NJ: Princeton University Press.

Phillips, D. (1977), *The Choice Is Always Ours*. Chicago, IL: Re-Quest Books.

Rapaport, D. (1958), The theory of ego autonomy. *Bull. Menn. Clin.*, 22:13–35.

Read, H. (1967), *Art and Alienation*. London: Camelot Press.

Rhodes, M. (1961), An analysis of creativity. *Phi Delta Kappan*, 42:305–310.

Rogers, C. (1964), Toward a modern approach to values. *J. Abnormal & Soc. Psychol.*, 68:160–167.

Sartre, J. (1957), *The Transcendence of the Ego*. New York: Noonday.

Schachtel, E. (1959), *Metamorphosis*. New York: Basic Books.

Schneider, D. (1950), *The Psychoanalyst and the Artist*. New York: International Universities Press.

Shattuck, R. (1963), *Proust's Binoculars*. New York: Random House.

Stierlin, H. (1976), Liberation and self-destruction in the creative process. *Psychiat. & Humani.*, 1:51–72.

Stravinsky, I. (1962), *An Autobiography*. New York: Norton.

Underhill, E. (1911), *Mysticism*. London: Methuen.

——— (1919), *Practical Mysticism*. New York: Dutton.

Upanishads (1926), trans. F. Mueller. Oxford: Oxford University Press.

Van Gogh-Bonger, J. & van Gogh, W., eds. (1959), *The Complete Letters of Vincent van Gogh*, 3 vols. Greenwich, CT: NY Graphical Society.

Wild, C. (1965), Creativity and adaptive regression. *J. Personal. & Soc. Psychol.*, 2:161–169.

Winnicott, D. (1955), Metapsychological and clinical aspects of regression. *Internat. J. Psycho-Anal.*, 36:16–26.

——— (1957), Transitional objects and transitional phenomena. In: *Collected Papers*. New York: Basic Books, 1958, pp. 182–204.

——— (1965), *The Maturational Processes and the Facilitating Environment*. New York: International Universities Press.

— 3 —

The Patient Who Was Touched By and Knew Nothing About God

STEVEN H. KNOBLAUCH

It is likely that Kohut (1984) was referring to his own experience when he wrote, "one of the conditions for the maintenance of a cohesive self as one faces death is the actual or at least vividly imagined presence of empathically responsive selfobjects" (p. 19). The general applicability of Kohut's insight is here illustrated in the treatment of a dying patient. The value of a tie with the therapist facilitates a selfobject experience, which, in turn, provides a sense of cohesion and continuity that helps to contain, manage, and buffer emotional suffering at the same time that it facilitates the recognition and understanding of psychic conflict.

In his most thorough description of selfobject experience, Kohut (1984) explained, "Throughout his life a person will experience himself as a cohesive harmonious firm unit in time and space, connected with his past and pointing meaningfully into a creative-productive future, only as long as, at each stage in his life, he experiences certain representatives of his human surroundings as joyfully responding to him, as available to him as sources of idealized strength and calmness, as being silently present but in essence like him, and, at any rate, able to grasp his inner life more or less accurately so that their responses are attuned to his needs and allow him to grasp their inner life when his is in need of sustenance" (p. 52). Having had 13 years to reflect on this statement, we now recognize from clinical and personal experience that a feeling of firm harmonious cohesiveness is quite illusive and fleeting in a world of multiple and discontinuous contexts. Nevertheless, for those times when it does occur, Kohut's formulation of the significance of responsiveness—along with contributions of others such as Balint (1968) and Winnicott (1958)—has been most helpful in our conceptualizations of this important self-state and the significance of the selfobject function to its precipitation.

An earlier version of this paper appeared as "The Selfobject Function of Religious Experience: The Treatment of a Dying Patient," in *The Impact of New Ideas, Progress in Self Psychology, Vol. 11* (The Analytic Press, 1995).

Kohut suggests a developmental line for selfobject experience and for a continuing need for such experience throughout life. Since his statement was published (1984), emphasis has been placed on the beginnings of such experience. Stern (1985), Lichtenberg (1989), and others have described infant development in terms of the emergence of self-structure through interactions with others who provide a sustaining context for the infant. How selfobject experience functions to facilitate a cohesive, continuous, and vital sense of self during other periods of life, particularly that of dying, is in need of further exploration and clarification. The following discussion provides a wider theoretical frame for the case to be discussed, in as much as it offers an understanding of the relationship between dying and religious experience from sociological and anthropological perspectives as well as from a self-psychological psychoanalytic view. Because this particular patient's experience of dying involved religious experience, the following discussion frames an understanding of the personal meanings the patient attributed to this time, and also the functions of the cultural context in which these meanings emerged.

RELIGIOUS EXPERIENCE AND DYING

The experience of religion and its accompanying cosmology has been described by Malinowski, Berger, and O'Dea as providing a person with meaning and an ordered surround. The onset of a life crisis can threaten disintegration of the predictability of this experience of self and surround. If a religious cosmology is not available when a life crisis disrupts this experience of meaning and order, then a person can experience what Kohut (1971) referred to as "disintegration anxiety." In the absence of such a religious function, a selfobject tie with an analyst can facilitate a process of recognizing and understanding conflicts and anxieties triggered by the life crisis. The tie can be experienced by a patient as restorative of meaning and order, in a sense, of integrity of the self-and-surround experience. Additionally, at times, the restorative function of the selfobject tie can be experienced, literally, in religious or spiritual terms. This occurred in the case to be described.

Religion is given the following definitions in *Webster's Third New International Dictionary* (1986): "a personal awareness or conviction of the existence of a supreme being or of supernatural powers or influences controlling one's own, humanity's, or all nature's destiny (only man appears to be capable of —) . . . the access of such an awareness or conviction accompanied by or arousing reverence, gratitude, humility, the will to obey and serve: religious experience or insight (in middle life he suddenly got —)." The idea that religion serves a cohesion-producing function for human beings has been expressed sociologically and anthropologically. An examination of these views, while relevant to the case to be described, is not intended to argue that other personal or social experience cannot also serve this function. Bronislaw Malinowski (1965) has written in the anthropological literature that

> Every important crisis of human life implies a strong emotional upheaval, mental conflict, and possible *disintegration*. Religion in its ethics sanctifies human life and conduct and becomes perhaps the most powerful force of social control. In its dogmatics it supplies man with strong *cohesive* forces, . . . death, which of all human events is the most upsetting and disorganizing to man's calculations, is perhaps the main source of religious belief [pp. 70–71].

Malinowski's explanation for the origin of religion in the human need for cohesion when faced with the disintegrating impact of the death experience is a theoretical construction that provides a basis for understanding the need for a selfobject tie in the absence of religion. The experience of one's physical and psychological disintegration can only be emotionally shattering and conflicted unless some kind of meaning and organization can be perceived as providing the cohesion necessary to buffer this experience.

Peter Berger, in his sociological analysis of religion (1969), has suggested that the human world has no order other than that constructed by humans. Thomas O'Dea (1966) has pointed to three types of human experience that represent a breakdown or failure of the order created by social life. *Uncertainty* concerns the loss in predictability of outcomes. *Powerlessness* concerns either loss of control or the absence of it in the first place. *Scarcity* concerns the experience of deprivation or frustration that occurs when a person's needs are not met. He addresses the function of religion in a human life in the following way.

> Religion, by its reference to a beyond and its beliefs concerning man's relationship to that beyond, provides a supraempirical view of a larger total reality. In the context of this reality, the disappointments and frustrations inflicted on mankind by uncertainty, and impossibility . . . may be seen as meaningful in some ultimate sense, and this makes acceptance of and adjustment to them possible. . . . Religion answers the problem of meaning . . . by providing a grounding for the beliefs and orientations of man in a view of reality that transcends the empirical here and now of daily experience. Thus not only is cognitive frustration overcome, which is involved in the problem of meaning, but the emotional adjustments to frustrations and deprivations inherent in human life and human society are facilitated [pp. 6–7].

Berger and O'Dea describe how religion creates a social context for the personal experience of crisis. The potentially disintegrating experience of the onset of death is thus characterized by failure of the social context to provide meaning and order to that experience, and even further, to press to the foreground experiences of uncertainty, powerlessness, and scarcity as defined by O'Dea. The authors seem to agree with Malinowski's analysis that religious belief emerges in the social context to function as a source of meaning and organization in the face of potentially disintegrating experience.

Leming (1979–1980) conducted an empirical study of the relationship between death anxiety and religious belief by surveying 372 subjects to compare their death anxiety with religious activities, beliefs, and experiences. He divided his subjects into four groups on the basis of a religious commitment scale and found that the least anxiety concerning death was associated with those subjects with the highest religious commitment. This finding is supportive of the views of Malinowski, Berger, and O'Dea. The description of the following case emphasizes self and selfobject experiences unique to the dying period of a patient as they emerged in treatment. Furthermore, how a selfobject experience interacts with and facilitates additionally needed selfobject experiences is examined.

The patient, Ms. L, had not experienced the kind of responsiveness in her surround that Kohut described. As a result, a significant impact of treatment emerged in the mirroring and idealizing selfobject transference dimensions. Transformations of Ms. L's self-experience were mediated such that she felt relief from her symptoms. She moved from a dreaded pattern of expecting nonresponsivity or constricting responses in her surround, accompanied by a sense of "arrogant" self-control, to one of expecting responsiveness, accompanied by feelings of "humility" and positive self-regard. In her dying days, she was able to feel good about herself and others. Central to these transformations was the understanding and interpretation of Ms. L's experiences of deity.

SELFOBJECT EXPERIENCE AND
HUMAN DEVELOPMENT

One question that this case study helps to address is how to conceptualize selfobject experience in developmental terms. Is the capacity for selfobject experience a linear phase-specific development or is it shaped by specific contexts irrespective of chronology? The answer seems to be that it is an interaction between certain sequential developmental accomplishments, particularly the capacity for representation, and the uniquely experienced contexts in which an individual is embedded as she or he develops. With this in mind, we examine the case of Ms. L and then construct an understanding of the specific developmental sequelae that contribute to the organization of her symptoms and their subsequent treatment. In framing an understanding of the case, the following observations from the self-psychological literature regarding selfobject experience are particularly relevant and helpful.

Fosshage (1992) has suggested that, "Within a more consistent field model self-generated and other-generated should be viewed as two poles on a continuum of selfobject experiences." Here Fosshage emphasizes contextual characteristics of the experience. Ms. L's experience of deity served a selfobject function that emerged in the treatment context but continued in other contexts in the absence of the therapist. What appeared to be facilitative was the acceptance and understanding of the unique meaning of her experience by her therapist.

Lichtenberg (1991) points out that selfobject experiences can be derived "from *ideation* associated with experiences that provide a powerful boost to vitalization and cohesion of the self. . . . Religion utilizes this recognition in its promise of an enduringly available protective deity" (p. 477). Lichtenberg's observation focuses on the vitalizing and cohering functions that can accrue from mental activity that substantiates the possibility of hope. Note that such ideation does not necessarily have to be derived from prior experience. It can be based in a faith emerging from a cultural context that holds out the promise of protection.

Basch (1988) describes religion as a "mature, abstract, internalized source of selfobject experiences" (p. 232). Implicit in this statement is the assumption that there are also immature, concrete, external sources of selfobject experiences. I infer from this perspective an assumption of a developmental sequence to selfobject experience, moving from the concrete and external to the abstract and internal. Whether this sequence can be conceptualized as linear or as a series of transformations that are context specific and reversible is not specified in the statement. Nevertheless, the idea that selfobject experience can be derived from an abstract and internal source implies the potential for such experience to emerge without the presence of another as a trigger or screen.

In short, all three theorists point to the use of experiences serving selfobject functions that (1) can occur without the use of another person, (2) are, therefore, self-initiated, and (3) are able to be sustained outside of the treatment relationship. This developmentally mature capacity utilizes experience for self-cohesion, self-sustaining, self-protecting, and vitalizing functions.

Ms. L could receive sustenance from the mirroring and idealizing selfobject dimensions of the treatment. These became the field for new relational experiences, both within and outside of the treatment context, that facilitated the transformation of a dreaded repetitive pattern originating in childhood to a new beginning (Ornstein, 1974). But, at the same time, these dimensions of selfobject experience were not able to transform the fear and loss of control generated by her current illness and anticipated death. In response to this fragmenting trauma, Ms. L utilized a developmentally mature selfobject experience precipitated by the therapist's understanding and acceptance of her sense of God. The following details illustrate the way in which this selfobject experience developed and functioned in the treatment context.

THE CASE OF MS. L

For Ms. L, life was miserable and she wanted to die. She first contacted me a year before entering treatment, while she was going through a long and harrowing divorce. During the divorce process she discovered that her cancer had recurred. Previously, Ms. L had a mastectomy and was believed to be in remission. Now her cancer had reappeared in her bone marrow. She indicated that she might soon be needing my services but did not call back again until a year later. She was then in a panic and asked to be seen immediately.

It should be noted that, at this time, the patient had a previously existing idealization of me. I inferred this idealization when the patient indicated, in her first phone contact, that she had heard of my work from a previous patient and held a strong belief that I would be able to help her with her current emotional suffering. In our first meeting, I learned of Ms. L's need for a supportive paternal figure and the disorganization and self-reproach that was triggered by the absence of such a figure. She expressed her hope that I would be able to help with her psychogenic dyspnea. This diagnosis had been given by an oncologist. As she talked, she exhibited difficulty breathing and distress, and described her state of panic and despair over the recent discovery that her initial prognosis had been incorrect. Previously, she was told she would live for about six more months. This period of time had expired.

Now, just prior to our first meeting, Ms. L was informed that the expectation for the length of time she would live with the disease had changed. The expectation was open ended. She described her horror of having prepared to die, of having "stepped out onto the edge, waiting for the angel of death to come and take [her], only to be told that there was a mistake and that no angel was coming and that, for that matter, it was not clear when the angel was coming." As she spoke, her breathing became more shallow. She began to gasp and wheeze with each breath she struggled to capture. Then, she let out a blood curdling scream, followed by several more, which she muffled with a handkerchief cupped over her mouth. She explained that this gave her temporary relief.

As Ms. L initially struggled with her breathing and then screamed, I observed how she watched me. She seemed to be waiting for me to do something to stop her or to give her a sign or command to stop. I refrained from intervening during this tense episode, sensing an important communication unfolding on a nonverbal level. After she screamed and explained, in part, why she did this, I noted the pain of the moment for both of us, her discomfort as well as mine in witnessing and accompanying her in her suffering. I suggested that as our work progressed, we might understand this "breathing problem" better.

Ms. L seemed somewhat relieved by my response and went on to describe the treatments she had undergone, which were based on the "theory" that she could be healed by "physical work." Recent efforts to seek relief from her symptoms through such "body work" treatment had been unsuccessful. Born of Jewish immigrant parents, Ms. L described her mother as very resourceful and her father as distant and depressed. She did not experience her parents as in love. She had a sister, three years younger, who was a happy, even jolly child in contrast to her. As a child she had suffered from colic and had cried a great deal. Her mother's typical response to her crying, which continued long after the colic, was to slap a hand over Ms. L's mouth so as to muffle her crying. Ms. L's reaction as a child was to hold her breath. This was her attempt to control her crying and to hold back the flow of her emotions, which were unacceptable to her mother. As she recalled these memories, I listened quietly to her. She began to feel even greater relief and her breathing improved. I asked her if she saw a connection between the content of her memories and the scene we had just enacted. She speculated that her state of panic may have been a way of communicating her memory and wondered if this were a pattern she had been unconsciously repeating throughout her adult life until this very moment when, now for the first time, she was getting an understanding of what this pattern might mean. She added jokingly that she knew I was the right man for her when she heard my name was "Dr. No Block."

In the next session, Ms. L described a new "symptom," frequent crying spells, some of which seemed to last for hours. She stated "I haven't permitted myself to cry for the last nine years." She associated her mother's slaps in the face to a series of slaps in the face that life had given her: her bouts with cancer, her divorce from her husband, and her difficulties raising her children. We recognized another unconsciously repeated pattern of Ms. L's: not giving herself permission to cry was an attempt to control her experience of "life circumstances . . . out of control." As she described her attempts to control her feelings, she added "Time is up." I noted the annoyance in her tone of voice and inquired whether these words might also refer to her experience of the treatment hour. I wondered if she felt robbed of a sense of control with me. She responded with a memory of a struggle with a former therapist who tried to get her to do some physical exercises to combat "her holding on to stress." In particular, she remembered a dream experience of "letting go," followed by three days in which she felt free of her pattern of holding in her pain. She described a kind of mystical sense of being at one with the universe. Then it stopped. She explained to me that she pushed it away. "I pushed God away. God had really touched me. I almost understood God. I've totally forgotten by now. I know nothing about God."

Ms. L's response to her therapist's impositions was to turn to God for relief. I wondered if now she was unconsciously experiencing her relationship with me as restrictive and reconfiguring the organizing themes of slap-in-the-face and withdrawal of needed support; or was describing the memory her way of unconsciously communicating to me how desperately she needed to find a way to reexperience the support and soothing relief that being touched by God could bring, and an acknowledgment of her need for my help to reexperience that support and relief? My speculations focused on the unconscious meanings of our exchange as constituted within the relational dynamics enacted between the two of us. I asked Ms. L about her religious beliefs and how she pushed God away. She indicated that she had never been religious and had pushed God away "By saying let's just stop all this breathing business for now. And all this flowing. I don't know why I did this. I think it overwhelmed me. I was arrogant enough to think I could switch this on and off at my own control. The simple fact is that I have no control of anything. . . . The ship is the captain. I don't know anything about the captain. It isn't given to me to know. If I sound religious, believe me, that's just about the extent of my knowledge."

I chose not to pursue my questions about the unconscious meaning of our relationship and the time restriction to her, but rather to stay with her experience of God and the possible meanings of this association. The intervention seemed to repair the rupture between us that the time issue had created momentarily and to allow additional associations and fantasy to unfold.

She described the struggle she had been in with her therapist for a sense of control: "I've been fighting the pleasure of "letting go" since I was a little girl, slapped hard in the face, telling herself—don't breathe out. It's too dangerous. I'm repeating that pattern now. The most effective way to hold emotions back is to hold your breath. It's horrible, but it works. That's what I did physically and emotionally; I held my breath and looked around for more trouble coming at me."

The strategy of staying with associations to God at this point in treatment facilitated a conscious integration for the patient of the unconscious meanings of her patterns of not breathing and experiencing feelings as a dangerous lack of control. We then examined this trouble she was anticipating. She described the uncertainty and fear of her unpredictable dying process. Together we constructed a set of possible meanings to the experiences she was thus far able to articulate. Her need to control blocked her ability to have the deific experience she once had and that she now needed in her time of despair to help her cope with feeling out of control. She added that, for her, life was dangerous. She couldn't control what was happening to her: not her dying, nor me, nor my rules about treatment. Her attempts to control were arrogant. She explained, "I need to know humility. If I don't learn humility, I'll be stripped bare. My breasts will be ripped off. I'll be poisoned. Everything I cherish will be torn away." I wondered with Ms. L if by humility she meant giving up the illusion of control and thus liberating herself from the arrogant and self-defeating patterns of not breathing, not feeling her emotions, not experiencing a connection to God, to me, or to any others with whom she might need to feel connected in order to feel safe enough to overcome, in part, her fear and anxiety.

From this point on in treatment, Ms. L's struggle with these issues became a central theme of treatment. While she verbally acknowledged the value of having her experience accepted by me, she seemed to need more in order to feel cohesive and vitalized in the face of her painful dying process. Her experience of God seemed to provide this additional organizing function for her, particularly when, as was often the case, I was unavailable to help her contain and express her feelings. In subsequent sessions, we further explored the co-constructed narrative that holding back had contributed to her suffering, and that her "arrogance" blocked her feelings of flowing, which she characterized as the presence of God in her life. She explained, "In all of this stuff that's happening to me now, I feel close to it again. It feels infinitely far away, as though I'll never get there again. But I'm not as far as it feels. When I cry, this all can dissolve again, and I feel hints of it. . . . Then I tighten up again . . . and hold back the crying. . . . So I'm in an unstable place, shaky on my feet, scared to death, blocked as hell."

In the next phase of treatment, Ms. L struggled in her words, to "humbly accept" her feelings, to flow, and thus to "know God." She began to experience relationships with others in a new way. She described a conflict with her daughter in which Ms. L was now able to express her feelings and needs, which at prior times would have eventuated in another "slap-in-the-face" episode. In subsequent months, the content of sessions centered on conflicts in other significant relationships with her son, ex-husband, friends, relatives, and the physicians who managed the treatment of her illness. As we examined these conflicts, the dynamic meanings associated with repetitively holding in her breath and blocking affect continually reemerged.

Increasingly, she expressed her feelings rather than holding them back. She began to feel understood by others and to express anger and resentments associated with past disappointments and rejections. As she reordered the meanings of past as well as present conflicts, she reported that she began to have a sense of resolution and acceptance. She attributed these feelings to her newly found connection to God. With this religious organization of events and relationships, she could understand and transform the repetitive pattern of holding back and articulate her affective experience.

Ms. L described her newly evolving self state as "really beautiful. And a time of intense suffering. And of almost, almost reaching whatever it is—let me say it—I'm almost reaching God. I'm purifying myself, making myself clean. Making myself worthy of whatever it is that's coming. I want to be ready for it."

Ms. L's sense of order and meaning in deific terms contributed to an increasing sense of coherence and stability for her states of self and associated affectivity. At this point in treatment, she introduced the poignant conflict over self-worth with which she struggled, particularly as it pervaded her sense of inadequacy as a parent to her children and as a wife to her husband. She felt she had let them all down and felt apologetic to me about her lack of strength for our sessions, or for boring me. But, as we examined this conflict and how it unconsciously had organized her transference feelings with me, her descriptions of self-experience began to shift from this sense of inadequacy toward an increasingly more positive self-concept and sense of hope.

For example, in regard to her home, Ms. L stated, "This house is becoming a sanctified place. I'm finding myself in this house. . . . I need this place in the woods to cry and yell and bathe in and be alone. I suddenly appreciate this unstable house I thought was such a burden. It's a gift to me at this time." She described a visit by a person to her home, which reflected the degree to which she had now organized her experiences in religious terms. She explained how every moment had become meaningful to her in this way. The visit was by a man of foreign descent whose name, in his language, meant the same as her's, "Praise God." Their visit, though ostensibly for a quite mundane purpose, was experienced by Ms. L as spiritual and timeless. She explained to me, "All of this is what God is to me." Investigation of these statements about events in her home led me to the interpretation that her words were also communicating feelings about her self-concept and about our relational space as a safe place for her analytic work.

As treatment continued, Ms. L further elaborated her encounters with others, particularly with men and with me, not in dangerous terms in which the other would be unresponsive—as with father, husband, son, and previous therapists—but as safe and sanctified with religious meaning. In one association, she described how she had cried in bed, remembering how she had prayed for something to ease her daughter's suffering over her illness. She described her prayers being met as her daughter's husband "fell from heaven." Now her prayers had brought my responsiveness to help ease her suffering. Her use of deity as selfobject experience met her need for support in the face of death. Ironically, she could experience feelings and connection to others more in her dying than any time previously in her life. Her immediate need was for the continuing presence of God and the affect integration facilitated by this presence.

Over time, Ms. L's physical condition deteriorated. Problems with medication, as well as periods of extreme fatigue and difficulty concentrating, undermined the frequency, duration, and focus of our sessions. During the last five months of Ms. L's life, we did not have regularly scheduled sessions. Periodically, she or I would initiate a brief phone call. She would catch me up on current events concerning her relationships with family members and the increasing deterioration of her body. Although physically exhausted, she was personally engaged up through our last contact. A few weeks before she died, she told me she could feel that death was close. The night before she died, she called her son to prepare him. She had made her preparations and accepted the transition with a sense of readiness for "what comes next."

DISCUSSION

Ms. L presented with panic attacks associated with the shock of her misprognosis. She had been a patient in numerous previous psychotherapies. Her history suggests difficulties managing affects, particularly anxiety. But it is probable that she also suffered episodes of dysthymia, though she did not indicate that she was so diagnosed or treated for this disorder. Her preexisting idealization of me impressed me as an important factor that contributed to the rapid unfolding of transference material so early in the treatment, as did the fact that she was facing the possibility of a short time of treatment with me, should she deteriorate quickly. In light of these factors, it is not surprising that the model scene (Lachmann and Lichtenberg, 1992) organizing and facilitating our understanding of the array of symptoms she was exhibiting in the first session was, in fact, part of the material produced in that session. It seemed that Ms. L's need for someone to listen and respond to her cries for help without slapping her in the face had been revived in the developing idealizing transference. In fact, the events of the first session may have created a new beginning (Ornstein, 1974) or mirroring selfobject experience for her.

The subsequent unfolding of meanings associated with this model scene led to a recognition that for Ms. L, humility meant giving up attempts to be in control of her emotional display by holding her breath. She was able to give up that control in treatment with me because I appeared willing to listen to and accept her experiences without imposing my own meanings or behavioral requirements upon her, something she had experienced with previous therapists. So, Ms. L's struggle for control could be considered as the repetitive dimension of the transference configuration, having been organized by her experiences with mother and previous therapists. In material not reported, we were also able to trace how she experienced this pattern in many other relationships, such as with husband, children, and physicians treating her illness. At the same time, her experience of my responsiveness to her feelings represented a new beginning (Ornstein, 1974).

Yet, while her breathing improved and tears began to flow, the anticipation of death remained as a source of uncertainty and helplessness for Ms. L. This danger could not be removed in treatment. Thus, the selfobject tie that unfolded as part of the treatment relationship did not serve only as a context for the transformation of the repetitive pattern of holding back emotions. In fact, it became clear that Ms. L's need for continuity and coherence could only be met by "an enduringly available protective deity" (Lichtenberg, 1991). Because Ms. L had repudiated her religious heritage as part of her controlling pattern, she not only needed to stop holding back emotions, but also needed some way of experiencing God. She was able to access her conflict with authority in the transference as the issue of time constriction emerged. Her associations to this episode allowed us to see how she had coped with such a conflict with a previous therapist, through what was initially dream ideation and later a kind of merger experience with her surround. This allowed her to feel, for three brief days, freedom from her constricting pattern of holding back emotions. In the treatment with me, she retrospectively characterized this as an experience of God. We can only speculate that this was Ms. L's personal way of reconnecting to a protective deity, that it was her hypomanic defense against a fear of reexperiencing with me the failure in responsiveness of father and previous therapists, or that it was both. Because I could not protect her from death, she needed me to help her re-create her sense of connectedness to this greater source of protection—one that she had briefly been able to experience once before when she felt endangered and out of control.

There was an interesting intersubjective resonance to the relationship between the two selfobject experiences described above. With my understanding and responsiveness, Ms. L could begin again to experience the needed presence and protection of God. With God's presence, Ms. L. could work with me in the transformation of a central life problem that had previously organized her experience—the holding back of emotion for fear of punishment and rejection, and the concomitant narcissistic wounding she felt in these moments. Hence, each dimension of experience for this patient contributed to the configuration of a context that made the other possible. This provides a wonderful illustration of a dialectical relationship between two dimensions of experience, constituting intrapsychic contents out of an intersubjective context. The contents were (1) the new potential for experiencing affects and relationships and (2) the experience of protection in the face of imminent demise.

This understanding can be compared to Meissner's (1984) conceptualization of belief in a religiously based moral order, which he states "can be seen as a creative effort to reinforce and sustain the more highly organized and integrated adaptational concerns" (p. 131). Meissner goes on to point out that "The religious concern may serve as a vital psychological force that supports the individual in his attempts at self-definition and realization" (p. 133). This understanding is consistent with the deific selfobject function that I understood Ms. L's experience to be, as compared with the speculation I earlier identified, which is an understanding of religious experience in Freud's terms as transference repetition. Here, the understanding would be of her religious experience as a defense against a retraumatization of constriction, of punishment, rejection, or both by a male authority figure. (See Freud, 1939, pp. 134–135, for a review of his argument that religion serves a guilt-inducing or punishing function.) This explanation is problematic because it reduces the patient's experience to one meaning that completely ignores the self-organizing function being accomplished, a recognition that is encompassed both in Meissner's perspective and in my understanding of the dialectical relationship between the two selfobject experiences illustrated in this case.

SUMMARY

The treatment of a dying patient is presented as an illustration of how a selfobject tie, configured on idealizing and mirroring dimensions, functioned to facilitate a selfobject experience of a protective deity. The dialectical resonance of these two selfobject experiences sustained the effects of each, facilitating a transformation of the patient's repetitive pattern of holding back her emotional display for fear of punishment or rejection, and providing continuity to the experience of safety and security provided by the presence of God. This case illustrates how the patient would not have been able to experience either of these selfobject dimensions isolated from the context of the other, and, furthermore, how this understanding shaped the subsequent unfolding of participation in treatment by both patient and therapist.

In the treatment of dying patients, impending loss of all ties and relatedness is universal. During such a period of dying, the critical dimension of selfobject experience for the patient is the acceptance and understanding of her need to sustain herself. For Ms. L, my acceptance and understanding of how religious experience functioned to serve that need was crucial.

REFERENCES

Balint, M. (1968), *The Basic Fault*. London: Tavistock.
Basch, M. (1988), *Understanding Psychotherapy*. New York: Basic Books.
Berger, P. (1969), *Sacred Canopy*. New York: Doubleday.

Fosshage, J. (1992), The selfobject concept: A further discussion of three authors. *New Therapeutic Visions: Progress in Self Psychology, Vol. 8.* Hillsdale, NJ: The Analytic Press, pp. 229–239.

Freud, S. (1939), Moses and monotheism. *Standard Edition,* 23: 7–137. London: The Hogarth Press, 1964.

Kohut, H. (1971), *The Analysis of the Self.* New York: International Universities Press.

——— (1984), *How Does Analysis Cure?* ed. A. Goldberg & P. Stepansky. Chicago, IL: University of Chicago Press.

Lachmann, F. & Lichtenberg, J. (1992), Model scenes: Implications for psychoanalytic treatment. *J. Amer. Psychoanal. Assn.,* 40:117–137.

Leming, M. R. (1979–1980), Religion and death: A test of Homan's thesis. *Omega,* 10:347–364.

Lichtenberg, J. (1989), *Psychoanalysis and Motivation.* Hillsdale, NJ: The Analytic Press.

——— (1991), What is a selfobject? *Psychoanal. Dial.,* 1:455–479.

Malinowski, B. (1965), The role of magic and religion. In: *Reader in Comparative Religion,* ed. W. A. Lessa & E. Z. Vogt. New York: Harper & Row, pp. 83–88.

Meissner, W. W. (1984), *Psychoanalysis and Religious Experience.* New Haven, CT: Yale University Press.

O'Dea, T. (1966), *The Sociology of Religion.* Englewood Cliffs, NJ: Prentice-Hall.

Ornstein, A. (1974), The dread to repeat and the new beginning: A contribution to the treatment of narcissistic personality disorders. *The Annual of Psychoanalysis,* 2:231–248. New York: International Universities Press.

Stern, D. (1985), *The Interpersonal World of the Infant.* New York: Basic Books.

Winnicott, D. W. (1958), The capacity to be alone. In: *The Maturational Processes and the Facilitating Environment.* New York: Basic Books, 1975, pp. 29–36.

— 4 —

Formulation, Psychic Space, and Time

New Dimensions in Psychoanalysis and Jewish Spirituality

DANIEL J. ROTHENBERG

For many years, the dialogue between religion and psychoanalysis has been both frozen and polarized. The interaction reached a point of hostile stasis not merely because of Freud's dismissive treatment of religion as "illusion" (1927) nor because of his depiction of *homo religiosis* as essentially irrational, weak, and dependent (1907). Rather the schism and subsequent estrangement emanated from the very conceptual structure of psychoanalysis, then founded upon a metapsychology that enshrined drives, causality, and determinism as the exclusive motivational underpinnings of an emerging science of the mind.[1]

Notions of individual choice and will, so central to most Western religious philosophies, were viewed as little more than artifacts of a regressive need to view man as other than drive dominated. The psyche itself was seen as unitary and self-contained, rather than shaped in an interpersonal field (Sullivan, 1953) or as unfolding in a relational matrix (Mitchell, 1988). Religions, even those that value the empirical and the rational but also address the inchoate and the ineffable, were nevertheless anathema

[1]I would like to acknowledge a number of individuals who gave generously of their time and ideas during the preparation of this chapter; first among them are the editors of this volume, Charles Spezzano, Ph.D. and Gerald J. Gargiulo, M.A. Edgar Levenson, M.D. read the text carefully and offered a number of important insights that guided me toward the completion of this paper. Philip Bromberg, Ph.D. provided particularly cogent and thorough comments regarding the text, in addition to the ongoing mentorship and friendship that have been an inestimable source of strength and joy over the years. Stephen A. Mitchell, Ph.D. has my profound gratitude for the intellectual inspiration and deep personal friendship he has extended to me. Finally, I wish to acknowledge Ms. Judith Drayton's fine technical and editorial assistance at all stages of this work. This paper is dedicated to Kiki Hollander Rothenberg for her patience, substantive insights, and ongoing support. Without her constant interest and care this paper could not have been completed.

to a psychoanalysis that sought to capture and cure everything with reason, the veridically interpretive, the language based, leaving as little as possible "unformulated" (Stern, 1983). Communal or group aspects of religious experience, seen in spiritual terms as vitally important and, at moments, transforming (Soloveitchik, 1973), were eschewed in the then new psychoanalytic context as both atavistic and authoritarian (Freud, 1921; Fromm, 1950) and as obscuring the essential primacy of the lone, empowered psyche.

Recently, psychoanalysis has moved to reconsider the hydraulics of the drive model (Stolorow and Lachman, 1980; Mitchell, 1988; Greenberg, 1991) and, in some circles, the monolithic implications of the "one-person psychoanalysis." In their place, more complex and interactive theoretical models have been developed, and with them, notions of multiple narratives (Schafer, 1976, 1983; Spence, 1982) and multiple self states (Mitchell, 1993; Bromberg, 1993) have been introduced. In this new context, the self is conceived of as neither spatially situated nor temporally fixed at some endpoint of stratified, archaeologically accrued development. Experiential space, too, has been extended beyond the exclusively intrapsychic, beyond a mechanically construed two-person schema, and even beyond formulations that encompass "intermediate" or transitional space (Winnicott, 1971; Bollas, 1992). In their place, in the spirit of Loewald's (1980) "atonement structures," conceptualizations are proposed that set aside bifurcated notions of inside and outside, fantasy and reality, conscious and unconscious, past, present, and future and that consider experience in terms of multiple self states (Bromberg, 1993; Mitchell, 1993).

These theoretical and clinical developments do not represent a sea change in psychoanalysis alone. They also hold the potential to redefine the bases of its relationship with other world views, including religious ones. It is tempting at this point to become expansive and to sketch the terms of rapprochement between religion-spirituality and psychoanalysis in general. Instead, however, it seems both more accurate and more measured to speak of possible new *points of contact* and, at this juncture as well, to narrow the focus of discussion that pertains to religion and to speak of one particular manifestation of it with which I am most familiar: Judaism.

It is my hope that in refocusing the discussion, the potential for parallels with other expressions of spirituality will not be forfeited. My purpose here is to be more rooted, in order to engender authenticity and avoid the kinds of elisions and overgeneralizations that often vitiate writings of this kind. Further, while an attempt will be made to cite a number of primary Jewish sources—contemporary, medieval, and ancient—I recognize as well that this is not the place for detailed and extended exegeses. The aim is to introduce a framework within which the several "points of contact" addressed here can be explored and to clarify the ways in which they diverge, as well as the ways in which understanding of one may deepen appreciation of the other.

I. REASON, FORMULATION, AND LANGUAGE

It is useful to begin this exploration of the interplay of religion and psychoanalysis with the area of rationality. This aspect of experience encompasses the logical and the realm of secondary process, as well as that of language and formulation. To begin here is seemingly to begin at the site of the greatest polemics between Jewish spirituality and psychoanalysis. So much of the classical and postclassical negation of religion has to do with its supposed incompatibility with the scientific, the objective, and the logical. And paradoxically, from yet another direction, Judaism has often been seen as hyperrational, as overly concerned with "Talmudic" detail, as given to obsessionalism and experiential constraint.

Like most polemics, the results have led more to caricature than to clarification. Some of the claims of "irrationality" seem ironic in light of the fact that major currents of Jewish religious thought stress "knowledge" of G–d and maximization of man's capacity to articulate, grasp and cognitively organize his relationship with the divine. In this regard, the Maimonidean tradition in particular places "knowledge" of G–d at the center of its axiology.[2] From another angle, the Jewish mystical-kabbalistic tradition, or even its more mainstream emphasis upon "*Chukim*" (superrational commandments), provides ample reason to question attributions of experiential narrowness to Judaism.[3] The picture is undoubtedly a more complex one than that captured by polemics alone.

Stating these points clearly, however, in many respects does more to obscure than it does to elucidate. It reinforces a dichotomy that resides in polemics but in no way inheres within Judaism itself. It is, instead, far more meaningful to speak about an *interpenetration* of the rational and the superrational within Judaism. Loewald's (1978) terms, articulated in more general comments about spirituality, may perhaps be applied to a Jewish ethic that promulgates an interplay of primary and secondary process as "a mutual appropriation of conscious and unconscious modes of thinking" (p. 77).

---

[2]See, e.g., Maimonides' Code of Law (*Yad Ha'Chazakah*), Fundamentals of Torah (*Yesodei Ha'Torah*) 1:1. See also his *Guide to the Perplexed*.

[3]See the medieval writings of Yehuda Halevi, *The Kuzari*; those of Saadia Gaon, *Emunot V'Deot*, and more contemporarily, works of S. R. Hirsch, such as *Horeb*.

To bring religious experience into this context is not to be dismissive of its potential for defensive, or even pathological, use (Leuba, 1896; James, 1902; Allison, 1968; Cavenar and Spaulding, 1977; Loewald, 1978; Rothenberg, 1986). What it does do is set aside the kinds of dichotomous categorizations whose reductionism evinces a blindness to the potential for spirituality to be both mature and experientially encompassing (Allport, 1950; Elkind, 1970; Spero, 1980; Ulman, 1982; Rothenberg, 1986; Loewald, 1980, 1988). This view of religious experience is very much in keeping with some voices within both the classical and relational schools of psychoanalysis. Apart from Loewald's forceful reframing of rationality, writers like Bromberg (1993) and Mitchell (1993) call into question the clinical usefulness of stratified concepts of the mind, not only those which separate primary from secondary process, but also those which impose temporal separations of past, present, and future upon individual experience. In addition, they cast doubt upon those who promulgate notions of self that are monolithic and linear, instead of viewing self in terms of subnarratives, each requiring attention on its own terms. To take this view is to accept linearity as an important, perhaps often compelling approach to organizing psychological data. At the same time, it is to recognize that this is not the *only* approach; perspectives that are dialectical, or alternatively, that emphasize simultaneity, the "transtemporal" (Loewald, 1980), or the interplay of co-creating systems may, at times, shed more light upon psychic reality.

No less a Jewish religious figure than Joseph B. Soloveitchik, writing as he did out of a post-Maimonidean-Aristotelian tradition, was deeply committed to rationality within Jewish law and lore.[4] Quintessentially, however, Soloveitchik did not view religion as recognizing or engendering a separation between that which we call the "rational" and the "superrational." In fact, for him, the process of what he calls "objectifi-

---

[4]Although the scope of this paper attempts to encompass more than the views advanced by Loewald and Soloveitchik, the two writers do emerge here, seemingly often in intense "conversation," highlighting ideas that lie at the core of this chapter. Clearly, the lives and ideational thrust of these two individuals are quite disparate, yet the complementarity or convergence of their perspectives is, at points, striking—all the more so since, to my knowledge, they neither knew each other nor one another's works.

Because Soloveitchik is likely to be unknown to most psychoanalytic readers, a brief orienting comment seems in order here. Joseph B. Soloveitchik (1903–1993) was this century's preeminent rabbinic-philosophical authority within what is known as Modern Orthodox Judaism. The breadth of his knowledge spanned Talmudic and rabbinic literature, as well as the substance of general and Jewish philosophy. Although he was a member of a distinguished rabbinic family, he pursued training in the secular academic world and completed a doctorate in philosophy at the University of Berlin in the early 1930s. From there, Soloveitchik continued on a course, which, while moored within the Orthodox Jewish tradition, was fiercely independent and richly innovative.

cation," which takes place through the establishment of norms within "*halacha*" (Jewish Law), perhaps paradoxically seizes the subjective flow converting it into fixed principles and universal norms (Soloveitchik, 1983, 1985). Thus, subjectivity is momentarily set aside in favor of access to "objective" behavioral norms defined by *halacha*. Nevertheless, he insists that what he calls "re-construction" (i.e., post hoc relinking with individual subjectivity) is not merely allowed. It constitutes, instead, a religious duty to formulate personally meaningful connections to religious acts. In this regard, Soloveitchik, known as "The Rov," retains an axiology, that is, a hierarchy of values that enables the individual to connect up with the intrinsic power of a given *mitzvah* or commandment. He then creates a conceptual bridge that demands, or at least enables, the religious devotee to erect rational or subjectively meaningful links to it.

Soloveitchik's stance in this regard emanates from a view that recognizes the crucial role of language and formulation, even as it confronts their inherently limiting, and at times experientially hollowing, impact. He contends that while language and rationality may expand individual understanding, it may, at times, attenuate and dilute experience. For "The Rov" then, *halacha*'s autonomy must be maintained, not merely for the preservation of the inchoate and the ineffable, but more importantly, in order to maintain the experiential link between selfhood and the divine. This link places G–d "outside" man, "inside" him or her, and neither at one and the same time.

Donnell Stern (1983) came to a similar conclusion regarding the potentially reductive impact of language. While mindful of Sullivan's (1953, 1956) admonition that much of what is called "unformulated" is merely the end product of the simple defense of "not thinking about it," Stern (1983) notes that all formulations derive initially from the unformulated. More powerfully, he asserts that while language is "constitutive of experience" (Arieti, 1976), it also "seduces us into easily accepting a mythology

---

Soloveitchik's primary self-identification was as a "*mechanech*," a teacher of tens of thousands of students and rabbis throughout North America. His public lectures during the 1950s, 1960s, and 1970s drew thousands of people from across the spectrum of backgrounds and political orientations. The bulk of his efforts, however, focused upon the teaching of Talmud and philosophy at Yeshiva University in New York City and to the Jewish community in Boston, Massachusetts.

An intellectual architect and exemplar of an approach to Jewish learning and life known as "*Torah U'Mada*," Soloveitchik espoused a "synthesis" of Jewish and general knowledge. In this context, he ascribed axiological primacy to the former, emphasizing the centrality of rigorous commitment to *halacha* (Jewish law), even as he insisted upon openness of inquiry in areas of science and the humanities. (For more extensive treatment of Soloveitchik's life and work see Lichtenstein, 1963, pp. 281–297; Goldberg, 1989; Rakeffet-Rothkoff, 1996.)

of a world around us based circularly on the properties of language itself. In these ways language and culture set limits beyond which even creative disorder cannot survive" (Stern, 1983).

As a counter to the narrowing seduction of language, Soloveitchik's view of Judaism preserves the experiential "space" necessary to enable fluid movement between "objective" *halacha* and inner or subjective elaboration upon it. In this respect, his view echoes that of Maimonides in *Guide to the Perplexed*, in which the author exhaustively infuses rationality into every aspect of Jewish experience, even as he concludes that, at moments, only *silent contemplation*, devoid of the intrusion of language, provides the most personally vital access to spiritual experience.

Such a view is echoed by Loewald in his landmark essay "Primary process, secondary process and language." There he argues against both the bifurcation of primary and secondary process experience and the casting of the realm of the spirit as "illusion" (see also Loewald, 1978, 1980). Like Soloveitchik, Loewald views such conceptual dichotomizing as depleting: sapping the very passion, vitality, and felt-authenticity from experience. Instead, Loewald calls for a "reconciliation" with "the primordial oneness" and a relinking of "thing" and "word" presentation—all in a context that retains a psychological capacity to differentiate and hold these aspects of experience as separate. Loewald (1978) concludes:

> In the course of the development of civilization . . . the primordial power and concrete impact of language became attenuated and relatively neutralized. In most creative forms of language, such as in its authentic religious use, in oratory, poetry and dramatic art, the primordial power of language comes again to the fore . . . there is an *interweaving* of primary and secondary process by virtue of which language functions as a *transitional mode encompassing both.* . . . It ties human beings and self and the object world, and it binds abstract thought with the bodily concreteness and power of life. In the word primary and secondary processes are reconciled [p. 204].

II. PSYCHIC SPACE

It should be clear from the previous section that both Judaism and psychoanalysis are interested in "the word": spoken, written, and thought. They are, however, perhaps equally interested in what Levenson (1994), citing the kabbalistic tradition, refers to as "the spaces between the words and the letters." For Levenson, these spaces beckon for inquiry into the details, the unattended, the unspoken and therefore mystified. For the spiritually minded, however, inquiry into these spaces provides heightened awareness and felt nearness to that which is at times unspoken and, at other moments, that which may be fundamentally unspeakable because it touches upon G–d's ontological otherness. This means that questing curiosity regarding *narrative* space may have as its partner searching inquiry into interpersonal and ontological space. In psychoanalysis such inquiry often occurs in a wordless place, shared perhaps in looks exchanged between analysand and analyst or, more likely, in the uncertain twilight *pregnance* of silence. It emerges, as well, in the silent gaze of the individual in search of G–d.

Some of the most difficult problems for analysts working and writing in the postclassical era derive from Freud's conceptualization of psychic space. For him, all psychological events occur "inside" the individual— there alone not only encompassing but exhausting the dimensions of experience. Reactions against purely intrapsychic formulations introduced "objects," the interpersonal field, and the relational matrix in order to broaden the analytic account of the human being's world. Winnicott (1971, 1975), grappling with, perhaps rebelling against, the tyrannizing constraints implicit even within self-other schemas, introduced the concepts of intermediate and "transitional space," which are meant to give recognition to what might be called the twin realms of "neitherness" and "bothness." Psychologically, this refers to the domain of experience that draws upon both self and other, but is neither occupied nor fully encompassed by either.

Religionists may have been appropriately encouraged by this expansion of a bed whose previously Procrustean proportions gave them no place to rest, let alone to dream. While the conceptual expansion that emanates from ideas such as transitional space may be of significant value, Spezzano (1994), among others, rightfully gives a withering review to proliferating attempts to find surcease for all theoretical problems— religious and psychoanalytic—in the boundlessly sheltering expanse of transitional space. Several problems *do*, of course, remain. One issue seems particularly salient in the context of the current discussion regarding psychological space: the problem of *transference* embedded in Freud's position, and even within the views of some proponents of the object-relations viewpoint, in which religious sentiments are reduced to vestigial remnants of "G–d the Father" (Freud, 1927) or G–d the enhanced, creatively elaborated Teddy Bear (Rizzuto, 1979). Neither the expansion of psychic space beyond the intrapsychic nor its relocation into transitional space does away with the trivializing, reductionistic, and anthropomorphizing impact of these formulations.

This problem is trenchantly articulated by Jones (1991) in his critique of Anna Maria Rizzuto's ground-breaking work, *The Birth of the Living God* (1979). He states that Rizzuto focuses too much on the transitional *object* and not enough on transitional *experience*. Thus she often makes God sound like a supernatural version of the teddy bear and then speculates on why the deity is not discarded like other such "objects" (pp. 45–46).

In a novel, and at turns, audacious, attempt to deal with the issues raised by both the Freudian and object-relations views, Ernest Becker (1973) suggests that transference, rather than being the problem with religion, may instead be among its greater contributions. Writing as he did at the intersection of religious and Rankian psychoanalytic thinking, Becker showed religious transference to be among the most mature available to the individual, potentially least embedded in the psychologically and religiously limiting contexts of the intrapsychic (G–d as illusion), interpersonal (G–d as Father), and the object-relational (G–d as Teddy Bear). In the process, he also addressed the philosophical problems of corporealization, anthropomorphism, and anthropopathism, which have troubled theologians for a long time. Becker states:

> We have to look for the answer to the problem of freedom where it is most absent: in the transference, the fatal and crushing enslaver of men. The transference fetishizes mystery, terror and power; it holds the self bound in its grip. Religion answers directly to the problem of transference by expanding awe and terror to the cosmos where they belong. . . . The personality can truly begin to emerge in religion because G–d, *as an abstraction*, does not oppose the individual as others do, but instead provides the individual with all the powers necessary for independent self-justification. . . . If G–d is hidden and intangible, all the better: that allows man to expand and develop by himself" [p. 202; italics added].

Whereas the limitations of transitional objects and experience have been amply demonstrated here, this does not negate their valuable contribution to the broadening of the concept of psychic space. Clearly, notions of transitionality provide an important bridgepoint or link between religious and psychoanalytic thinking, allowing what are seen as more experientially encompassing and ideologically acceptable ways of talking about the inchoate and the ineffable. Such formulations also provide language that is more tangible and experience-near, albeit personified, in contrast to Becker's nonanthropomorphizing but stark vision of a transference-free sphere. For this reason, it is worthwhile to elaborate briefly upon the concept of transitional space here, if only to mark its important role in the expanding dialogue between psychoanalysis and religion.

Ogden (1990), invoking Winnicott's work, considers this "third space" as the site of "playing and creativity, transitional phenomena, psychotherapy and 'cultural experience'. . . . Potential space is an intermediate area of experiencing that which lies between the inner world and the actual external reality" (p. 204). Whereas Winnicott freely makes the connection between creative access to transitional, including religious, experience, analysts such as Bollas (1992) do so with some trepidation, fearing that extension of psychoanalytic discourse to the realm of the spirit could lead to "a kind of mystification . . . [and] an indifference to investigation of thought itself." In this regard, he poses a cogent question, that is, "whether it is possible for spirit to enter into the language of psychoanalysis without falling in love with its suggestive power? Or will it herald the movement of neo-surrealistic romanticism in which the ungraspable, the seeming essence of experience, displaces the effort to dissect, to deconstruct, indeed to de-spiritualize?"

Apparently Bollas is haunted by the very sense of dichotomy, that is embedded in all of the responses to the problem of transference presented thus far. He attempts to resolve this problem by finding a "middle ground, a midworld in which the vector of idiom signified by 'spirit' is allowed its contribution to the mulling over of self experience as is the vector of objectivity signified, say, by the word 'empirical' or 'observational' " (Bollas, 1992, p. 64) In advancing this view, Bollas cobbles out a sector of experience, much like intermediate or transitional space, in which empirical and rational processes can interact freely with spiritual ones, without compromising either. By taking this position, he finds an expanded, although still bifurcated, area of experience, one that represents a site of more encompassing possibility, even as it emerges as one fraught with tension.

Bollas's work retains the very sense of dichotomy, which in the view of many psychoanalytic thinkers is both inevitable and unresolvable, even for those who subscribe to transitional concepts. For them the split between inside and outside, conscious and unconscious, and in metaphysical terms, "*holy*" and "*profane*," is not truly and decisively resolved by its relocation to a "place" defined as intermediate. It is not apparent whether Bollas is ambivalent about the interplay among what he refers to as "spirit," "idiom," and "intermediate space," or whether he sees the tension among them as both necessary and inevitable. Clearly, however, many theorists retain this split and the accompanying sense of dichotomy as a principaled stance, integral to their worldview.

The previous reference to the distinction between "holy" and "profane" might seem surprising, if not jarringly out of place, even within this fairly varied discussion regarding psychic space. Nevertheless, the realm of *Kedusha* (roughly translated from Hebrew as "holiness," "sanctity," or perhaps "separation") is suggestive of a nexus of transitional experience par excellence: ineffable or "unformulated" (Stern, 1983) in its essence; simultaneously potentiating interplay, dissolution, or interpenetration of spatial and temporal boundaries. Here, demarcations of self and other (including G–d The Other), inside and outside, wax and wane, even as separations of past, present, and future may be telescoped, may collapse altogether, or may be stridently maintained.[5]

In fact, the discourse regarding "internal" and external" contents of experience with respect to *kedusha* did not escape the attention of Jewish philosophers and exegetes—contemporary and medieval. One reading of the views of Rabbi Solomon ben Isaac, known by the acronym "RASHI" (ca. 1040–1105), for example, highlights the latter's insistence upon just such a "dichotomy-as-necessity" schema. In his biblical commentary, RASHI equates access to holiness, as requiring its peremptory separation from that which is profane. By contrast, Rabbi Moses Ben Nachman (ca. 1240), known as Nachmanides or "RAMBAN," dissents, insisting upon the fluid interplay between these two metaphysical realms.[6] In contemporary times, Soloveitchik (1985) comes down powerfully in the latter philosophical camp, insisting upon rootedness in *halachic* observance even as he rejects demarcations between inside and outside, holy and profane. In this regard, he states: "The religious *telos* finds its full realization in the passionate religious life, permeated with enthusiasm and rapture. . . . The dualism that is so prevalent in other religions, namely, the division of a profane and sacred domain, is transcended. The entire universe is con-

---

[5]These ideas are presented in a speculative or suggestive mood, meant to evince discussion and exploration rather than to generate "answers." To frame them otherwise would be presumptuous, or worse, boring. It would also carry the unwitting residual impact of being both reductive and experientially depleting. Soloveitchik (1983), among others, raises this very concern. Nevertheless, in his view, once the ineffable quality of *kedusha* (or other superrational elements of Jewish spirituality) is established as *primary*, there is meaning, perhaps overarching value, in human attempts to develop subjectively validating connections to experiences that in the end are not fully encompassed by formulation and language.

Notions of transitionality, applied in this limited way, seem particularly apt and potentially transforming. In this extended context, *kedusha* emerges as a state or experience that is neither truncated nor eviscerated by the imposed limitations of spatial or temporal metaphor (see Loewald, 1980; Mitchell, 1993). Such metaphor may instead give way to notions of dialectics, simultaneity, or interpenetration, concepts whose applications are developed more fully later in this chapter.

Shabbat, the Jewish Sabbath, for example, may be framed, but, again, not fully captured or expressed in terms of its transitional qualities. It emerges via the designation of a weekly 25-hour period involving temporary disruption, renunciation of/withdrawal from specific materially based actions/experiences. *Shabbat*, in this regard, is seen as enabling a *different* kind of creativity and spirituality, one that is less available while grappling with the pressures and constraints of daily life. It affords a prescribed occasion to renew dimensions of personal, interpersonal, and spiritual experience which may otherwise be usurped by the pace, technological content, and spiritual *hubris* of life. For some, at the most mundane level, it provides surcease in the face of the overreaching access of "everyone" to one's personal time and space. Temporally, it evokes the past beginnings of life and the origins of the world, while providing experiential nearness to a sense of timelessness or perhaps the eternal (see Loewald, 1980, pp. 138–47; Grunfeld, 1954).

[6]See commentaries of RASHI and RAMBAN to Leviticus 19:1.

verted into one monistic realm, the domain of G–d. Street and home, the synagogue and the shop merge" (1985).

Here, the problems of *transference* and of *space* with which we began first fade, then dissolve. Boundedness is seen as giving way to interpenetration because, in The Rov's words, G–d is "not transcendent, mysterious and unapproachable but our *immediate* Companion." The individual need not meet G–d as the Father, although he might;[7] she/he certainly need not encounter Him in some third or intermediate space because, Soloveitchik (1985) continues:

> We live *in* G–d and experience Him in his *full immediacy*. As the settler experiences his home, as man intuits space, so does [he] intuit G–d. . . . He does not repose *in* me; He is not just one phase of my world perspective; He envelopes all. If the universe is unthinkable without a space frame (and this indeed is the crux of Kant's *a priori* concept) so much more so is the Jewish World incomprehensible without an all-embracing G–d [p. 20ff].

In a similar vein, for Loewald (1988) just such a notion lies at the core of his dismissal of dichotomized accounts of psychological space. Although expressing respect for object-relational formulations of transitionality, he seems to view them as unnecessary and, perhaps, one step removed from experience. Instead, his view, like Soloveitchik's, underlines the immediate, that is, the *not* mediated, the instantaneous and permeable encounter between self, G–d, and other. By contrast, Sorenson (1994) views access to transitional experience as preceded by what he calls "hesitation"; this is similar to the view of RASHI, for whom it is adumbrated by withdrawal, in hebrew, "*prisha*." Yet, according to Loewald, Soloveitchik, and perhaps recently, Ogden (1994), the experience is immediate—not even as divisible a process as that described by a dialectic. It is instead one that is marked by the unmediated interpenetration of "inside" and "outside."

Speculatively, it is possible that the cadre of theorists and Jewish religious writers who insist upon notions of *inter*mediacy (as opposed to *im*mediacy) and transitionality may do so in order to preserve a modicum of *boundedness* within human experience. Thus, while religion, creative endeavors, and the like may be seen as potentially productive of transitional experience, they also may require this somewhat more demarcated schema as a crucial bulwark against excessive concretization and anthropomorphism

---

[7]The Jewish religion does not, in my view, require eradication or sanitizing of such transferences, recognizing instead that people might draw upon representations of mother, father, or others in their most intense moments and relationships. Nevertheless, the highest, most mature forms of relating to G–d appear to be ones that prevail on an intrinsic or "*l'shma*" level (see Maimondes, *Laws of Repentance*, Chap. 10, Yeshiva University, New York, NY).

on the one hand, and on the other, as a stopgap against excessive mystification and reliance upon the ineffable and the unformulated. Thus Bollas and others may have found it important to locate the transitional in a "midworld" whereas Loewald, Soloveitchik, and perhaps writers like Mitchell and Bromberg, would feel constrained even by such notions of space, preferring instead to subscribe to concepts of interpenetration and Loewald's "appropriation"—beyond sublimation—concepts that transcend the language of the temporally and spatially bound. Regardless, each of these approaches provides an expanded framework within which previously dichotomized accounts of space may be mitigated and, perhaps, set aside.

III. HISTORY, REMEMBRANCE, AND TIME

Psychoanalysis first enshrined history, then recoiled from it, seeking to shuffle off its constraints in favor of the here and now (Sullivan, 1953), a focus on the transference (Racker, 1968), or on the dyadic interaction (Gill, 1982; Hoffman, 1983). For other writers, the effect, if not the intent, was to relativize history, installing narrative coherence where veridicality was once the prevailing value (Spence, 1982). Often these changes were driven by ideological or cultural shifts within the *Zeitgeist*, mandated by the ascendancy of operationalism or pragmatism or, later, by experiential immediacy, all of them seen as preferable to more illusive encounters with history. These changes were also prompted by analysts' experience doing work that, at points, thrust history to center stage, for instance, when clinicians encountered evidence of "seduction" or trauma, and at other points relegated history to fringe relevance. In this latter regard it was observed, for example, that a focus upon history could be clinically "off," that is, it could miss the point or deflect attention away from more salient analytic data (Levenson, 1972, 1983).

Among psychoanalysts of the interpersonal and relational schools, the problems emanating from preoccupation with the past have been voluminously written about. In this spirit, Mitchell (1993) has cogently noted the limitations introduced by what he describes as the "developmental tilt" within psychoanalysis. In a clinical context, Bromberg (1993), among others, has written elegantly about dissociative experience as a "lifelong cathexis of the archaic and an unconscious romance with a dead past which is far preferable to the felt banality of the 'real' present." Other writers across the psychoanalytic spectrum (Levenson, 1972, 1983; Gill, 1982; Jacobs, 1991) have recognized the potential for history to be used to deflect patients' experience, shield the analyst, and reinforce defensiveness between both participants within the psychoanalytic dyad.

Religion, at least that of the Judaic variety, brings similar concerns about history and time to the table—albeit in enhanced form and perhaps from a different direction. Judaism, too, is troubled by an overemphasis upon history. From one perspective, the Jewish tradition eschews concepts that relativize history as well as those that rob individual experience of its sense of continuity and rootedness. Yet, at the same time, it also rejects approaches that make for an unwanted "tilt" in a direction which, by implication, minimizes man's capacity to effect change.

The Jewish concept of *Teshuva*—literally "return," more broadly repentance or atonement—provides an apt illustration not merely of the centrality of change within the Jewish motif, but also of its very conception of time. In this context, Soloveitchik (1985) asserts that the Jewish concept of time, far from being linear, is actually *reversible*; that is, past may become present, present may become past, future may recast both past and present. He states:

> Yet the religious time awareness is so paradoxical as to register both becoming and reversibility. As to "becoming" the idea of creation introduces it metaphysically and the religious norm with its associated postulate of freedom sponsors it ethically. Nevertheless, the *reversibility* of time and the causal order is fundamental in religion. Otherwise the principle of conversion would be sheer nonsense. The act of reconstructing past psychic life, of changing the arrow of time from forward to retrospective direction, is the main premise of penitence. Sin and remorse frequently explore not only traces of a bygone past retained in memory, but a living past which is consummated in . . . emergent time consciousness [p. 49ff].

Other important elements of Judaism, particularly communal ones, can find no place within truncated conceptions of time that emphasize linearity. The Passover *Seder* and marking of the Jewish exodus from Egypt three thousand years ago, for example, take on a sense of *current* actualization beyond mere recollection when seen in the context of the Talmudic dictum that states "Humankind is commanded (in each generation) to view itself as having gone out of Egypt" (Babylonian Talmud, Tractate Pesachim). Again, Soloveitchik sees these not as mere reminiscences or reenactments, but as literal and actual implementations of historic experience in contemporary times. In another, perhaps more arcane example, the Jewish *mitzvah*, or commandment, to both remember and simultaneously banish from memory the actions of the now-extinct nation of Amalek makes no sense in the context of a conception of time or memory that follows a progression from past to present to future. For how is it possible to expunge Amalek from memory, even as one is bidden to recall and reinvoke its heinous actions? This too, by implication, points to embedded concepts of time and of memorial activity that are fluid, permeable, and reversible. It also reflects a concept of remembrance that encompasses the complex, the paradoxical, and the contradictory, rather than placing it out of bounds on the putative basis of the force of linear logic.

Perhaps more poignantly, cutting across communal and individual experience, notions of timelessness, which according to some elements of the tradition are central to the Jewish experience of the Sabbath, are all but meaningless when the language of causality is imposed upon them. In fact, the Jewish approach to time itself treats it as animated, capable of acquiring an imprint, that is, of becoming "holy" or "profane." Such an approach makes no sense whatever within a conceptual framework that treats time as the neutral and inert accretion of moments of the past.

It appears, then, that the Jewish tradition attempts to preserve history against its being recast in relativistic or experientially remote terms, even as it attempts to guard against a preoccupation with the past, a romance with the archaic, which can usurp the primacy of present action and future initiative. Perhaps most interestingly, Judaism seems to be about instilling conceptions of time that are both animated and permeable: at turns bidirectional, at times "linked" (Bion, 1993), at times dissolving entirely the very boundaries that separate past from present from future.

A close look at some of the writers on the contemporary psychoanalytic scene reveals surprising common ground with elements of the Jewish tradition presented here. Ogden's writings on the depressive, or what he calls "historical position," represent a good fit with the writings of Maimonides regarding the penitential process. In this regard Ogden (1990) writes:

> Mourning rather than depression is the psychological process by which previous object ties are relinquished. Historical memory is itself a form of mourning in that it acknowledges the fact that the past events no longer exist in their earlier forms. As Freud points out . . . transference is an act of repeating instead of memory. . . . Analysis of transference is in part a process of transforming a repetition into a memory and is in this sense an attempt at expanding the historicity of the depressive position. . . . The process of transforming enactment into remembering and the sustaining of those feelings over time is at the heart of what Freud meant by "*Wo es war, soll ich Werden*"—where *it* was there shall *I* be [p. 82; italics added].

Contrast this with writings in the Maimonidean Code of Law known as *Yad Ha' Chazakah* and their elaboration much later by Soloveitchik. Maimonides requires the individual engaged in repentance to revisit and confront the past, breaking with it to the point that his very *persona* is viewed by the individual as new. Penitential expressions that lack this component are viewed as incomplete, because they are seen as leading inevitably to repetition. Yet at the same time, the Jewish tradition decries a disowning of the past and insists that, in the name of continuity, an experiential link with it be maintained.

Soloveitchik (1983), expanding upon the Maimonidean rendition of the penitential process, characterizes the individual relationship with his past and with remembrance as follows: "*Halachic* man does not indulge in weeping and despair, does not lacerate his flesh or flail at himself. . . . He does not regret an irretrievably lost past but a past still in existence, one that stretches into and interpenetrates with the present and future" (pp. 113–114). As in transference, the past in penitential experience is not merely revisited. It is reanimated in a manner that provides it with the immediacy to enable a mutative process, that is, a decision to change. Only such a confrontation with memory can give way to its decisive relegation to the past. For Soloveitchik, this does not mean that from that point onward we arrive at a notion of the penitent *cum* amnesiac. To the contrary, true repentance, according to him, involves a capability to recall, even fondly invoke, the past, drawing upon its value but not being impelled to repeat it (Soloveitchik, 1974). Here again, Ogden's (1990) language dovetails with this line of thought:

> The form of transference possible in the depressive position allows one to perpetuate, have again, important aspects of what was experienced with people who one has lost through absence, death . . . psychological change. . . . The transference experience makes possible the pain of loss. . . . One may have to give up people whom one has lost but one does not have to give up entirely one's experience with those people" [p. 90].

From this standpoint, change may transpire in a manner that achieves renunciation even as it maintains the individual's sense of inner cohesion and continuity. For such an individual, "history is not re-written as it is in splitting, rather history is buried and thereby preserved" (Ogden, 1992, p. 92).

Psychoanalytic theorizing that emphasizes temporal rather than spatial metaphor permits conceptual and clinical movement in a direction that highlights linkage of self states, rather than stratified or bifurcated notions of self. Such movement also engenders a view of self that evinces a sense of timelessness—one that links past, present, and future versions of self— instead of viewing it as the mere end product of accrued experience. In Mitchell's (1993) view, "selves change and are transformed continually over time; no version of self is fully present at any instant and a single life is composed of many selves" (p. 102).[8]

---

[8]Elsewhere, Mitchell vividly evokes the felt timelessness of psychoanalysis (see Mitchell, 1993, p. 115ff).

In this same context Bromberg (1992) provides the following elaboration:

Further, I suggest that the way analysts are conceptualizing reality in terms of past and present is also changing. The clinical focus is not as much on discovery of past roots of current problems, as though past and present experience are discretely stratified in the memory bank of a unitary "self," but on exploring the way in which self states comprising a patient's personal identity are linked—linked to each other, to the external world and to the past, present and future. [Echoing the words of Loewald, Bromberg concludes:] "We encounter time in psychic life primarily as a linking activity ... past, present and future woven into a nexus ... the individual not only has a history which an observer may unravel but he *is* history and *makes* history by virtue of memorial activity in which past, present and future are created as mutually interacting modes of time [pp. 4–6].

History in such a context is not viewed as a distant element of a buried past. Future, for that matter, is not seen as events that have yet to "happen" or accumulate. Rather, when they become experientially linked—animated in the present—all dimensions of time are immediate, albeit with varying degrees of affective salience, vividness, and urgency.

These ideas are brought to full expression in what emerge in this essay as the conceptually parallel writings of Soloveitchik and Loewald. Clearly they do not say the same thing, and the purpose as well as the scope of elaboration of each is quite different. Nevertheless, the commonalities in their ideas about time, and about religious experience itself, take on a kind of synergy when they are read concurrently. In fact, Loewald (1978) rejected the recasting of religious experience by psychoanalysis as mere sublimation. Although he saw the concept of sublimation as an advance over other, more belittling characterizations of religious experience as "regressed," infantile, or fundamentally immature, he called the term *sublimation* "reductionistic," overly suggestive of defense; he preferred instead to speak of "appropriation of experience leading to a responsive interplay between id and ego" (p. 68). Acknowledging the potential use of religious experiences for defensive purposes, he spoke boldly of religious concepts of time and intimations of eternity as

Bringing us in touch with levels of our being, forms of experiencing and of reality that may be more deeply disturbing [and] anxiety provoking to common sense rationality of everyday life. They [religious concepts of time] go against our penchant for objectifying and distancing our experience and our world in order to make and keep it manageable and tolerable. . . . They evince another mode of reality. I am not speaking of a realm of being beyond or above this universe, of a spiritual world located elsewhere, but of a different form of reality. . . . This form is more-or-less ignored in modern Western thought, insofar as we are dominated by narrow Scientism [pp. 69–70].

In Loewald's view, then, a schism developed within psychoanalytic thinking which mirrored that of Western culture at large and led to an intellectual culture in which "forms of religious experience . . . [and] aspects of unconscious mentation . . . are [currently] more deeply repressed than 'sexuality' is today" (pp. 69–70).

In similar terms, notions of timelessness, temporal reversibility, and interaction—as opposed to concepts like regression, based upon linear succession—are at the heart of what Loewald conceives the analytic process to be about. Accordingly, he took the view that for analysis to be vital it must engage and potentiate a linkage of temporal states. Inattention to such linkage renders the analytic process iatrogenic in some fundamental way because it cuts individuals off from the vitalizing interplay of primary and secondary process, as well as from access to a full range of temporal experience. In tapping this encompassing range of experiential reality, Loewald (1978) treats religion, not as a useful "illusion," but as potentially lying at the nexus of the memorial activity that, in his view, comprises experiential wholeness. In this regard he states:

> Neither the felt version nor the verbalized version, it seem to me, should be called an illusion. If we acknowledge the undifferentiating unconscious as a genuine mode of mentation which underlies and unfolds into secondary mentation (and remains extant with it although concealed by it), then we regain a more comprehensive perspective—no doubt with its own limitations yet unknown. Such a perspective betokens a new level of consciousness, of *conscire*, on which primary and secondary modes of mentation may be *known together* [p. 65; italics added].

Soloveitchik's writings on *teshuva*—repentance—again serve to illustrate the parallels between current psychoanalytic thinking and at least one man's rendition of Jewish thought regarding temporality. Echoing, or perhaps anticipating by several decades, the conceptual schema advanced by Loewald, Soloveitchik (1983) writes:

> From this perspective we perceive the past not as "no more" nor the future as "not yet" nor the present as a "fleeting moment." Rather past, present and future merge and *blend together* [emphasis added]. . . . The past is joined to the future and both are reflected in the present. . . . The law of causality, from this perspective, also assumes new form. . . . We have here a true symbiotic, synergistic relationship. . . . The future transforms the thrust of the past. This is the nature of that causality operating in the realm of the spirit if man as a spiritual being, opts for this outlook on time, time as grounded in the realm of eternity. However, the person who prefers the simple experience of unidimensional time—time, to use the image of Kant, as a straight line—becomes subject to the law of causality operating in the physical realm [pp. 54–59; pp. 114–115].

From Soloveitchik's standpoint, only an individual who is capable of viewing himself as being at the nexus of time, rather than as its causally impelled object, is capable of repentance. Only such an individual can view himself as capable of asserting autonomous will.

Here, the writings of Soloveitchik and Loewald come full circle. Loewald's ultimate depiction of human experience involves what he calls "atonement structures," which first alienate man from the undifferentiated matrix of primal experience and then hold out an opportunity for individuation and for later mature return. For Loewald, atonement connotes potential for unification or "at-one-ment" in the same way as Soloveitchik's unhyphenated atonement presents the individual with the possibility of "return"—*Teshuva*. For the Rov, as for Loewald, such unification may follow a dialectical course. It may, as well, be the instantaneous product of an *immediate* and decisive act of will that potentiates change. Regardless, for both writers, it draws upon all aspects of man's creative faculties—conscious, unconscious, and preconscious; secondary and primary process—as well as upon the full range of that which comprises the dimensions of time in a human context.

Loewald's writings, those of Soloveitchik, and the ideas of the other writers cited here mend together what, under the press of classical metapsychology, led first to attenuation, and later to the fraying, of both psychological experience *and* what might have been the natural exchange between religion and psychoanalysis. These authors, some knowingly others implicitly, have amply demonstrated that spirituality—in this essay, Judaism—on one hand and psychoanalysis on the other, when adapted as interacting modes of inquiry and thought, may engender *linkage* where once only a sense of dichotomy prevailed. This is not to suggest that the goal of either system is or should be to obviate contradiction, conflict, paradox, or doubt. Nor should it mean the engendering of a process that, in Donnell Stern's phrasing, seeks to cast a cloak of familiarity over that which is essentially illusive or unfamiliar. To the contrary, the presence of tension and, at times, wrenching and unremitting conflict, are essential to both—perhaps most trenchantly because they are an inescapable part of human experience (Soloveitchik, 1983; Lamm, 1972). These "facts of life" notwithstanding, however, the expressions of Judaic and psychoanalytic thinking presented here emphasize (1) the interpenetration of primary and secondary process; (2) the intermediate or "transmediate" rather than the exclusively intrapsychic or interpsychic, and (3) the transtemporal rather than the linear, the successive, or even simultaneous. All comprise what is hoped will provide experiential "space" in which religion and psychoanalysis can meet. And although an "atonement"—that is, expectations of an *at-one-ment* of religion and psychoanalysis—may prove to be ultimately illusive, a mutually enriching encounter of the two now seems possible. For both patients and practitioners, and for the many analysts and analysands who are both, the need for such reconciliation, or at the very least, for an interplay possessed of intellectual and experiential integrity, is by now an urgent, long-awaited event.

REFERENCES

Allison, J. (1968), Adaptive regression and intense religious experiences. *J. Nerv. & Mental Dis.*, 145:452–463.

Allport, G. W. (1950), *The Individual and His Religion.* New York: Macmillan.

Arieti, S. (1976), *Creativity.* New York: Basic Books.

Babylonian Talmud, English trans. London: Soncino Press.

Becker, E. (1973), *The Denial of Death.* New York: Free Press.

Bion, W. R. (1993), *Second Thoughts.* Northvale, NJ: Aronson.

Bollas, C. (1992), *Being a Character.* New York: Hill & Wang.

Bromberg, P. M. (1992), Shadow and substance: A relational perspective on clinical process. *Psychoanal. Psychol.*, 10:147–168.

Cavenar, J. & Spaulding, J. (1977), Depressive disorders and religious conversion. *J. Nerv. & Mental Dis.*, 165:209–212.

Elkind, D. (1970), The origins of religion in the child. *Rev. Religious Res.*, 12:35–42.

Freud, S. (1907), Obsessive acts and religious practices. *Standard Edition*, 9:115–129. London: Hogarth Press, 1959.

——— (1921), Group psychology and the analysis of the ego. *Standard Edition*, 18:69–143. London: Hogarth Press, 1955.

——— (1927), The future of an illusion. *Standard Edition*, 21:5–56. London: Hogarth Press, 1959.

Fromm, E. (1941), *Escape From Freedom.* New York: Holt, Rinehart & Winston.

——— (1950), *Psychoanalysis and Religion.* New Haven, CT: Yale University Press.

Gill, M. (1982), *Analysis of Transference.* New York: International Universities Press.

Goldberg, H. (1989) *Between Berlin and Slobodka.* Hoboken, NJ: KTAV.

Greenberg, J. (1991), *Oedipus and Beyond.* Cambridge, MA: Harvard University Press.

——— & Mitchell, S. A. (1983), *Object Relations in Psychoanalytic Theory.* Cambridge, MA: Harvard University Press.

Grunfeld, I. (1954), *The Sabbath.* New York: Feldheim.

Halevi, Y. (1905), *The Kuzari*, trans. H. Hirschfeld. New York: Schocken, 1964.

Hirsch, S. R. (1962), *Horeb*, trans. I. Grunfeld. London: Soncino Press.

Hoffman, I. Z. (1983), The patient as interpreter of the analyst's experience. *Contemp. Psychoanal.*, 19:389–422.

Isaac, Rabbi Solomon ben (*The Pentateuch and RASHI's Commentary*), linear trans. Philadelphia: Jewish Publications Society, 1949.

Jacobs, T. (1991), *The Use of the Self.* New York: International Universities Press.

James, W. (1902), *The Varieties of Religious Experience.* New York: Macmillan, 1961.

Jones, J. W. (1991), *Contemporary Psychoanalysis and Religion.* New Haven, CT: Yale University Press.

Lamm, N. (1972), *Faith and Doubt.* New York: KTAV.

Leuba, J. (1896), *A Psychological Study of Religion.* New York: Macmillan.

Levenson, E. (1972), *The Fallacy of Understanding.* New York: Basic Books.

——— (1983), *The Ambiguity of Change*. New York: Basic Books.

——— (1994), Beyond countertransference. *Contemp. Psychoanal.*, 30:4.

Lichtenstein, A. (1963), Rabbi Joseph Soloveitchik. In: *Great Jewish Thinkers of the Twentieth Century*, ed. S. Noveck. Clinton, MA: Bnai-Brith Department of Adult Jewish Education.

Loewald, H. (1978), *Psychoanalysis and the History of the Individual*. New Haven, CT: Yale University Press.

——— (1980), *Papers on Psychoanalysis*. New Haven, CT: Yale University Press.

——— (1988), *Sublimation*. New Haven, CT: Yale University Press.

Maimonides, M. *Yad Ha'Chazakah* (Code of Jewish Law).

——— *Guide to the Perplexed* (English rendition of *Moreh Nebukim*, trans. S. Pines). Chicago: University of Chicago Press, 1963.

Mitchell, S. A. (1988), *Relational Concepts in Psychoanalysis*. Cambridge, MA: Harvard University Press.

——— (1993), *Hope and Dread in Psychoanalysis*. New York: Basic Books.

Nachman, Rabbi Moshe ben (n.d.), *RAMBAN's Commentary on the Torah*, trans. C. Chavel. New York: Shilo, 1973.

Ogden, T. (1990), *Matrix of the Mind*. Northvale, NJ: Aronson.

——— (1994), *Subjects of Analysis*. Northvale, NJ: Aronson.

Racker, H. (1968), *Transference and Countertransference*. Madison, CT: International Universities Press.

Rakeffet-Rothkoff, A. (1996), Rabbi Joseph Dov ha-levi Soloveitchik: The early years. *Tradition: A Journal of Orthodox Jewish Thought*, 30:193–209.

Rizzuto, A. (1979), *The Birth of the Living God*. Chicago: University of Chicago Press.

Rothenberg, D. J. (1986), Psychological dimensions of rapid religious change. Unpublished doctoral dissertation, Ferkauf Graduate School of Psychology, Yeshiva University.

Saadia Gaon (n.d.), *Emunot V'Deot* (The Book of Beliefs and Opinions), trans. S. Rosenblatt. New Haven, CT: Yale University Press, 1948.

Schafer, R. (1976), *A New Language for Psychoanalysis*. New Haven, CT: Yale University Press.

——— (1983), *The Analytic Attitude*. New York: Basic Books.

Soloveitchik, J. B. (1944), *The Halachic Mind*. New York: Seth Press, 1986.

——— (1972), The unique experience of Judaism. In: *Shiurei Harav*, ed. J. Epstein. New York: Yeshiva University (Hamevaser).

——— (1973), The covenantal community. In: *Shiurei Harav*, ed. J. Epstein. New York: Yeshiva University (Hamevaser).

——— (1974), *Al ha' Teshuva* (On Repentance), ed. P. Peli. Jerusalem: The World Zionist Organization, Torah Education Department.

——— (1983), *Halachic Man*. Philadelphia: The Jewish Publication Society of America. (Originally published in Hebrew under the title "Ish ha-Halakhah" in *Talpiot* I, nos. 3 & 4, New York, 1944.)

——— (1985), Sacred and Profane (Kodesh and Chol). Reprinted in the *Torah U'Mada Reader*, Yeshiva University, pp. 20–32.

Sorenson, R. L. (1994), Ongoing change in psychoanalytic theory. *Psychoanal. Dial.*, 4:631–660.

Spence, D. P. (1982), *Narrative Truth and Historical Truth*. New York: Norton.

Spero, M. H. (1980), *Judaism and Psychology*. New York: KTAV.

Spezzano, C. (1994), Illusion, faith and knowledge: Commentary on Sorenson. *Psychoanal. Dial.*, 4:661ff.

Stern, D. B. (1983), Unformulated experience. *Contemp. Psychoanal.*, 19:71–99.

Stolorow, R. D. & Lachmann, F. M. (1980), *Psychoanalysis of Developmental Arrests.* New York: International Universities Press.

Sullivan, H. S. (1953), *The Interpersonal Theory of Psychiatry.* New York: Norton.

——— (1956), *Clinical Studies in Psychiatry.* New York: Norton.

Thouless, R. (1923), *An Introduction to the Psychology of Religion.* New York: Macmillan.

Ulman, C. (1982), Cognitive and emotional antecedents of religious conversion. *J. Personal. & Soc. Psychol.*, 43:183–90.

Winnicott, D. W. (1971), *Playing and Reality.* London: Tavistock.

——— (1975), *Through Paediatrics to Psychoanalysis.* New York: Basic Books.

— 5 —

Psychoanalysis Is Self-Centered

JEFFREY B. RUBIN

Psychoanalysis is arguably the preeminent discourse in the 20th century for investigating the nature and vicissitudes of self-experience. From Freud's account of self-unconsciousness, to Jung's description of self-division and self-integration, to Winnicott's depiction of compliance and authenticity, to Kohut's discussion of self-depletion and self-restoration, psychoanalysis has explored many facets of self-experience with lapidary precision.

The vast majority of psychoanalysts—with the exception of Lacanians—agree that a fundamental aspect of analysis is an expanded and nuanced experience and understanding of "I-ness." In his synthetic overview of postclassical psychoanalytic views of the self, Mitchell (1991) suggests that each school of psychoanalysis illuminates a different aspect of selfhood. Mitchell distinguishes three views of the self: the Freudian view of the self as separate and integrated, the object-relations and interpersonal view of the self as multiple and discontinuous, and the self-psychological view of the self as integral and continuous.

But the dialogue between Freud and his friend Romain Rolland concerning religion implicitly suggests that there is more in the nature of selfhood or "I-ness" than these accounts of selfhood imply. Responding to Freud's (1927) critique of religion in "The Future of an Illusion," Rolland, a poet and student of the Indian saint Ramakrishna, indicated that it had much merit but that it neglected the most important source of the religious sentiment, a "sensation of 'eternity,' a feeling of as something limitless, unbounded" (p. 65). In "Civilization and Its Discontents" Freud (1930) admitted that he could not discover this "oceanic" feeling in himself and voiced discomfort in coping with these "obscure modifications in mental life" (p. 73). Subsequent psychoanalysts, with such rare exceptions as Loewald and Kovel, have followed Freud's lead and also neglected and pathologized this facet of self-experience.

Whereas psychoanalysis has elucidated pathological facets of oneness experiences, for example the characteristic boundary problems of schizophrenics or the way fusion experiences may ward off feelings of disappointment, loss, or oedipal conflicts (Silverman, Lachmann, and Milich, 1982), it has neglected its adaptive possibilities, particularly what I shall term *non-self-centered subjectivity*. Non-self-centered subjectivity is a psychological-spiritual phenomenon that is implicated in a range of adaptive contexts, from psychoanalytic listening to creating or appreciating art to emotional intimacy.[1] It is something many people have experienced, for example, creating art, participating in athletics or religious experiences, or in love. It is characterized by heightened attentiveness, focus, and clarity, attunement to the other as well as the self, non-self-preoccupied exercise of agency, a sense of unity and timelessness, and non-self-annulling immersion in whatever one is doing in the present.

The adaptive dimensions of non-self-centered subjectivity raise important questions for psychoanalysis: Do such self-transformations as may occur, for example, in this state of being, ever enrich self-experience? Might such experiences aid analysts and analysands in envisioning selfhood in new and more expansive ways?

In this essay I suggest that there is more in the nature of subjectivity than is dreamt of in psychoanalytic psychologies. More specifically, I argue that the fertile, authentic subjectivity that contemporary psychoanalysts of every stripe have so ably illuminated and facilitated eclipses a vital facet of self-experience, non-self-centered subjectivity. The neglect of non-self-centric subjectivity and of the spirituality of which it may be a part, leads, I believe, to an impoverished view of self, a narcissistic conception of relationships, and an incomplete account of morality. Freed from a picture of the self that may have held analysts captive, we might be encouraged to conceive of subjectivity in more expansive and less self-alienating ways.

In the first section I briefly contextualize psychoanalysis within the culture of individualism that underlies it; I then explore some of the consequences for its view of self, relationships, and morality. In the second section I put psychoanalysis "on the couch" and highlight certain problems with analytic conceptions of subjectivity. The third section uses clinical material from a psychoanalytic treatment with a Buddhist meditator to examine some of the strengths and limitations of psychoanalysis and Buddhism. In the concluding section I explore how a *contemplative psychoanalysis*—a therapeutics that draws on the partial truths about self and morality of psychoanalysis and Buddhism and recognizes the reality of

---

[1]Silverman, Lachmann, and Milich (1982) illuminate the adaptive as well as the pathological possibilities of oneness experiences, although from a slightly different perspective than I adopt in this chapter. They emphasize the way the absorptive union of oneness fantasies can enhance therapeutic success, as long as the sense of self is not threatened, while I emphasize the self-expansiveness (and relatedness) of non-self-centered subjectivity. Identity is not "sublated," as Hegel might put it, but extended and enriched. Jones (1995) has helped me articulate this.

human agency while not eclipsing the capacity for non-self-centered subjectivity—might be more ethically responsive to the challenges confronting postmodern selves-at-risk than either psychoanalysis or Buddhism pursued alone.

PSYCHOANALYSIS AND INDIVIDUALISM

Four character ideals have vied for center stage in the history of Western life, according to sociologist Phillip Rieff (1963): the "political" subject of classical antiquity, who participates in public life; the "economic" subject who retreats into a search for private fulfillment while enjoying the fruits of citizenship; the Hebraic and Christian "religious" person who substitutes faith for reason; and the late 19th- and 20th-century "psychological" subject who eschews any redemptive external doctrine or creed—whether political or religious—and attends to the workings of his or her own private universe of thoughts, feelings, dreams, and symptoms.

Psychoanalysis arose from the soil of the modern period in which there was a "despiritualization" of subjective reality (see Kovel, 1991), by which I mean, a devaluation, marginalization, and pathologization of the spiritual. The "psychological" subject monopolizes the stage of intellectual life in the West during the formation and development of psychoanalysis.

"In the age of psychological man, the self," notes Rieff (1963) "is the only god-term" (p. 23). Selfhood, according to Baumeister (1987), became a problem in the modern period.

> During the Victorian era (roughly 1830–1900), there were crises with regard to . . . four problems of selfhood . . . how identity is actively or creatively defined by the person, what is the nature of the relationship between the individual and society, how does the person understand his or her potential and then fulfill it, and how and how well do persons know themselves . . . early in the 20th century, themes of alienation and devaluation of selfhood indicated concern over the individual's helpless dependency on society [p. 163].

For psychological man, self-maximization, not participation in the polis, is the chief vocation. Interest in the workings of one's psyche replaces commitment to the life of the commons. Psychotherapeutic concern for the meaning of symptoms replaces questions about meaning or "ultimate concern." Better living, not the Good Life, becomes the main psychoanalytic preoccupation (Rieff, 1963).

Analytic assumptions about the self—arguably, even within relational schools—are based on Western values, particularly the "Northern European–North American cultural values and philosophical assumptions involving individualism" (Roland, 1995, p. 4). The individual in individualism is sacred: "the supreme value in and of itself, with each having his or her own rights and obligations. . . .

Society is considered to be essentially subordinate to the needs of individuals, who are all governed by their own self-interest (p. 6).[2] Psychoanalysis is an exemplary psychological version of Western individualistic thought. In the next section I reflect on some relational and moral consequences of psychoanalytic individualism.

BEYOND PSYCHOANALYTIC INDIVIDUALISM

The psychoanalytic conception of subjectivity that arose in response to 19th-century Victorian Europe was particular and partial. The emphasis in psychoanalysis on the development of the psyche of the "psychological" subject offered psychological grounding and comfort for the psychologically dehumanized and alienated early 20th-century citizen. But in overemphasizing a reified, egoistic individualism, psychoanalysis necessarily promotes excessive self-centeredness and eclipses certain possibilities and features of subjectivity, such as self-transcendence and spirituality, or non-self-centric modes of being. The concept of a separate "I" is, as Bateson (1972) claims, *the* epistemological fallacy of Occidental civilization. Individuality and the "uniqueness of personality" are arguably, as Fromm (1941) suggests, "the greatest achievement of modern culture" (p. vii). Individualism has fostered such things as the importance of human dignity and rights, even as the "limits of individualism" (Gaylin, 1988, p. 59), the materialism, greed, and xenophobia it also bequeaths us, cry out to us on a daily basis. It could be argued that narcissism is at the root of the pervasive intolerance, oppression, inequality, and injustice in the world. Narrow and narcissistic conceptions of self seem to be implicated in many contemporary crises, ranging from resistance to utilizing available resources that might remedy world hunger to the scapegoating of the oppressed.

Rampant fundamentalist thinking, racial and religious scapegoating and bigotry, and ecological insensitivity in our world suggest that the narcissistic and disconnected sense of self is dysfunctional—both a cause and a result of much of the suffering and disharmony in late 20th-century life. Psychoanalysis has caused neither the narcissistic or disconnected sense

---

[2]Roland's (1988) characterization of the Western self as essentially individualistic may be more true of men than women. Male individualism takes for granted, and is indissolubly linked to, the support and service of nonautonomous and nonindividualistically oriented women and less privileged men.

Interpersonalists such as Harry Stack Sullivan have usefully critiqued the self-contained individual. Yet, as I attempt to demonstrate in my discussion in the next section on psychoanalytic views of relationships and morality, certain endemic problems with individualism may exist in and haunt even relationally oriented schools of thought.

of self, nor the mayhem in our world. But its self-centered conceptions of self may have contributed to viewpoints that perpetuate self-constriction, suffering, and alienation from self and others.

If "infantilism" was the malady afflicting the unreflective, pre-self-conscious, proto-individual symbiotically immersed in the tribal mind (see Houston, 1980, p. 27), then narcissism, disconnection, nihilism, and anomie may be the pathology characterizing the autonomous, self-sufficient, atomized, Promethean man of our hyper-self-conscious, individualistic society. Threats to the social order may thereby not lie, as Freud (1933) claimed, in conquering instinctual aggression through rationality and renunciation, but in mollifying narcissism and increasing understanding and tolerance of the other.

Because autonomous, differentiated identity—which is a more self-centered aspect of subjectivity—has been traditionally viewed as the apex of human development by most psychoanalysts (except Kohutians), non-self-centric modes of being have been interpreted by most psychoanalysts as symptoms of psychopathology. From traditional analytic perspectives, such experiences are most often viewed as a regressive attempt to merge with the preoedipal mother. In the self psychology tradition, permeability of self-boundaries and alterations in self-cohesion—such as might occur in self-transformative moments of non-self-centric subjectivity—appear to be viewed as symptoms of a vulnerable, besieged, or under-structuralized self.[3]

But experiences of self-transcendence, in which there is non-self-centricity and at least a transient loss of self-differentiation, may embody a nonpathological, expanded sense of self[4] that is quite different from archaic states of nondifferentiation. Although the non-self-centric is usually conflated in psychoanalysis with pathological self-loss, there can be an expansion of self-structure that is not necessarily indicative of an ego defect or a boundary problem and that is self-enriching and not self-annihilating.[5]

It is difficult to paint a picture of such experiences because, in authorizing us to "think and speak in terms of single, stable self-entities" (Schafer, 1989, p. 159), the English language offers an impoverished vocabulary for evoking non-self-centric states of being. When we are open to the moment

---

[3]Atwood and Stolorow (1984) view permeability of self-structure as a sign of a healthy self, provided one also is experiencing self-stability.

[4]It would take me far afield to discuss Ogden's (1991) suggestive reworking of the Kleinian notion of positions. The non-self-centric mode of being I am pointing toward here is, among other things, the positing of a *fourth* state of being, a corrective to the emphasis on the regressive and the primitive in the autistic-contiguous, paranoid-schizoid, and the depressive positions.

[5]Karen Peoples's (1991) unpublished summary of a paper-in-progress enriched this section.

without a sense of time, un-self-conscious but acutely aware, highly focused and engaged yet relaxed and without fear, in non-self-centric subjectivity, we experience a sense of self-vivification, self-renewal, and self-transformation, and we live, relate, and play with greater creativity, joy, and efficacy than we normally experience. Non-self-centered subjectivity is a source of rejuvenation, sanity, and health. Loewald (1978) depicts some manifestations of these self-enriching facets of non-self-centered subjectivity that nonmeditators, as well as meditators, have probably experienced.

> We get lost in the contemplation of a beautiful scene, or face, or painting, in listening to music, or poetry, or the music of a human voice. We are carried away in the vortex of sexual passion. We become absorbed in . . . a deeply stirring play or film, in the beauty of a scientific theory or experiment or of an animal, in the intimate closeness of a personal encounter [p. 67].

In non-self-centric states of being there is a nonpathological, dedifferentiation of boundaries between self and world: a self-empowering sense of connection between self and world that results in a lack of self-preoccupation, a sense of timelessness, efficacy, and peace. Moments of non-self-centricity—whether surrendering, merging, yielding, letting go—seem to be part of most spiritual traditions.

There are at least three reasons why spirituality may have been either neglected or pathologized by psychoanalysts. First, religion, as Freud (1927) emphasized, has been guilty of many "crimes" and "misdemeanors" (p. 27) in its attempts to ward off and make tolerable human existential feelings of helplessness; these range from rationalizing authoritarian behavior and intolerance to physical and psychological persecution of dissenters. Second, oneness experiences may stir up various internal and interpersonal anxieties and dangers, including fears of engulfment and self-loss. Finally, exploring the realm of spirituality opens up a question that Winnicott recognized that psychoanalysis—with its essentially "tragic" world-view (Schafer, 1976), its recognition of the inescapable mysteries, dilemmas, and afflictions pervading human existence—has rarely addressed: "what is life about, apart from illness?"[6]

The plethora of analysands and analysts who are pursuing various forms of spiritual practice, the increasing number of conferences and articles on spirituality and psychotherapy, and, perhaps also, the burgeoning attention to subjectivity and relationship issues in psychoanalysis, suggest that we may be witnessing a hunger for, and a return of, the (spiritually) repressed in contemporary psychoanalysis. In the spring of 1994, for example, over 500 therapists and Buddhists participated in a conference on Healing the Suffering Self at the Harvard Club in New York City.

---

[6]There seems to be a greater interest in this question in the last decade and a half.

Might many analysands and analysts turn to the meditation cushion (or yoga ashram) in addition to the psychoanalytic couch, because psychoanalysis may not fully nourish their spiritual needs or hunger?

The egocentric conception of "I-ness" in psychoanalysis fosters a type of self-blindness and self-impoverishment. Thinking of the self as the center of the psychological and moral universe can foster a narrow and problematic way of seeing and relating to ourselves and others. For example, it encourages an inflated sense of self-importance and may thus promote ethnocentrism and xenophobia. "Every spirit," says Emerson at the end of *Nature*, "builds itself a house and beyond its house a world, and beyond its world a heaven." "Know then," he continues, "that the world exists for you. For you is the phenomenon perfect. What we are, that only can we see." While every person may be at the center of his own world, no one is the center of the whole world. Thinking that we are—which individualism encourages—may compromise empathy and tolerance, foster disconnection from others, and engender self-alienation.

The impoverished view of relationships fostered by psychoanalysis may be related to its narcissistic view of the self. It may not be accidental that psychoanalysis calls the other an "object" and relations with others "object relations." The word "object" connotes a thing and predisposes one to adopt a depersonalized view of (see Buccino, 1993, p. 130), and a narcissistic relation to, others, in which one focuses on what the other needs to do for the self, rather than what the self might do for the other. The other tends to be viewed, in psychoanalysis, as an *object*, not as a *subject*. The narcissistic view of relationships emerges in the psychoanalytic vocabulary of "bad objects," "part-objects," "need-satisfying objects," and "self-objects." It is not surprising that psychoanalysis lacks a nuanced and compelling account of emotional intimacy among egalitarian subjects. For how could there be an adequate account of intimacy when the other is seen mostly in terms of what it does (or does not do) for the self? In a theoretical world in which "relationships are secondary phenomena and emotions are derivative," writes Gaylin (1988) "love will never be discovered" (p. 44). The complexity of intimacy and love cannot be adequately explained when there is a valorization of humans as self-centered and hedonic monads, accountable only to the dictates of their own personal tastes and dispositions.

From Thai Buddhists irritated about religious demands of Muslims in Thailand, to Californians who resent the influx of immigrants, the claims and strains of otherness are a central facet of the world. Understanding and getting along with the other, whether in or outside of analysis, becomes more crucial in a world of shrinking, shifting borders and globalized communication, in which we all confront increasing scarcity, selfishness, intolerance, disconnection, alienation, and nihilism.

The psychoanalytic neglect of otherness affects its view of morality as well as its conception of interpersonal relationships. In this section I attempt to demonstrate that psychoanalysis both compromises our understanding of morality and complicates and enriches spiritual perspectives.

Psychoanalysis may now be very far from Heinz Hartmann's (1960) assertion that it is a clinical procedure without moral considerations. Hartmann's position seemed to echo Freud's (1933) claim that psychoanalysis does not posit any values beyond those within science as a whole. Nonetheless, moral questions pervade it, from value lacunas of patients seeking our help (Panel, 1984) to the implicit and explicit values in our theories and practices. From the metapsychologies we utilize to the decor of our offices, values impinge on psychoanalytic theories and clinical work. Once it is recognized that the moral neutrality extolled by Hartmann is neither possible nor desirable, the question becomes, "what values are operative in psychoanalysis?"

There seems to be an ambivalence within psychoanalysis concerning values and morality. Let me cite two examples. Conscience, ideals, and values are within the terrain covered by the concept of superego—one of three pillars of self-experience since Freud. The rigidity and harshness of the superego is presumably lessened in the course of successful treatment. Value neutrality, on the other hand, is still deeply held by many analysts who believe in the possibility of, and aspire to being, scientific. And yet, to know what a cure is—to know what recovery would look like—the analyst must already have a vision of what the good life is (Phillips, 1994). Such a vision places us squarely in the land of morality. Secondly, psychoanalysis, writes Gedo (1986), does not "espouse a single ethical point of view" (p. 214) and lacks normative criteria for comparing competing systems of morality, yet it can bring more reason to bear on one's asocial, self-centered drivenness, lessen irrational conscience, and improve our standard of conduct (p. 207).

Because ethics and tolerance also involve decentering from the centrality of our own cherished viewpoints and taking into account those of others (Varela, 1984), psychoanalysis offers a necessary, although insufficient, perspective for thinking about morality. The greater self-acceptance and lessened narcissism that often develops as a result of analytic treatment exists without the larger perspective fostered by spiritual perspectives, wherein one's own experience is viewed as a *part* of a more encompassing reality. A psychoanalytic view of morality based on an individualistic sense of self leads to a morality rooted in the neglect of the other, which does not provide an adequate framework for ethics. Given these difficulties with the individualistic view of self, psychoanalysis seems to underestimate human possibility.

Moralities rooted in religious thinking—whether in the form of the ethic of Christian fellowship or love, or of Buddhist egoless compassion—may encourage less self-centered views of self and more humane conduct. But Freud (1917) complicates the moral landscape and the vocabulary of moral reflection at one's disposal with his monumental "de-centering" of self-mastery resulting from psychoanalysis' demonstration that the ego "is not master in its own house" (p. 143). The availability of a richer vocabulary of moral distinctions fosters greater sophistication and sensitivity in our moral deliberations. It is more difficult—if not more self-deceptive—to take religious claims about doing good and acting benevolently at face value in a world in which generosity may hide self-aggrandizement and self-deprivation. Nonpsychoanalytic spiritual conceptions of self and morality tend to neglect the psychological complexity of selfhood and ethics, for example, the multiplicity of conflicting motives that may underlie a particular action.

Clinical case studies of religion in general and Buddhism in particular are rare in psychoanalysis. There is, thus, a dearth of clinical data in psychoanalysis regarding Buddhism (Rubin, 1993). In this section, I present material from a psychoanalytic treatment with a Buddhist meditator in order to explore the possibilities and liabilities of psychoanalysis and Buddhism. My focus will be on only those aspects of the case material that relate to psychoanalysis and Buddhism. This is the only clinical data about this topic I am aware of in the psychoanalytic or Buddhist literature, except for my own earlier work (Rubin, 1991, 1993, 1996).[7]

"East is East and West is West" wrote Kipling, "and never the twain shall meet." More recently, Salman Rushdie (1994) stated, "I too have ropes around my neck, I have them to this day, pulling me this way and that, East and West, the nooses tightening, commanding choose, choose. . . . Ropes I do not choose between you. . . . I choose neither of you and both. Do you hear? I refuse to choose" (p. 211).

Let us consider the case of a man I shall call Albert. He is an affable humanities professor in his late 20s who suffered from conflicts over individuation and success, excessive self-judgment, diminished self-esteem, inauthenticity, compliance, and a pervasive sense of directionlessness and meaninglessness. His refusal to choose between East or West, between Buddhism or psychoanalysis, or rather his choice of *both* (and his discovery of where the twain did or did not meet) has made all the clinical difference.

Albert was an only child who was raised as an agnostic. His parents were agnostic. In the early stages of treatment he described his mother as intelligent, caring, and devoted. As treatment progressed, other images of her emerged. He experienced her as a rigid person who was more concerned with everyone conforming to her view of reality, which included how people in general, and her son principally, should act and be. She was deeply committed to foreclosing, if not banishing, subjective life and she

---

[7]Roland (1988) has done short-term analytically oriented work with Indians and Japanese patients who are not Buddhists.

demanded that everyone live in accordance with her narrow view of reality, which was composed of preestablished rules and "shoulds."

He felt that she lived in a "fortune cookie" universe in which cliché responses—"you must have felt badly when so and so died"—replaced genuine affective engagement. Albert felt impactless and nonexistent in her presence. His mother was like a "fencer who parries everything I say." Instead of being affirmed and validated by her, he felt nonengaged and invisible.

From Albert's account, he had a distant relationship with his father, who he experienced as intelligent, detached, critical, and passive. His father submissively went along with his wife's way of living and relating. His father's blind loyalty to his wife resulted in Albert's never feeling understood or supported by him. His father could not sustain interest in him. Albert repeatedly cited numerous examples of his father's changing the subject whenever Albert shared some athletic or academic accomplishment. Albert gradually realized that although his father had made him feel incompetent and inadequate, in actuality his father avoided many areas of life for which he let his wife take responsibility.

As Albert described the way his parents laundered communication of all subjective meaning, vaporized conflict, and nullified authentic selfhood, while appearing to exude empathy and significance, I was reminded of Bollas's (1987) suggestive account of "normotic illness" (p. 135). Such people are "fundamentally disinterested in subjective life" (p. 136). They have a "disinclination to entertain the subjective element in life whether it exists inside . . . or in the Other. The introspective capacity has rarely been used" (p. 137). Normotics are invested in "eradicating the self of subjective life" (p. 156). "The normotic flees from dream life, subjective states of mind, imaginative living" (p. 146).

Albert's parents did not see themselves or him as subjects capable of introspecting, feeling, desiring, or playing. Rather, he was coerced into accommodating to their preexisting viewpoint on reality. To stay connected to his parents he needed to hide his subjective life. He "harmonized" with his parents' normotic view of reality—so as not to be like "an astronaut cut off from home base in outer space"—because that was the only way of keeping the hope alive that he could be emotionally related to them.

His parents were sorely unresponsive to his inner reality and failed to encourage his uniqueness to emerge or flourish. In fact, they encouraged false-self compliance with their narrow mode of being by emotionally rewarding submissiveness and conventionality, and discouraging authenticity and individuation.

He felt like a powerless pawn in their play that was designed to whitewash reality and his subjective life. Albert developed a private subjective world of depth and richness, but he had great difficulty believing in its validity and sustaining his commitment to it. The price of accommodating and conforming to his parents' wishes was to bury his own sense of how he should live. He kept alive the tenuous hope of being accepted by his parents by banishing huge parts of his self through subverting and obscuring his own "voice." This led to an excessively limited view of himself and his capabilities. What he wanted lacked significance to him, and he felt that his life was not his own. He experienced himself as an "ellipsis-virtuality," with certain important parts of his potentialities dormant. This left him feeling self-doubtful and directionless.

He had what sounded, at first, like vital and interesting male friendships, characterized by openness and depth. As time went on, material emerged suggesting that several of these friends were either narcissistic or emotionally needy. His male friendships seemed organized so that he would provide a great deal of psychological sustenance. Relationships with women were often characterized by a great desire to be related, a self-nullifying attention to their emotional needs—which left out his own needs—and a stance of pseudo-incompetence. He dove into the world of scholarly pursuits and Buddhist practice, avoided the world of practical affairs, and set it up so that the women he was involved with would take care of these matters, which secretly left him feeling incompetent and unable to have the kind of partnership he desired.

His competence and expertise were also carefully hidden from others in his academic work. He assumed that his competence would either be disregarded by those he valued or be threatening to less able colleagues. He was afraid that competence and self-assertion would result in his being shunned and "orphaned." He simultaneously complied with the needs of others and related to them in a deferential manner while he secretly pursued interests and avocational pursuits, such as Buddhism, that did not fit in to the mainstream of the familial, professional, and social worlds he inhabited. That his abilities were not appreciated fed his sense of invisibility. He tended to become involved in projects with colleagues who were not his equal, which reinforced his sense of deprivation.

We observed in his life what Pontalis termed a dialectic of "death work" in which "parent and child develop a reciprocal preference for maintaining an unborn self" (in Bollas, 1987, p. 144). He described the process of denying his own needs, subordinating himself to what others wanted, and neglecting his own goals as "Albertlessness." It involved both deferring to the needs of others and "straitjacketing" himself. In later stages of analysis he described this as being "buried alive."

In the beginning of treatment, Albert was affable and compliant. Initially he did not talk about Buddhism. As we explored his tendency in the transference to conform to me by attempting to speak my language, his fear that he would be alone and invisible if he did not accommodate to those around him, including me, emerged. As we understood two of the dangers he anticipated—that I would be like his critical father or like his usurping mother—material about Buddhism emerged. After several months in treatment, Albert reported on his recent experiences with

Buddhist meditation. He had just returned from pursuing intensive meditation practice at a Buddhist retreat center and found it enlightening and inspiring. He practiced Vipassana meditation, in which one attends to whatever one is experiencing—thoughts, feelings, fantasies, sounds, bodily sensations—without selection or judgment. This practice is said to cultivate refined awareness that eventually leads to heightened perceptual acuity and attentiveness, deepened insight into the nature of mental and physical processes, selfhood and reality, the eradication of suffering, and the development of compassion and moral action.

He described the way meditation practice cultivated heightened attentiveness and self-awareness. The heightened attentiveness helped him begin to be able to know his own reactions more easily and steadily. This aided him in not accommodating as readily to the needs of others.

He also emphasized the way ethics seemed more central in Buddhism than in psychoanalysis. From what he had observed, the three teachers of meditation that he had studied under seemed to have a more expansive view of the world and morality than the therapists he had encountered socially and professionally. He illustrated the more panoramic perspective on ethics by a story about Gandhi. A man went to a talk that Gandhi gave, with the goal of assassinating him. Moved by the power of Gandhi's teachings, he shelved his plan. After the talk, he prostrated himself in front of Gandhi and told him of his change of heart. Gandhi's response to this man, a potential assassin, was "how are you going to tell your boss about your failed mission?"

Albert felt that the view of self and morality in psychoanalysis was partial, and thus the view of health in psychoanalysis was an arrested state of development. He felt that possibilities for health existed—and were cultivated in Buddhism—that Western psychology in general, and psychoanalysis in particular, had not yet tapped.

My own stance toward his involvement with Buddhism, which was never stated explicitly but was probably implicit, was to approach it with neither unequivocal reverence nor defensive rejection. Heeding Freud's (1921) warning to avoid "two sources of [interpretative] error—the Scylla of underestimating the importance of the repressed unconscious, and the Charybdis of judging the normal entirely by the standards of the pathological" (p. 138), I attempted to avoid the twin dangers of a priori pathologizing, which would reject Buddhism automatically, or unconstrained idealization, which would accept it without critical examination. If psychoanalysis has too often been reductionistic in pathologizing religious phenomena, then challenges to psychoanalytic reductionism within religion and nonanalytic Western psychologies have often fallen victim to a reverse pitfall, accepting religious experience too uncritically and simplistically. The complexity and depth of religious phenomena is eclipsed in both approaches, and both religion and psychoanalysis are then impoverished.

The Eurocentrism that pervades psychoanalysis, by which I mean the tendency to treat European standards and values as the center of the intellectual universe, has often blinded analysts to the potential clinical value of Buddhism and other spiritual traditions. In our clinical work it became evident that Buddhist meditation practice helped Albert in several ways. It was quite helpful in cultivating enhanced self-observational capacities—for instance, it increased his attentiveness and self-awareness. When he discussed relationships, for example, he demonstrated great subtlety of insight as to the possible patterns of interaction and the hidden meanings and motivations that might be operative. This enabled him to do such things as track his reactions to me and others and often to detect inchoate perceptions and fantasies. While meditating, for example, he became aware of his formerly disavowed feelings of betrayal at the way his mother "gaslighted" or mystified him.

His self-introspective abilities seemed to increase as his involvement with meditation deepened. Because such self-awareness is also central to psychoanalysis, it seems impossible to ascertain the relative influence of each tradition in promoting it. One factor suggested to me that meditation practice played an important role: several times Albert returned from meditation retreats the day of our session, and he seemed unusually attentive to nuances of his inner life, such as latent motives, formerly disavowed intentions, and so forth.

Not only did his receptivity to internal and interpersonal life increase, his attitude toward his experience changed. The meditative spirit of attending to experience without judgment or aversion gradually replaced the self-critical stance exemplified by his father.

Not only did he become significantly less self-critical, he also became less "attached" to experience—less addicted to pleasing experiences and less afraid of painful ones. Attachment, as Buddhism tirelessly emphasizes, causes suffering. Albert, like the rest of us, suffered when he was attached, when he wanted things to be his way, when he tried to control experience. As he meditated more, he seemed to become less attached. He accepted change. He let things happen. He flowed with experience, rather than demanding it be his way or prereflectively utilizing habitual coping strategies. For example, after he had meditated for some time, he reported the following incident while visiting his parents for dinner. He witnessed the same disturbing dynamics that had permeated his childhood. He experienced rage at his father's belittling treatment and his mother's deadening normotic behavior. But instead of reacting by either tuning them out or mindlessly fitting in, as he had before he meditated, he was able to experience the anger and deprivation without either resorting to avoidance or to self-hurtful or self-anesthetizing behavior. Detachment helped him become less caught in habitual or conventional reactions and attitudes. This resulted in decreased defensiveness and more openness to experience.

He had a highly developed capacity for tolerating and living in and through a range of affects, without having to foreclose or simplify either the confusion or the complexity. He was able, for example, to examine such things as ambivalence, anger, and perplexity without judging himself, reducing the complexity of these experiences, or clamoring after premature understanding. As he accepted himself more—emotional warts and all—he developed deeper acceptance of others.

He then experienced a fluidity, an openness of being, that was very different from the normotic rigidity of his parents in which experience was foreclosed. His lightness of being was not simply born of accommodation and submission, although parts of both may have been operative.

As a result of all this, his suffering decreased—both the "neurotic misery" that Freud felt psychoanalysis addressed *and* the "common human unhappiness" he claimed psychoanalysis could not resolve.

Buddhism's dereifed conception of subjectivity was also liberating for Albert. By continually revealing to him, on an experiential level, the fluidity and self-transformative facets of self-experience, the way consciousness changes moment after moment, the practice of meditation offered him a more fluid way of experiencing subjectivity. Meditation taught him that the apparently unified narrative he and his parents constructed about his self was, in part, illusory. This homogeneous image of the self hid its heterogeneity: the discontinuities, fissures, and anomalous perceptions expressed in the transient and episodic mental states that arise from moment to moment. Meditation facilitated, to borrow Foucault's (1977) terminology in a different but not incompatible context, an "unrealization" (p. 160) of his taken-for-granted, unified identity based teleologically on past experiences and conceptions of himself. An unreified and unconstricted sense of subjectivity was thus facilitated. By offering a less reified view of self, Buddhism helped Albert challenge the deadening clutches of his parents and his own preset, one-dimensional, normotic view of himself.

My own knowledge of Buddhism's view of self-experience alerted me to the dangers of self-reification, which helped me recognize and avoid the subtle self-commodification that occurred in his family, his relationship to himself, and periodically in his previous analysis and our analysis. In these four situations he was made into a thing, a means rather than an end, an it rather than a Thou. Self-commodification happened in his family when he was narcissistically viewed as an extension of his parents. His parents were more concerned with making him into the sort of person they needed him to be, so that they could feel better about themselves, than with facilitating his own differentiated development.

In our analysis, a pattern emerged that had apparently shadowed his previous analysis and probably our work in which he would almost instantaneously bury negative feelings—for example, the feeling that I had not fully appreciated a particular accomplishment—and shift the analytic focus onto understanding what *he* had done wrong. His self-bashing was sometimes quite subtle and not easy to detect because it was so automatic and because the shift in focus he initiated had some plausibility; in other words, he would direct us toward areas that seemed to be troublesome for him. For example, after one session, in which he had discussed what he had learned from both Buddhism and psychoanalysis, he suggested that we examine the way in which he sometimes undermines himself and hides his intellectual potential. He suggested that his convoluted presentation of his ideas during the previous session could provide a clue to what he needed help with in this area. He suggested that his presentation was symptomatic of a difficulty he sometimes had in his intellectual work. My experience of the previous session was that he had made some subtle and important points about both psychoanalysis and Buddhism but that some of his ideas were still inchoate. I also felt that I had not offered him much assistance in further clarifying the material. After I commented in the current session about one of his ideas that I believed was quite interesting, he realized, through the contrast between my more zestful response in today's session (compared to the previous session), that the previous session had been disappointing for him. Further exploration revealed that he was disappointed that I had not been more effusive about his ideas. He realized this when he suggested, at the beginning of the current session, that we examine the negative way in which he thinks that he was both obscuring his disappointment in me for not being more enthusiastic about his intellectual work and making himself into a "commodity" to be worked on and improved. He indicated that he felt that this kind of process pervaded his previous analysis. The Buddhist dereifed view of subjectivity—particularly Buddhism's appreciation of the fluidity of consciousness and the importance of the transient, episodic mental states that arise moment after moment—helped both of us be sensitive to the way self-commodification occurred in our work and in his life outside analysis, which led to a more unconstricted view of himself.

Non-self-centric moments of consciousness and experiences of self-transcendence, in which there is a loss of self-differentiation, became more apparent as attention was paid to the fluidity of subjectivity. Non-self-centricity may refer, as I suggested earlier, to nonpathological, expanded states of consciousness qualitatively different from more archaic states of nondifferentiation. Because psychoanalysis lacks a psychology of transcendent states, these modes of being do not appear on its map of human development and are assumed to be pathological. The ways they might enhance self-experience are thereby eclipsed.

With its more expansive, less self-centered view of self, Buddhism suggested possibilities of selfhood and morality that went beyond the narrower views of either psychoanalysis or his family. That psychoanalysis—even relational versions—treats the other reductively is suggested, as I mentioned earlier, by its notion of the other as an *object*, its failure to articulate a workable theory of intimacy, and its egocentric conception of responsibility. The word *responsibility* rarely appears in the *Standard Edition* of Freud and is usually absent from psychoanalytic discourse. Despite the relational turn in psychoanalysis in the last 15 to 20 years, the morality underpinning psychoanalysis—even a relational one—is based on a one-person, nonrelational model of human beings. While contemporary psychoanalysis charts relational influences on development and treatment, it discourages a relational perspective on moral responsibilities. In contemplating action-moral decisions, we unconsciously import a one-person perspective on morality. For example, when patients struggle with ambivalence about a relationship or moral dilemma—should I remain with or leave my partner? Should I allow my aging parent to move in?—we psychoanalysts usually don't ask "what is right?" but rather what do *you* feel, or want, or need?" Our very question about what the lone individual wants or needs predisposes us to think of single individuals, not of people inextricably involved in a network of relations.

In asking not what the other can do for the self—the question his parents and psychoanalysis focused on—but rather, what the self might do for the other, Buddhism offered Albert an alternative vision to the solipsistic, normotic world of his parents. Albert tended to view morality in a more complex and nuanced way because of his concern with the other as well as the self.

Psychoanalysis needs Buddhism in order to become less excessively narrow, less self-centered, less focused on the needs and wishes of the separate self. Buddhism teaches us that when we think about action, choice, moral commitment, and relational affiliations, we need to focus on the other as well as on the self.

Narcissism, Buddhism has taught us, is at the root of both human suffering and evil. It has recently been theoretically claimed (Epstein, 1995), although never clinically demonstrated, that "meditation is a means of indefatigably exposing this narcissism, of highlighting every permutation of the self-experience so that no aspect remains available for narcissistic recruitment" (p. 134). In recent years there has been a rash of scandals in Buddhist communities involving grossly self-centered and exploitative sexual and financial behavior among Buddhist teachers (Boucher, 1988), those individuals presumably selected by enlightened Buddhist masters as teachers in part because they represent the highest level of spiritual realization and ethicality among Buddhist practitioners. The prominent teacher of Tibetan Buddhism, selected by a renowned Tibetan Buddhist master to be his successor, who slept with a number of unsuspecting students while knowing he had AIDS, and the Zen Buddhist master who expropriated funds from the community that he led, raise telling questions that Buddhists and Buddhistically sympathetic Western mental health professionals have rarely, if ever, addressed or illuminated. Why is there so much unconsciousness, egocentricity, and amorality in a tradition that prizes and focuses on self-awareness, selflessness, ethicality, and compassion? Why do years of meditation practice not prevent this sort of exploitative conduct? Is narcissism really eradicable?

If the Eurocentrism permeating psychoanalysis resulted in a pathologizing of Buddhism, then Buddhists and Western mental health professionals and scholars writing about psychoanalysis and Buddhism have often fallen victim to the reverse danger, what I have termed *Orientocentrism* (Rubin, 1993), the tendency to deify "the East" and denigrate "the West," to view the former as the apex of civilization, as somehow transparently true and devoid of self-deception and self-blindness. Orientocentrism precludes thoughtfully examining Buddhism. It is dangerous to treat Buddhism (or any human creation) as if it is exempt from critical scrutiny and somehow free from self-interest, illusion, and corruption. Orientocentrism also insures that what psychoanalysis might offer Buddhism is neglected.

One of the unconscious functions of viewing Buddhism uncritically and ignoring what psychoanalysis might offer it is that it allows the partiality and flaws in Buddhism to remain unscrutinized. That Buddhism has pockets of unconsciousness is suggested by such things as the residues of pathology found in enlightened meditators (Brown and Engler, 1986), the plethora of scandals in spiritual communities, and the nature of unconsciousness. One reason for the resistance to psychoanalysis is that the idea of the unconscious, as Phillips (1994) aptly notes, makes a mockery of the belief in self-mastery (p. 117). After Freud, the notion of transparent self-awareness and unfettered liberation seems psychologically and morally naive. Psychoanalysis teaches us that actions and motivations that spiritual disciplines may only view from a conscious viewpoint may be riddled with more complex unconscious intentions and effects. For example, a sense of nonentitlement, self-abasement, and self-sabotage can masquerade, as it sometimes did for Albert, as spiritual nonattachment.

While exposure to Buddhist practice gave Albert the experience of dereified, decommodified, and non-self-centric subjectivity, psychoanalysis revealed some of the unconscious limitations of Buddhism.

Psychoanalytic perspectives on subjectivity helped me realize the way Buddhism unconsciously contributed to the self-nullification of Albert, what he termed "Albertness." Analytic investigation revealed that Albert's attraction to the no-self doctrine of Buddhism had at least three possible meanings. First, the doctrine of no-self had an important emotional resonance for Albert because it captured his experience of nonexistence that was so pervasive in his life. It embodied the subjective sense of selflessness he felt about his self-nullified life. Second, the problem of self-assertion—being orphaned—was avoided by embracing this doctrine. If there was no *self*, then there was no self-*assertion*. If there was no self-assertion, then there was no threat of being ostracized and abandoned by the other. Third, the doctrine of no-self relieved the emotional pain of Albert not being who he could have become: being what he called "Albertfull." If we follow Christopher Bollas (1989) in *Forces of Destiny*, all humans share a desire to discover and actualize their "destiny"—their unique, personal idiom. Embracing the no-self doctrine of Buddhism anesthetized Albert's excruciatingly painful sense of having missed out on his potential.

Psychoanalysis not only clarified some of the possible origins and meanings of Albert's attraction to the Buddhist doctrine of (no-)self, it illuminated some of the unconscious consequences. Buddhist meditation can mollify egocentricity and decrease narcissism, even as it can foster what I would term an *evasion* of subjectivity, which has self-betraying and self-endangering consequences. With its microscopic attention to consciousness, Buddhism helped Albert experience the texture of his inner life with greater sensitivity, even as its self-negating view of subjectivity eclipsed the baby of his subjectivity in the act of throwing out the bathwater of his egocentricity.

Selves, like civilizations, are built on the twin pillars of what they *exclude* and what they *include*. What Kristeva (1982) terms the "abject," that which we find loathsome and other, may be a central part of what is excluded. From its place of "banishment" it exerts an uncanny significance and force. The abject is "what I permanently thrust aside in order to live. . . . Not me. Not that" (p. 2). Culture and individual identity rest upon it. It is "something rejected from which one does not part . . . the place where I am not and which permits me to be" (p. 4).

"[A]bjection," according to Kristeva (1982), "is the other facet of religious, moral, and ideological codes on which rest the sleep of individuals and the breathing spells of societies. Such codes are abjection's purification and repression" (p. 209). Buddhism's telling ambivalence about emotional life may partake of the "abjection of the self" (p. 5). On the one hand, the meditative method counsels acceptance of whatever one is experiencing. On the other hand, the purpose of meditation, according to many Buddhist texts, is to "purify" the mind of "defilements" such as greed, hatred, and delusion. Does the tension in Buddhism regarding emotions—and the emphasis on cleansing impurities—signal that the *self* itself, in Buddhism, is viewed as *abject*?[8]

---

[8]This may be less true of Tantric and Mahayana Buddhism. Tantra, for example, is based on "the affirmation of life in all its forms and the validity of the phenomenal world" (Stevens, 1990, p. 60). In Tantra, "passions" are viewed as "the raw material of enlightenment—not obstacles but true building blocks" (p. 62), with sexuality as the "most powerful aid in the quest for liberation" (p. 60). The stance toward self-experience underlying Buddhism, however, still leads to the abjectification of self, even in strands of Buddhism in which the view of emotions and the world is relatively less negative.

Buddhism's attempted circumvention of human subjectivity does not eliminate its shaping power. A sense of nonattachment to subjective life does not mean that one will not be deeply shaped and delimited by it. The fact that sociopaths may be "detached" suggests that detachment is not freedom. One can disidentify from a troubling character trait without necessarily being free of its pernicious hold. A spiritual teacher or guru can deeply feel that the self is an illusion and that he or she is thus not the "owner" of any accomplishments and yet still unconsciously bask in and encourage the self-betraying submissive adulation of his or her students.

By attending to the evasion of Albert's subjectivity fostered by Buddhism, we were able to ascertain where he had unwittingly become its prisoner by perpetuating certain self-betraying modes of self-care—such as subverting and obscuring his voice—as well as reenacting restrictive relational configurations of childhood, such as burying his discontent and engaging in compliant and depriving relationships, which left him feeling alone and neglected.

By cultivating heightened attentiveness, detachment, and equanimity, meditation practice helped Albert more easily know what he was feeling, and this reduced his automatic tendency to accommodate to the needs and wishes of others. But it also anesthetized his emotional pain and deprivation, which stifled his affective discontent. Momentarily decentering from troubling affect inadvertently inhibited Albert from feeling the need to address some of the imprisoning aspects of his existence, which perpetuated his passivity and thereby hindered him from challenging and more fully extricating himself from the captivity of the normotic prison. We came to understand that while he had increasingly found the normotic mode of being of his parents—which he called "the House"—vacuous and unsustaining, he had not yet built an alternative universe. Detaching from his emotional pain compromised his motivation for working on this dimension of his life.

Albert could not heal the fault line in his personality without a therapeutic relationship in which fears of individuation and self-depriving ways of caring for self and organizing relationships could be reenacted and understood, and a self that reflected his values and ideals could be cultivated and developed. The Eastern literature has anecdotes of teachers and masters interacting with students and disciples in ways that are designed to help them recognize characterological patterns. But the use of transference is sporadic and unsystematic. By systematically analyzing transference phenomena and relational reenactments, psychoanalysis can illuminate ways of being that may either go unnoticed or be submerged in Buddhism—such as Albert's idealization of his teachers and his concomitant self-submissiveness (Tart and Deikman, 1991). In Buddhism, this dynamic may remain unexamined, as it did with Albert, and the student's self-devaluation and deferentiality may never get resolved and may play itself out in various other relationships. This seemed to be the case with Albert in many of his relationships, with both men and women.

As the crucible for the reemergence of archaic transferences, the psycho-analytic relationship can aid in the process of aborted development being recognized, reinstated, and worked through. Because Albert had only an inchoate sense of self, the Buddhist focus on deconstructing the self left him directionless, even as it fostered greater awareness and tolerance of thoughts, feelings, fantasies, and so forth. Since it omits the crucial task of self-construction, Buddhism's model of working with self-experience was a necessary but incomplete way of healing the fault line in his personality. He needed what I would term self-creation and self-amplification more than self-deconstruction. Since his life was haunted by absence, emptiness, and virtuality, not by misplaced desires and attachments, he needed to build a *new* life, one based on his own relational and avocational values and ideals, not simply to detach from a bad one based on attachments to illusory notions of self and reality. He thus needed psychoanalysis as well as meditation in order to work through his directionlessness and build an alternative life to the normotic world.

Self-construction necessitates a somewhat different and more active role for both the analyst and the analysand than he experienced in Buddhist practice.

I shall focus on four aspects of the process of facilitating authenticity that were involved in my work with Albert: (1) the importance of the ana-lyst providing a "self-delineating selfobject function" (Stolorow, Atwood, and Brandchaft, 1992; Stolorow and Atwood, 1992), by which I mean aid-ing the analysand in articulating and validating his or her subjective expe-rience; (2) the therapeutic exploration of Albert's experience of my inevitable impingements; (3) sustained investigation of his subtle affective discontent, which may signal the first faint pulsings of authenticity; and (4) attention to my experience of therapeutic *contentment*, which signified Albert's unconscious compliance in the treatment.

The sense of self of certain, if not all, patients who, like Albert, struggle with inauthenticity, is tenuously held. They have scant belief in the valid-ity of their perceptions or judgments about themselves or others. They may doubt or dismiss their own emotional reality. Their experience of emotional deprivation, for example, may be denied or minimized.

People's sense of, and confidence in, the reality and substantiality of their subjective experience develops as a result of parental attunement to their subjective world, including their positive and negative affect states. There was an absence of this in Albert's life. In their designation of the "self-delineating selfobject function," Stolorow and Atwood (1992) stress the "developmental importance of a selfobject function contributing to the articulation and validation of a child's unfolding world of personal experience . . . the self-delineating selfobject function, [which] . . . may be pictured along a developmental continuum, from early sensori-motor forms of validation occurring in the pre-verbal transactions between infant and caregiver, to later processes of validation that take place increasingly through symbolic communication and involve the child's awareness of others as separate centers of subjectivity" (p. 27).

Knowledge of, and belief in, one's own subjective reality is deeply compromised, as we saw in Albert's case, when such parental attunement is absent. Albert struggled, for example, with self-mistrust and was prone to take on the viewpoints of others. He subordinated—to the extent of negating—his own sense of self and the world to his parents in order to maintain a sense of connectedness to them. This was a breeding ground for compliance and inauthenticity.

For analysands such as Albert, who experienced absent or faulty parental responsiveness to their affective states, including parental denial or defensiveness about their affective malattunement, traumatic repetition of parental misattunement with the analyst is an ever-present danger. Albert assumed, for example, that sharing his inner world would lead to either enraging usurpation or hostile attacks. It is in this context that I understood his fears with me and his compensatory attempts to "speak my language."

An attuned and nonimpinging environment is essential in working with such issues. Impingements foster compliance and false self-proclivities. Nonimpingement safeguards the analysand against a compliant sense of being *for* the analyst.

Unless an analyst possesses total self-consciousness and no counter-transference—which is impossible—therapeutic influence and impingement are inevitable. Analyzing their impact is thus essential. Otherwise, the perpetuation of compliance and inauthenticity goes underground. The interesting therapeutic question is not how to eliminate misattunement and impingements—which is a quixotic enterprise—but how to understand the analysand's *experience* of the impact of the misattunement or impingement. What is thus needed is the analyst's self-delineating self-object function, his ongoing clarification and validation of the analysand's subjective experience, including reaction to the analyst's inevitable impingements and misattunements.

The analyst's attunement to the analysand's experience, from within the latter's own vantage point, is crucial to the process of clarifying and further consolidating the analysand's inchoate subjective reality. This may well include the analysand's experience of the analyst's impingement, the analysand's affective discontent about the analyst or the analysis, and the analysand's vulnerability and ambivalence about experiencing and articulating a tenuously held affective reality because of fear of traumatic affective misattunement.

Once this sort of analytic environment is established, and when necessary, reestablished, it is somewhat less dangerous for the analysand to experience and articulate a range of affect. This may then lead to the emergence of formally disavowed or warded off affective states.

The analysand's subtle affective discontent—for example, Albert's irritation and muted disappointment in me for not affirming his ideas—can represent the first faint pulsings of authenticity, which will probably be experienced by him or her as unfamiliar, trivial, strange, or silly. The analysand may (1) not believe in, (2) dismiss, or (3) devalue moments of authenticity, just as important caregivers failed to value and encourage the expression of, and belief in, those aspects of the analysand's subjective world at earlier stages of their development. Albert experienced all three at different times in our work together. My interest in these intimations of authenticity aided in their further expression and clarification. This, in turn, eventually led to Albert's strengthened recognition of, and belief in, their existence and validity.

Attunement to the *analyst's* experience—particularly his or her sense of therapeutic *contentment*—as well as the analysand's discontentment, can sometimes also aid in facilitating the emergence of the analysand's authenticity. For example, my sense of excessive efficacy and ease at various points in the treatment signaled, not that the analysis was proceeding in an unequivocally successful manner, but that it was permeated by Albert's unconscious compliance with me. Exploring moments in which Albert tried to "speak my language" because of the emotional dangers that he anticipated, eventually opened up the pattern of self-submissiveness inculcated with his parents that permeated his relationships, professional life, and the treatment. The feeling that I had that I was in tune with Albert hid the way in which he was sometimes accommodating to me. My sense of therapeutic success was periodically an artifact of his conformity rather than the result of my correct interpretations. Attention to this dimension of my experience aided me in reexamining subtle aspects of compliance in the therapeutic interaction, which encouraged transference analysis of this formerly neglected area. Albert described our work in an association during this period of treatment as "a crane pulling the buried coffin out of the earth."

We were then able to begin to address other issues, such as the obstacles to intimacy and professional fulfillment that he experienced and established, which are often suppressed or dealt with abstractly in Buddhism. These topics are often not addressed directly by meditation teachers. Clear guidelines about how to deal with them are rarely offered.

As Albert was more able to be authentic with me, his personal and professional relationships also began to change. He formed more reciprocal social and intellectual partnerships and his friendships and his primary intimate relationship were more fulfilling.

His professional work was also enriched. As he valued his own needs more, he became more comfortable with self-assertion and his writing, like his life, became more "Albertful." Tired of keeping his potential under wraps and seducing others into diminished views of his academic work, he was able to put his best intellectual foot forward, which resulted in his receiving acknowledgment by those he valued in his field for his academic talents.

What psychoanalysts and Buddhists "discover" about selfhood is often an artifact of the way they investigate it. The substantiality, self-centricity, and historicity of a subject shaped by a particular history of relationships and self-experiences is evident to a psychoanalyst utilizing a diachronic psychoanalytic method. On the other hand the fluidity, non-self-centricity, and spiritual aspects of selfhood—the way humans are shaped and created anew, moment after moment, by the rising and passing away of fluid and discontinuous mental states—seems self-evident to someone examining selfhood meditatively with the synchronic Buddhist method.

In a popular formulation Engler (1986) has claimed that the way these two senses of self can be reconciled is to realize that non-self-centeredness is a higher state of being than self-centeredness and that *both* a sense of self and a sense of no-self are necessary for experiencing optimal psychological health and leading a full life: "you have to be somebody before you are nobody" (p. 24). I agree with his claim that psychoanalytic concern with building a cohesive and integrated self is a "precondition" of the subsequent developmental task of disidentifying from restrictive self-representations and reducing excessive self-involvement. One certainly cannot disidentify from what one is not. Albert, for example, could not become unattached to the virtuality of his self.

But it is incorrect to conceive of non-self-centricity as a *higher* or final stage of being, because a consolidated sense of self and a sense of non-self-centricity are interpenetrating aspects of human experience; they are alternating positions of being, as Ogden (1991) might put it, rather than hierarchically ordered stages. The privileging of non-self-centeredness, and the consequent devaluation and repression of self-centeredness, ultimately engender the egocentric behavior sometimes acted out in Buddhist communities. For as Jung emphasized, when one aspect of subjectivity is consciously overemphasized, its opposite takes on increased unconscious importance.

The experience of non-self-centered subjectivity and self-centered subjectivity exist in tension in everyone's psyche. It is affectively difficult to keep this tension alive. Collapsing this core dialectic in human psychology by valorizing either experience of self—as is the case in Eurocentric (Alexander, 1931) or Orientocentric perspectives (Epstein, 1995)—affords psychic relief even as it impoverishes our understanding of human psychology.

As I hope my work with Albert has suggested, psychoanalysis and Buddhism were both necessary to keep alive his tenuous hope for a life that might feel more authentic and alive. Buddhism's view of non-self-centric subjectivity tempered the egocentricity of psychoanalysis and widened its moral purview. Psychoanalysis illuminated some of the deleterious psychic consequences of Buddhism's evading of subjectivity. Buddhism challenged the integrated self that psychoanalysis attempted to promote, by demonstrating that in eclipsing the always unfinished and open nature of the self the notion of self-unity can be a limiting and imprisoning type of self-experience. In fostering self-restriction and self-alienation, the ideal of the integrated self might thus represent what Erich Fromm (1941) termed an "escape from freedom"—the ever-renewing possibility and responsibility for creating who we are. But psychoanalysis taught Buddhism that there is a hidden and pernicious cost to absolutizing its view of the fictionality of the self, especially a "return of the repressed" in spiritual practices, communities, and relationships that generates pain and corruption in its wake.

The expanded conception of subjectivity that I am advocating involves thinking more dialectically; granting both psychoanalytic and Buddhist viewpoints a range of applicability; recognizing the two perspectives as alternative tools, useful for different purposes, rather than as contradictory claims. In my Loewaldian conception of selfhood, the self can be likened to a symphony composed of a variety of instruments—consciousness and unconsciousness, self-centeredness and self-lessness, rationality and imagination, and so forth—each with its own idiosyncratic sound and application. The self is impoverished if certain instruments are not played. The best music occurs when no instrument dominates or is excluded, and when there is communication and cross-fertilization between them.

Albert's experience of allowing psychoanalysis and Buddhism to cross-pollinate suggests that psychoanalytic and Buddhist conceptions of subjectivity would be enriched if the understandings obtained from their different ways of investigating subjectivity were integrated into a more encompassing and inclusive framework, one that values the unique insights into different facets of subjectivity they each elucidate, while avoiding their limitations. Such limitations might include the "nearsightedness" of Buddhism, with its synchronic focus on the change and flux of consciousness in the present moment, and the "farsightedness" of psychoanalysis, with its diachronic emphasis on the historical nature of human lives, the way, to quote Wordsworth, in which the child is father to the man (or the mother to the woman).[9]

---

[9]Freud (1895), in his concept of "deferred action"—that is, the past is active in the present and the present can alter and "retranscribe" memories from the past (p. 356)—and his metaphor of the "mystic writing pad" (1925), in which the mind is likened to a writing tablet composed of traces from both the past and present, presented a dual-track model of mind in which both the past and the present are formative. The implications of this model seem not to have been fully elaborated.

A more encompassing model of subjectivity would illuminate a more complete range of the multiplicity that is the self than either pursued alone. By adopting such a complementary bifocal viewpoint, Albert and I were able to recognize that states of self-centricity and un-self-consciousness were both part of his attempts to live a full and meaningful life. The former was necessary to help him fixate the self and view it as a concrete, substantial entity. This helped him to reflect upon his life and conduct, delineate what he felt and valued, assess situations, formulate plans and goals, and choose among potential courses of action. It ultimately helped him to find an alternative to the suffocating normotic world of his parents. Sensitivity to states of non-self-consciousness enabled him to live less self-centeredly, more fluidly and gracefully. The view of the self as a process facilitated his appreciation of art, his capacity to listen to his students, to participate in athletics, and eventually to experience love.

A complementary view of subjectivity helped us avoid the far-sightedness of Buddhism and the near-sightedness of psychoanalysis, neither eclipsing the view of self-fluidity, non-self-centricity, and self-transcendence suggested by Buddhism, nor the self-substantiality, historicity, and agency revealed by psychoanalysis. In the next section, I attempt to paint a picture of a contemplative psychoanalysis, a therapeutics that draws on the valuable facets of psychoanalysis and spirituality.

TOWARD A CONTEMPLATIVE PSYCHOANALYSIS

A contemplative psychoanalysis of the future might explore both what psychoanalysis might contribute to spiritual traditions *and* what spirituality might teach psychoanalysis. A therapeutics that judiciously draws on spiritual practices of training attentiveness such as Buddhism offers (Rubin, 1985) and psychoanalytic modes of investigating self-experience and interpersonal relatedness might enable us to distinguish between, and reconcile the possibilities and pathologies of, self-centered *and* non-self-centered subjectivity. It would thus *deabsolutize* the self-centered self and *deprovincialize* the non-self-centered self.

In terms of the former, detaching from a hypertrophied, overly self-centric sense of self may free us from the prison of a self-alienating egoism, enhance our capacity for empathy and tolerance, and foster a sense of connection with, and compassion for, others. Loosening the grip of excessive self-preoccupation, as occurs when one is deeply immersed in playing a musical instrument, watching an engrossing cultural event, participating in athletics, or making love, often leads to a heightened sense of living. Such a view of subjectivity opens subjects up to the possibility of greater intimacy, for friendship and love necessitate that we unconstrict and sometimes transcend our normally more restrictive sense of separateness from others and the world.

Non-self-centered subjectivity might also enrich analytic treatment in several ways. In a less bounded, non-self-preoccupied, non-self-centric state, the analyst can more easily engage in transient identifications with subtle affect experiences, access somatic knowledge,[10] and decenter from habitual and limiting psychological conditioning. In this state there is sometimes "an easy commerce of the old and the new" (Eliot, 1963, pp. 207–208), resulting in what the Indian philosopher Krishnamurti termed a "freedom from the known," in which we are able to spring from familiar patterns of thinking and relating and experience newness. This is illustrated by the analyst who makes a creative interpretation or intervention—saying something she was not consciously aware that she knew, or relating in an unfamiliar yet creative and facilitative manner—instead of reiterating something unoriginal that she already knows. These states are likely to promote in the analyst increased capacity to listen creatively and respond to the exigencies of the clinical moment in a less fettered manner.

Analysands who experience non-self-centered subjectivity may have less difficulty alternating between what Modell (1989) terms the "multiple realities" of the analytic setting and process—such as past and present, transference as "real" *and* illusory—that are essential to change. The analysand's capacity for psychic fluidity would probably also facilitate the capacity to free associate.

The non-self-centered subjectivity that characterizes Buddhism might become deprovincialized when Buddhism welcomes the questions analysts might have about such things as the pathologies of nonattachment, self-evasion, and spiritual idealization and submissiveness. Self-betraying facets of Buddhism, including the abjectification of self and emotions, the self-compromising facets of the hidden authoritarianism of the teacher-student relationship, and the potential countertransference of Buddhist teachers, might then become grist for the meditative and psychotherapeutic mills.

The moral iniquity and vacuity of current civic and public life, and the absence of thoughtful and substantive dialogue about how education, media, families, and public and religious institutions might celebrate diversity, strengthen bonds between peoples, and nourish life-affirming modes of being and relating all demand progressive responses.

In facilitating our recognition of the reality of moral complexity and human agency, while not eclipsing the capacity for non-self-centered subjectivity, a contemplative psychoanalysis might be more ethically

---

[10]Somatic knowledge is illustrated when we "remember" the pin number or gym lock combination we have momentarily forgotten. Remembering occurs, not when we try to think about the number, which only seems to generate more frustration and temporary amnesia, but when we "let our fingers do the walking" and thinking.

responsive to the moral challenges humans now face than either psycho-analysis or a spiritual discipline such as Buddhism pursued alone. A new and expanded sense of I-ness that would foster links between people, rather than a privatist, individualist ethos, might be one such beacon in our collective darkness. A spiritually attuned contemplative psychoanalysis might see the needs of fellow citizens and the polis as crucial organizing principles for the conduct of human lives.

Out of a contemplative psychoanalysis we could fashion a permeable but bounded postindividualistic "species self" (Lifton, 1993), for whom both individuation and non-self-centricity are seen as interpenetrating facets of what it means to be a human being. The sphere of empathy of a species self would reach beyond oneself and those significant others within one's circle of concern to include fellow citizens of the world and the dispossessed. Seeing oneself in a more expansive and interconnected yet differentiated way—as a self-in-community, instead of a selfless spiritual self or an isolated, imperial psychological self—might foster both connectedness to the polis and self-enrichment, thus decreasing alienation and anomie.

There is a growing and disturbing disparity in the 1990s between the haves and the have-nots. By fostering a sense of connection with and tolerance for the other, spirituality may be a crucial aspect of our collective mental health—as long as it is open to the questions of psychoanalysis. When the spiritual is no longer delegitimized—as it has traditionally been in psychoanalysis[11]—then there might be a "widening scope" of psychoanalysis that might encourage analytically informed examinations of issues that adversely effect the health of individuals as well as cultures: the seductions of materialism and consumerism and the psychology of greed, authoritarianism, submissiveness to fanaticism, racism, sexism, homophobia, and ageism. Questions about such things as the nature of creativity, health and intimacy, constructive and engaged citizenship, and the process of fostering psychological decolonization might then be seen as more germane to our field. A psychoanalysis that was not *only* self-centered might contribute to a civilization with less discontent.[12]

---

[11]There are notable exceptions. The more sympathetic non-Eurocentric work of Horney (1945, 1987), Jung (1958), Kelman (1960), Fromm, Suzuki, and DeMartino (1960), Roland (1988), and myself (Rubin, 1985, 1991, 1993), for example, has pointed to various aspects of Buddhism's salutary dimensions, including its ability to enrich psychoanalytic listening (Rubin, 1985); promote "well-being," being fully awake and alive (Fromm et al., 1960), and expand analytic conceptions of subjectivity (Roland, 1988; Rubin, 1993, 1996). But the cross-pollination that might mutually enrich both disciplines tends to be lacking even in approaches that avoid Eurocentrism and Orientocentrism. Elsewhere (Rubin, 1993, 1996, 1997) I explore this topic from different angles than in this present essay.

[12]Dialogues with George Atwood, Gerald J. Gargiulo, James Jones, Marilyn Saur, Charles Spezzano, Deborah Tanzer, and Mary Traina enriched this paper. A revised version of this paper appears in Rubin (1997).

REFERENCES

Alexander, F. (1931), Buddhistic training as an artificial catatonia: The biological meaning of psychological occurrences. *Psychoanal. Rev.*, 18:129–145.

Atwood, G. & Stolorow, R. (1984), *Structures of Subjectivity*. Hillsdale, NJ: The Analytic Press.

Bateson, G. (1972), *Steps to an Ecology of Mind*. New York: Ballantine Books.

Baumeister, R. (1987), How the self became a problem: A psychological review of historical research. *J. Personal. Social Psych.*, 52:163–176.

Bollas, C. (1987), *The Shadow of the Object*. New York: Columbia University Press.

———— (1989), *Forces of Destiny*. London: Free Associations.

Boucher, S. (1988), *Turning the Wheel*. San Francisco, CA: Harper & Row.

Brown, D. & Engler, J. (1986), The stages of mindfulness meditation: A validation study. In: *Transformations of Consciousness*, ed. K. Wilber, J. Engler & D. Brown. Boston, MA: Shambhala, pp. 161–283.

Buccino, D. (1993), The commodification of the object in object relations theory. *Psychoanal. Rev.*, 80:123–134.

Eliot, T. S. (1963), Little Gidding. In: *Collected Poems (1909–1962)*. New York: Harcourt, Brace & World, pp. 207–208.

Engler, J. (1986), Therapeutic aims in psychotherapy and meditation: Developmental stages in the representation of self. In: *Transformation of Consciousness*, ed. K. Wilber, J. Engler & D. Brown. Boston, MA: Shambhala, pp. 17–51.

Epstein, M. (1995), *Thoughts Without a Thinker*. New York: Basic Books.

Foucault, M. (1977), Nietzsche, genealogy, history. In: *Language, Counter-Memory, Practice*. Ithaca, NY: Cornell University Press, pp. 139–164.

Freud, S. (1895), *The Complete Letters of Sigmund Freud to Wilhelm Fliess*, ed. J. Masson. Cambridge, MA: Harvard University Press, 1985.

———— (1917), A difficulty in the path of psycho-analysis. *Standard Edition*, 17:135–144. London: Hogarth Press, 1955.

———— (1921), Group psychology and the analysis of the ego. *Standard Edition*, 18:69–143. London: Hogarth Press, 1955.

———— (1925), A note upon the "Mystic writing-pad." *Standard Edition*, 19:227–232. London: Hogarth Press, 1961.

———— (1927), The future of an illusion. *Standard Edition*, 21:5–56. London: Hogarth Press, 1961.

———— (1930), Civilization and its discontents. *Standard Edition*, 21:64–145. London: Hogarth Press, 1961.

———— (1933), New introductory lectures on psychoanalysis. *Standard Edition*, 22:5–182. London: Hogarth Press, 1964.

Fromm, E. (1941), *Escape from Freedom*. New York: Avon Books.

———— Suzuki, D. T. & DeMartino, R., eds. (1960), *Zen Buddhism and Psychoanalysis*. New York: Harper & Row.

Gaylin, W. (1988), Love and the limits of individualism. In: *Passionate Attachments*, ed. W. Gaylin & E. Person. New York: Free Press, pp. 41–62.

Gedo, J. (1986), *Conceptual Issues in Psychoanalysis*. Hillsdale, NJ: The Analytic Press.

Hartmann, H. (1960), *Psychoanalysis and Moral Values*. New York: International Universities Press.

Horney, K. (1945), *Our Inner Conflicts*. New York: Norton.
——— (1987), *Final Lectures*. New York: Norton.
Houston, J. (1980), *Life-Force*. New York: Delacorte Press.
Jones, J. (1995), The real is the relational: Psychoanalysis as a model of human understanding. Unpublished manuscript.
Jung, C. (1958), *Psychology and Religion*. Princeton, NJ: Princeton University Press.
Kelman, H. (1960), Psychoanalytic thought and Eastern wisdom. In: *The History of Psychotherapy*, ed. J. Ehrenwald. New York: Aronson, 1976, pp. 328–333.
Kovel, J. (1991), *History and Spirit*. Boston, MA: Beacon Press.
Kristeva, J. (1982), *Powers of Horror*. New York: Columbia University Press.
Lifton, R. (1993), *The Protean Self*. New York: Basic Books.
Loewald, H. (1978), *Psychoanalysis and the History of the Individual*. New Haven, CT: Yale University Press.
Mitchell, S. (1991), Contemporary perspectives on self: Toward an integration. *Psychoanal. Dial.*, 1:121–147.
Modell, A. (1989), The psychoanalytic setting as a container of multiple levels of reality: A perspective on the theory of psychoanalytic treatment. *Psychoanal. Inq.*, 9:67–87.
Ogden, T. (1991), An interview with Thomas Ogden. *Psychoanal. Dial.*, 1:361–376.
Panel (1984), Value judgments in psychoanalytic theory and practice. S. Lytton, reporter. *J. Amer. Psychoanal. Assn.*, 32:147–156.
Peoples, K. (1991), The paradox of surrender: Constructing and transcending the self. Unpublished manuscript.
Phillips, A. (1994), *On Flirtation*. Cambridge, MA: Harvard University Press.
Rieff, P. (1963), Introduction. In: *Freud: Therapy and Technique*. New York: Macmillan, pp. 7–24.
Roland, A. (1988), *In Search of Self in India and Japan*. Princeton, NJ: Princeton University Press.
——— (1995), How universal is the psychoanalytic self? Unpublished manuscript.
Rubin, J. B. (1985), Meditation and psychoanalytic listening. *Psychoanal. Rev.*, 72:599–612.
——— (1991), The clinical integration of Buddhist meditation and psychoanalysis. *J. Integrat. & Eclectic Psychother.*, 10:173–181.
——— (1993), Psychoanalysis and Buddhism: Toward an integration. In: *Comprehensive Textbook of Psychotherapy Integration*, ed. G. Stricker & J. Gold. New York: Plenum, pp. 249–266.
——— (1996), *Psychoanalysis and Buddhism*. New York: Plenum Press.
——— (1997), *A Psychoanalysis for Our Time*. New York: New York University Press.
Rushdie, S. (1994), *East, West*. New York: Pantheon Books.
Schafer, R. (1976), *A New Language for Psychoanalysis*. New Haven, CT: Yale University Press.
——— (1989), Narratives of the self. In: *Psychoanalysis*, ed A. Cooper, O. Kernberg & E. Person. New Haven, CT: Yale University Press, pp. 153–167.
Silverman, L., Lachmann, F. & Milich, R. (1982), *The Search for Oneness*. New York: International Universities Press.
Stevens, J. (1990), *Lust for Enlightenment*. Boston: Shambhala.
Stolorow, R. & Atwood, G. (1992), *Contexts of Being*. Hillsdale, NJ: The Analytic Press.

———— & Brandchaft, B. (1992), Three realms of the unconscious and their thera-
    peutic transformation. *Psychoanal. Rev.*, 79:25–30.
Tart, C. & Deikman, A. (1991), Mindfulness, spiritual seeking and psychotherapy.
    J. Transpers. Psychother., 23:29–52.
Varela, F. (1984), The creative circle: Sketches on the natural history of circularity.
    In: *The Invented Reality*, ed. P. Watzlawick. New York: Norton, pp. 309–323.

— 6 —

Coming to Life

The Creative Intercourse of Psychoanalysis
and Zen Buddhism

JOSEPH BOBROW

We shall not cease from exploration,
And the end of our exploring will be
to arrive where we started,
And know the place for the first time

—T. S. Eliot, *Four Quartets*

Religion and psychoanalysis, with some exceptions, have been traditionally suspicious of one another, each tending to view the other
as a purveyor of illusion. Psychoanalysts' discomfort with religious
experience seems to have roots in a few key concerns. It can be an escape
from unpleasant experience, a soothing balm that postpones coming to
grips with reality, or worse, a self-deception. It may kindle fears of a
return to magic, to superstition.

Freud (1907) saw in religion a desperate turning to a powerful illusory
authority as an antidote to human helplessness, and a socially acceptable
form of obsessive neurosis: "One might venture to regard obsessional
neurosis as a pathological counterpart to the formation of religion, and to
describe that neurosis as an individual religiosity and *religion as a universal neurosis*" (pp. 126–127; emphasis added).

This speaks to a narrowing of the range of experience, and the diminution of the role of personal awareness, discrimination, and agency. It
reflects confinement within rigid rituals and prescriptions for what and
how to think and be. So it is both confinement and escape, not to mention
the specter of sin that may be conjured up. The God one fears is just

beneath the surface, a God who punishes for transgressions from the party line.

Religious objections to psychotherapy and psychoanalysis have been many and varied but a central concern is that they build up or ignore the tendency toward self-centeredness rather than encouraging its dissolution. This is seen as detrimental to the capacity to be in contact with and have concern for one's fellow humans, and to know God.

Fromm (1960) and Symington (1994) describe a religious motivation characterized not so much by primitive psychological mechanisms, but rather rooted in the search for fundamental self-knowledge, integrity, and core human values. Such a religious path views human beings as capable of responsibility, intention, and choice. Meditative practice can be part of such a path and, instead of imprisoning one in a rigid system of beliefs, can liberate rather than confine, reveal rather than obscure, foster openness, resilience, the kind of loosening up that analysts also look for. (Of course, it can also be put to other uses; it can have multiple functions.) In fact, genuine meditative experience is quite subversive. It is subversive to the core of our beliefs about ourselves, our relations with others, and the very nature of reality and human existence. It challenges our most profound and unconscious assumptions about "the way it is" and "the way it's supposed to be," the most cherished organizing concepts that give shape to who we take ourselves to be. Among these are our notions about the nature of mind, meaning, identity, and self. In so doing, meditative experience can facilitate a qualitatively different kind of exploration and deepening of these dimensions of our lives.

In a spirit of respect for the distinctiveness of both psychoanalytic and meditative traditions, I here examine some of their similarities and differences, with a view toward mutual enrichment. After all, both speak to the relief of suffering, emancipation from mental and emotional constraints, the freeing of human potential to love and learn through self-knowledge. I suggest what may be an innovative way to think about their interaction and place it in the context of work by Mitchell (1993), Ogden, (1989, 1993), Loewald (1980), Erikson (1966), Fromm (1960), Symington (1994), and Engler (1983).

I suggest that two dimensions of human experience—which I call letting go and coming forth, relinquishing and emerging—are common to both psychoanalysis and Zen though each is privileged differently in the respective disciplines. These dimensions, which infuse our experience and development, are not simply sequentially related but are intrinsically synchronous. A vital human life—a coming to life—involves the capacity to both fall away and gather together, to be somebody and to be nothing at all, to know and to not know. It involves the ability to move between the two, realizing moments where each activity is distinct, moments when they interpenetrate, and moments when (by virtue of being heuristic and fundamentally illusory organizing concepts) each falls away in direct, liberating, unmediated experience. I include a clinical vignette and discuss the notions of meaning, identity, self, and mind. I then explore the dynamic relation between the two disciplines and suggest a way to think about their interaction.

ZEN

The meditative tradition I describe, Zen Buddhism, is not a religion in the traditional sense. The practice of Zen is not worship as it is commonly thought of. There is no deity in the ordinary meaning of the word, no otherworldly, supranatural entity. Zen does not posit a soul, traditionally construed as an everlasting personal or transcendental essence that changes form over time and space. Rather, through the practice of sitting meditation or *zazen*, usually in the context of a mutually supportive community or *sangha*, through mindful awareness in the many moments of one's daily life, and usually through a relationship with a teacher, each person is deemed capable, like the historical Buddha Shakyamuni, of coming to know (*gnosis*) for him or herself the intersection of the sacred and the personal, the universal and the particular, by his own experience in this life.

Zen practice offers a path for addressing perennial human questions of identity, origin, meaning, and ethics: Who am I? Where do I come from? Where am I going? What is the meaning of my life? Why is there such suffering? What is it to live a good life, a wise life? The practice of Zen can productively help to engage what Mitchell (1993) calls "the struggle of people at the end of the 20th century for personal meaning and interpersonal connection." It offers an avenue for resolving what Loewald (cited in Mitchell) felt was the "compulsive separation between self and other, inside and outside, on different levels of organization" (p. 253).

Complementary Paths

The intention of each path is, in one sense, quite different. Psychoanalysis facilitates integration of the personality, a gathering together, particularly the integration of that which is unconscious, that which has been split off, dissociated, repressed, or otherwise excluded from awareness. Zen, on the other hand, offers the opportunity for fundamental ontological insight: What is the *essential* nature of the one who is born, lives and dies, loves and hates, laughs and weeps? From this vantage point, humans exclude from awareness not only split-off affects, wishes, perceptions, memories, conflicts, parts of ourselves, and conflicting self-organizations; *we also keep unconscious our fundamental insubstantiality, interdependence, and consequently, our own sacredness and that of our fellow beings, human and otherwise.*

I do not think the purposes of the two disciplines are mutually exclusive or ultimately divergent. Rather they are complementary and potentiating.

Psychoanalysis and Zen practice share various features. Each is a journey and a way of discovery: a process of inquiry, self-knowledge, and transformation. Each encourages the use, expansion, and ultimately the liberation, of attention. Each recognizes the tendency toward self-deception; each values truth, awareness, the depth dimension. Each acknowledges that things are not always what they seem, that indeed we ourselves and our fellows are not what we seem. What is not readily apparent does not lose value thereby; what does not make sense can be important and valuable. Ambiguity and uncertainty are not to be shied away from but can be a gateway. Knowing—understanding that is not discrepant from experience—leads in each to a kind of transformation. Each presumes that such direct experiential understanding is not synonomous with being smart, that unlearning is important. So each implies the activity of unknowing as well as deeper knowing. Curiosity activates, deepens, and energizes both processes. In each path, richer understanding leads to greater acceptance of oneself and one's experience and to what might be called a certain wisdom. This is cotemporaneous with openness to others and the world, to activity for the good. Wisdom, compassion, and virtue go hand in hand (Symington, 1994). Each path leads to an expanded sense of meaning and aliveness and in so doing places value in this. Individual development and freedom (arising from expanded perspectives, from seeing oneself and one's activity as one actually experiences and constructs it) is not alien to deepening feelings of connection and responsibility. Each values a process of tolerating paradox, holding discrepant experiences, letting things emerge, unravel, take shape, and give up their meanings.

Each situates its inquiry in, and values the cultivation of, the rich field of ordinary daily experience in its multifaceted dimensions. The lotus blooms in the mud; insight arises in the very field of pain, conflict, and confusion. It is from unhurried, gradually freed-up, skillful attention to *what is so* that understanding and growth emerge, not from chasing elsewhere, seeking to escape one's experiential and emotional field, or using willpower alone to forcefully make it other than it is. Another word for *buddha*, which means "awakened one" or "awakening," is *tathagatha,* which means "thus come," the "one who thus appears," or *intimacy with that which arises and passes.* Nyogen Senzaki, an early Zen pioneer in America, left this message to his students: "Trust your own head. Do not put on any false heads above your own. Then, moment after moment, watch your steps closely. These are my last words to you."

Each setting involves a stepping out of ordinary social norms of interaction. Fromm (1960) noted that people in our culture rarely speak truthfully and frankly to each other. Mitchell (1993) refers to "the protection and timelessness of the analytic situation" and how these conditions make "learning about and connecting with multiple self-configurations possible without having to account for oneself in the way one has to in ordinary life" (p. 115). Bion and others find the freedom to engage in reverie to be a central quality of the activity of both patient and analyst in the unfolding of a deep, genuine psychoanalytic process, as it is in the mother-child relationship. At the outset of every Zen retreat or *sesshin*, participants are encouraged to leave behind social graces and habitual modes of interaction and let themselves settle deeply.

Each path, each discipline, involves an intimate relationship over time with another person. The dyads of the analysand and the analyst on the one hand, and the Zen student and Zen teacher on the other, each struggle with and find some measure of experiential resolution to, two key and apparently paradoxical dimensions of human existence: namely, letting go and forgetting the self in direct engagement with one's experience, and bringing forth, maintaining, and affirming a sense of self, of personal agency and self-continuity. In one mode or dimension, self is multiple, relational, discontinuous, and ultimately nonexistent; in the other, self appears as singular, private, and continuous.

Letting Go and Coming Forth

Letting go and bringing forth constitute a fundamental rhythm of life, and may be useful metaphors for organizing our inquiry. As we shall see, they are neither entirely discrete nor simply sequentially related; rather, they are intrinsically synchronous.

I am using the term "letting go" in a rather broad way, attempting to bring together various psychical activities. I relate it to the falling away of outmoded understandings and the opening to new experience, new understandings. It originates as the encounter with difference, discrepancy, and dissatisfaction, with illness, death, loss, and mourning, with aging and impermanence. Things don't go our way. Who among us, patient or analyst, has not been touched by suffering, *duhkha*, the first of the Four Noble Truths of Buddhism? Who has not been exposed to sickness, old age, and death, to helplessness and loss in some form? Sickness, old age, and death are three of the four "signs" (the fourth was seeing a monk, a seeker for the way) that led the historical Buddha Shakyamuni, after a very protected early life, to search for resolution to the question of why there was such suffering. Ultimately, after many struggles, seated with firm resolve beneath a pippala tree, he came to his understanding of suffering, his experience of liberation, and a long career of teaching others. The awareness of our mortality and of not living as fully as we might, impell us. Each evening during Zen retreats, at the end of a long day of meditation and before retiring, the participants hear the following message: "I beg to urge you everyone. Life and death is a grave matter. All things pass quickly away.

Each of you must be completely alert, never neglectful, never indulgent" (in Aitken, 1993).

Letting go is facilitated by what in Zen is metaphorically called "the sword that kills," an aspect of wise action that cuts away delusive understanding and protective conceptual structures that prevent us from encountering our circumstances directly. Life itself functions in exactly this way if we can learn from it. None of us has escaped unscathed over the course of our experience. This experiential current relates to unpacking, destruction—to unintegration—and finally to the encounter with that which cannot be measured, and letting go of the idea of the immeasureable and simply being awake, in direct, moment-to-moment experience.

Bodhidharma, a Zen master who helped bring Zen from India to China, was asked upon his arrival by the emperor: "What is the first principle of Buddhism?" Bodhidharma replied: "Vast emptiness, nothing holy" (Cleary and Cleary, 1977). The emperor was unsettled, to say the least. Dogen, the teacher primarily responsible for Zen taking root in Japan, sheds light on the path to self-knowledge in Zen:

> To study the Way is to study the self.
> To study the self is to forget the self.
> To forget the self is to be enlightened by all things of the universe.
>   [transl. in Aitken, 1992]

Compare this with the view of a contemporary psychoanalyst (Mitchell, 1993):

> The basic mode within the object relations approach to the analytic process is the facilitation of a kind of unraveling. The protection and timelessness of the analytic situation, the permission to free associate, to disorganize, allows the sometimes smooth but thin casting around the self to dissolve and the individual strands that make up experience to separate themselves from each other and become defined and articulated [p. 107].

One can see here both the parallels in approach and the differences in intention of the two paths. Traditionally, in Zen it has not been of particular importance that "the individual strands of our inner experience become defined and articulated." Rather, the approach has encouraged getting to the bottom of things, directly experiencing our essential nature, becoming aware of thoughts, feelings, images, and bodily sensations as they arise—not examining in detail their patterning or personal meanings, conscious or unconscious, but instead focusing attention at a more fundamental level of inquiry.

As with "letting go," I am using the idea of "coming forth" to refer to a broad group of activities related both to emergence and gathering together.

This is the aspect of cohering and coalescing, of creation, personal agency, structure, stability, survival, and continuity—integration. It is the realm of things appearing, new schemata taking shape, of symbol formation and self-formation. This coming forth and its significance in a life is captured in *The Gnostic Gospels*:

> If you bring forth what is within you, what is within you will save you. If you do not bring forth what is within you, what you do not bring forth will destroy you [Pagels, 1979, p. xv].

This can be seen as what in Zen is metaphorically called "the sword that gives life," a bringing to life that makes us truly human. Desire, intentionality, meaning, even subjectivity itself: these relate to form, to coherence, agency, actualization, to the personal subject, to time. In this mode, we are and are becoming something, somebody. We have a point of view, perceptions, desire. This relates to knowing. It may not always be clear or pleasant, it may involve ambiguity or conflict, but there is a sense of some self-structure, someone knowing that which is known. Mitchell (1993) writes "People often experience themselves at any given moment, as containing or being a self that is complete in the present; a sense of self often comes with a feeling of substantialty, presence, integrity and fullness" (p. 102).

In letting go, letting be, there is nothing to become or attain and nothing left undone, nowhere to rush to. This relates to the timeless, to not knowing and to unknowing, a negating of sorts. The field is open, spacious, and clear.

Emptiness

Andre Green once told a seminar: "Two-thirds of the world's people practice religions which speak of emptiness and not sin. What significance does this hold?" An analyst reminds us of *shunyata*, the shining void, traditionally the domain of those sometimes referred to as mystics. Although this emptiness sounds barren, it is neither anomie nor vacuum, but rather the absence of self as absolute and continuous in time and space. Charged with potential, boundless, and without measure, this emptiness is the fundamental ground of Zen. In psychoanalysis we can see its action in generative, nondefensive silence, sometimes called the fertile void, a deep, cooperative mutuality into which pieces can gather, and out of which surprises, discoveries, new movement unfolds. Some think this is the goal of analysis, some think it underlies its method, free association. Perhaps both are true. If we are empty in this way, we are open to realizing our fundamental kinship not only with patients or our analyst, but with intimates, enemies, and the widening circle of life. We can allow and bear being constituted by, and co-constituting all beings and phenomena. We may even appreciate and be enhanced by it. Joanna Macy, a Buddhist scholar and teacher, said (1995):

> You are not a thing. You are not a substance or an essence separate from your experience of life. The juiciness of this, the wealth of the flowing river, is often left unsung, unappreciated. So the teachings can seem rather unappetizing. Selflessness can easily be misunderstood to mean that we are being erased. In truth, we don't erase the self. We see through it. Throughout our lives, we have been trying so hard to fix that "I" we have each been lugging around. So when we drop the endless struggle to improve it or punish it, to make it noble, to mortify it, or to sacrifice it, the relief is tremendous [p. 6].

Contemporary analysts too, appreciate this: Mitchell (1993) writes, "The rushing fluidity of human experience through time makes authenticity essentially and necessarily ambiguous. The fascination with and pursuit of that ambiguity lies at the heart of the analytic process" (p. 145). In a spirit not unlike Mitchell here describes, meditative inquiry into this ambiguity, this field of not-knowing, underlies Zen practice in general and *koan* study, an insight practice of disciplined curiosity, in particular.

Koans

Koans are meditative, metaphorical themes usually drawn from spontaneous, everyday encounters between students and teachers, the folk stories of Zen. A *koan* is literally a "matter to be made clear." *Koan* practice allows one to discover the sacred in the particulars of one's daily experience. Here is an example from a collection entitled *The Gateless Barrier* (Aitken, 1990):

> A monk asked Feng-hsueh, "Speech and silence are concerned with equality and differentiation. How can I transcend equality and differentiation?" Feng-hsueh said,
> I always think of Chiang-nan in March;
> Partridges chirp among the many fragrant flowers.

Feng-hsueh wasn't trying to be "in the present" nor was he avoiding remembering the past. That familiar conflict couldn't have been farther from his state of mind. Rather, he was coming forth unfettered and showing simply and personally just how speech and silence, equality and differentiation, are transcended.

First steps in Zen practice involve cultivating the ability to attend, usually to the breath, and to settle into our experience. Eventually, inquiry deepens and there is a qualitative shift as observer, observed, and observation are no longer separate entities. Yamada Koun Roshi (*roshi*: "old teacher") used to say that Zen is the practice of "forgetting the self in the process of uniting with something." Attentive to each moment as it is, we come to rest in the question itself.

Another *koan* is "Who hears?" (Who is the master of hearing that sound?) *Kuan-Yin*, the archetypal embodiment of compassion in Buddhism, means "the one who perceives the sounds of the world," the sounds of suffering. Yet there is also the laughter of children, and the crow of the rooster. The sensory apparatus in *zazen* is not in a state of deprivation, sounds are not shut out; to the contrary, we open ourselves and let them enter. But the question is "Who is the one who hears?" The Buddha's question was why there was suffering in the world. Our own deepest questions and those of our patients are not all that different. "Who am I?" "Why am I here?" "Why is life so hard?"—these are perennial human dilemmas.

Curiosity about origins is at work here. The question "where did I come from?" refers, of course, to the intercourse of one's parents, to the womb of the mother, the penis of the father, and the minds of both. In Zen, however, the *koan* "Show me your original face before your parents were born" speaks to another dimension of human curiosity. Children's questions— "Where do I come from?" or "I know I came from mommy and daddy but where did you, mommy and daddy, come from?"—although in part deflective, contain more than a kernal of real inquiry. Our response as parents, "from each of our mommies and daddies," leads us back to the mysteries of the beginnings of time and creation, which are animate in the present.

Practically speaking, the ability to split the ego and self-observe, though a crucial developmental achievement in psychoanalysis and meditation, may be a necessary, but not sufficient, condition for emancipation. Whereas *zazen* includes nonjudgmental observation of the arising and passing of thoughts, images, affects, and bodily sensations, inquiry begins in earnest when the subject, its object of attention, and the attending itself (in Buddhism, the Three Wheels) are no longer sharply distinguished; in fact, when they are not operative at all as discrete entities. The question itself is held in awareness, pregnant with curiosity, and attempts to figure it out intellectually fade away. Mental turmoil gradually dies down. We are less under the sway of constraining, conflictual, perceptual structures. Concentrated but not narrowly so, we become open and receptively absorbed.

Through continued, mindful practice we may come to experience the emptiness of all concepts, including the self. However, to be stuck in emptiness is not the object of Zen. "Take another step," the Zen teacher says:

> You who sit on the top of a hundred foot pole,
> although you have entered the way, it is not yet genuine.
> Take a step from the top of the pole
> and worlds of the Ten Directions are your total body.
> [Shih-shuang, in Aitken, 1990]

There are many stories of Zen students coming to awakening (*kensho*, *satori*, realization, seeing into essential nature) through hearing a sound or seeing an object, as if for the first time. The ground has usually been prepared by years of meditation and moment to moment attentiveness, perhaps working with a *koan*. The mind is focused yet free from preoccupation, open, unself-conscious in the usual ways. We gradually become able to attend, to settle body and mind, to sustain focused inquiry. We are surprised when we find that we are no longer thinking of attaining anything at all, no longer trying to breathe, but rather simply breathing, no longer speculating about an answer to a question, but somehow having become the question itself. Do we breathe or are we breathed? We begin to allow ourselves to become absorbed in what we do. We gradually stop "chasing out through the five senses" (Meister Eckhart). The mind is settled, empty, alert, and receptive, having come naturally to rest through self-awareness (not mind deadening). At such a moment, anything can serve to awaken. Sometimes it is the sound of a bell, one's own sneeze, the act of standing up, or in the Buddha's case, looking up at the morning star. All categorization— self-other, inside-outside, subject-object, enlightened-deluded—gives way, and there is an experience of coming alive which is not bound by such dualistic constructs. Bashō wrote a haiku that presents this:

> The old pond;
> A frog jumps in—
> The sound of the water.

This is not simply a matter of aesthetics; Bashō got *completely* wet. Nothing was missing, nothing left over. Sengai expresses this in his version (Aitken, 1978):

> The old pond!
> Bashō jumps in,
> The sound of the water!

Over the course of practice this insight or enlightenment is clarified, refined, deepened, personalized in our ordinary daily life, and let go, so as not to become a stale artifact and an impediment to further learning.

Yamada Roshi would speak, for purposes of explanation, of each moment, each frame of experience, as being like a fraction; the numerator is the particular phenomenon and the denominator is empty infinity. Each lived moment—laughing or crying, throwing a ball, sharing an ice cream with my child—is like this. This is the radical understanding of Zen, immanent, but needing to be realized personally, through practice. What obscures this realization are narrow, mistaken views of self, other, and mind that are based on an illusion of self as solid, substantial, and continuous in time and space. These mistaken views are rooted in subject-object duality.

CLINICAL VIGNETTE

What follows is an anecdotal account of a four-year, twice-a-week psychotherapy with a 35-year-old married woman, a graduate student in psychology and mother of three children. I will focus on the unfolding of a specific, shared experience.

Ellen wanted more from her relationship with her husband, more enjoyment from being a mother, more from life. Over time, we explored various aspects of her dissatisfaction, multiple and occasionally conflictual meanings of her sense of not getting what she wanted. This dynamic emerged in the transference and we examined it over many months, from different angles, in several configurations. After a turbulent period, Ellen began to wrestle in a qualitatively different way with her distress, its roots in her growing up, and her relations with her parents, especially an anxious mother. It began to occur to Ellen that she herself had become an obstacle to "getting it," that somehow the urgency itself was part of the difficulty; the more she wanted, the further away it got. Her entire life, it seemed to her, had been shaped, even distorted, by this search. She began to have a sense of the hollowness, the falseness of it. This observation came with surprise and sadness and was without self-blame. Periods of grieving followed; sometimes it was clear as to what was being mourned, sometimes not.

About two years into the therapy, halfway into a session, she drifted into silence and began to talk slowly about how hard it was for her to just let herself be. There was a fleeting image of her mother, then a long silence. Her eyes filled with tears but there was no struggling. Rather, there was a slow, meditative pace and quality to her reflections. I do not teach or speak about meditation to patients; this unfolded out of the work together. Silences lengthened and seemed to deepen. I felt a powerful shift in the affective climate. A cardinal was singing. It was bright and sunny that day, and light filtered into the office. After several minutes, she began to speak again in a very different way: "There is the tree," she said, gazing out the window at the avocados, " the bird is chirping, the light is shining through the leaves, it feels warm on my skin." This was not detachment as defense or escape; rather she was unanxious, deeply settled, alive in the present moment. Each statement seemed to arise from silence itself and not to be an observation at all. As I experienced this sense of peace that was simultaneously alive, I had the image of a child feeling held so that she could completely let go, completely come to rest, "fall into" each moment, and, utterly unconcerned about moorings, simply be. But that was my image, a relational one, and while I felt affected and drawn in to the experience, I also felt oddly in the presence of an absence, as if I were witnessing a transformation of sorts, albeit temporary, something bigger than the two of us. Each thing was just as it is. Just as it was, it filled the screen. What was absent was the sense of a separate experiencer, an observer apart from what she was observing. There was no trace of hollowness or pretense.

In the weeks that followed, as she reflected on what happened, material about dependence and control emerged that could be worked through and integrated. Ellen looked back and felt that although it was but one experience among many, it had been a turning point. A knot had loosened from within, which she felt had to do with being alive—quite in contrast to being nice, compliant, seductive, or frustrated, demanding, unsatisfied and hopeless. She could begin to let in—and to be more fully absorbed in—what she had been clamoring for but had realized she was afraid and conflicted about. The experience occurred 15 years ago, when I was several years out of graduate school, and although I didn't know quite what to make of it, I was intrigued because it was so moving, so helpful to Ellen, and also because it seemed akin to the type of experience that in Zen often precedes realization.

Whether or not there was a relational frame to this experience, such as the "being alone in the presence of the other" I had imagined, I want instead to highlight a different aspect. The experience itself involved a relinquishment; a limiting self-organization dropped away, making possible what Buddhists might call a glimmer of Suchness. In shedding her encrusted, familar but unsatisfying way of experiencing herself in the world, she came alive, and curiously began, slowly, over time, to feel more herself. Mitchell (1993) quotes Graham Bass who noted the "great irony of the psychoanalytic experience; that in some respects, the patient is actually less known at the end of an analysis than at the beginning" (p. 121). Mitchell writes that "one of the great benefits of the analytic process is that the more the analysand can tolerate experiencing multiple versions of himself, the stronger, more resilient and durable he experiences himself to be" (p. 116). I think this, in turn, facilitates a deepening exploration or "unraveling."

MEANING

Meaning—explicit, implied, conscious, unconscious, manifest, latent, conflicted, nonconflictual, constructed, discovered, intrapsychic, relational—is the bread and butter of analytic work. The vignette above, however, describes what seemed to be a nondual (though shared) experience. There was no meaning proper to it; rather, it was its own meaning. Inside and outside, subject and object, authentic and inauthentic, continuous and discontinuous: such polarities, such dialectical tensions themselves did not seem to be active. What could we say about the value of such an experience? Usually value is a relative notion, defined in operational terms according to a particular frame of reference: what can I do with it, or in Fromm's (1960) critique of contemporary life, what can I get from it or buy with it. Although valuation and utility were perhaps implicit, they were not experientially central to the experience. Yet it was not an esoteric exchange, something otherworldly. It disrupted, catalyzed and enriched her set of personal meanings and values.

Such experiences don't only represent, they *present* something fundamental. They don't only symbolize, they also just *are*. Fromm (1960) writes:

> If one follows the original aim of Freud, that of making the unconscious conscious, to its last consequences, one must free it from the limitations imposed on it by Freud's own instinctual orientation, and by the immediate task of curing symptoms. Then the aim becomes that of overcoming alienation, and the subject-object split in perceiving the world; then the uncovering of the unconscious means giving up the illusion of an indestructible separate ego which is to be enlarged and preserved as the Egyptian pharohs hoped to preserve themselves as mummies for eternity. To be conscious of the unconscious means to be open, responding, to have nothing and to be [p. 136].

There was not a separate experiencer standing outside of the experience, commenting, narrating, as is usually the case, imbuing it with particular meaning. The experience was not the object, nor were we the subjects. This shared coming alive was in a way not bound or justified by traditional meaning criteria at all. Such experiences of touching down in a dimension of no-meaning-proper can enrich one's sense of authenticity, aliveness, connection, and, paradoxically, the sense of meaning in one's life. They illuminate what is truly of value and enrich and deepen our value system. Our ability to see, understand, and relate compassionately, not only to ourselves but to others, as they are, is deepened. This reflects— in Zen as in psychoanalysis—a receptive emptying, a sloughing off of familiar me-you perceptual meaning-making grids. Mitchell (1993) writes that "Self refers to the subjective organization of meanings one creates as one moves through time. An experience of self takes place necessarily in a moment of time; it fills one's psychic space, and other, alternative versions of self fade into the background."

One can call what Ellen and I shared "an experience of self, in time, facilitated by alternate versions of self having faded into the background." But the question What does this mean? never crossed our minds. And while this was not a trance—either of us could have responded adequately to a mental status test if we had to—the coordinates of space and time which ordinarily anchor us were absent. Meaning-making per se or self-construction were not going on. Even calling it a variety of self-experience, as Stolorow does, introduces something whose very absence facilitates this kind of experience. In time, association, symbolization, remembering, integration began apace. But they were not intrinsic to the experience itself.

Making meaning presupposes, literally arises out of, tolerable and generative moments of no-meaning. An analytic teacher of mine suggested that Ellen's experience might be understood as a kind of "going on being" such as Winnicott wrote about, which necessarily takes place over time. However, it was not shaped or constrained by time coordinates at all; there was precisely no yesterday, tomorrow, or today for that matter; nor was it the stuff of thinking, planning, or reexperiencing. While this experience took place over time, it was not time bound; there was no past, present, or future to it. And yet it was not vacuous. I am reminded of Blake's verse:

> To see a world in a grain of sand
> And heaven in a wildflower,
> Hold infinity in the palm of your hand,
> And eternity in an hour.

The loosening, even the temporary absence of such temporal and meaning-as-symbol criteria, in fact, facilitates such experiences. Fogel (1991) writes:

Concepts, metaphors, symbols—all of these may function at varying degrees of distance from the realities they organize. The perfect, ideal symbol seems to, may express reality directly. Rather than standing for something true, it may function as a vehicle for the direct realization of truth [p. 187].

This points not only to symbolic meaning, rich and important as it is, but rather to a kind of presentational meaning, not unlike *koan* work in Zen.

Relinquishment, Emergence, and Identity

Although Zen practice has a long history of facilitating the realization of this coming alive in falling away, it is not the exclusive domain of Zen, but a perennial human experience. Over fifty years ago, when meditation was of less interest culturally, a college student, during a period of alienation and turmoil when she was searching for resolution to deep self-doubts and existential questions, was sitting in her room (Courtois, 1971).

There, alone in my room, sitting quietly on the edge of my bed and gazing at a small desk, not thinking of anything at all, in a moment too short to measure, the universe changed on its axis. The small, pale green desk at which I'd been so thoughtlessly gazing appeared now with a clarity, a depth of three-dimensionality, a freshness I had never imagined possible. At the same time, in a way that is utterly indescribable, my questions and doubts were gone as effortlessly as chaff in the wind. I knew everything and all at once. Yet not in the sense that I had ever known anything before. A luminous openness obliterated all fixed distinctions including "within" and "without." I found myself running along the street in joyous abandon. Sometimes when I was alone I simply danced as freely as I did as a child. The whole world seemed to have reversed itself, to have turned outside in. Activity flowed simply and effortlessly and to my amazement, seemingly without thought; nothing seemed to go out of bounds; there was no alternation between "self-control" and "letting go," but rather a rightness and spontaneity to all this flowing activity. This new kind of knowing was so pure and unadorned, so delicate, that nothing in the language of my past could express it. Neither sense nor feeling nor imagination contained it yet all were contained in it. In some indefinable way I knew with absolute certainty the changeless unity and harmony in change of the universe and the inseparability of all seeming opposites. A paradoxical quality seemed to permeate all existence. Feeling myself centered as never before, at the same time I knew the whole universe to be centered at every point. All was meaningful, complete as it was, each bird, bud, midge, mole, atom, crystal, of total importance in itself. As in the notes of a great symphony, nothing was large or small, nothing of more or less importance to the whole [pp. 30–35].

Flora Courtois, now in her eighties, came to describe what happened as "open vision." She was not using mind altering substances, had no previous meditation instruction, was not a member of a cult or active in any organized religion, and was not psychotic. While knowing more about this young woman would place this account in the context of a particular human life, and perhaps reveal multiple functions of such an experience, that is a task for another essay. Such information would not, however, detract from what she describes so vividly and inadequately.

Many years later she had occasion to speak about what happened that day to a respected senior Zen teacher. He acknowledged her experience and asked her to write it up. "You lost your way," he wrote in a poem to her, "and now the way has extended in all directions." While it is a direct, immediate, nonabstract, "knowing" which one can usually present to the teacher, to talk about it, however interesting, misses the mark.

In a culture and a context quite different from Bashō's Japan, it seemed that there was something about the work Ellen and I were doing that resulted in a gradual but deep reappraisal of her self-representation. It is significant, I think, that such experiences seem to occur over the course of considerable and painful contact with areas of experience not usually identified as self. In Zen practice, as in psychoanalysis and in our later self-analysis, there are rude awakenings to our familar yet constricting, incomplete, and perhaps illusory self-images. In Ellen's case, slowly and with difficulty she became able to experience herself not only as deprived, entitled, and seeking desperately, but also as obstructing. This enabled her to begin to become aware of the pain, the "consequences" (Grotstein, 1995) of her constricting and protective self-other representational structure and strategy for dealing with anxiety and suffering. Although her experience did not yield the kind of fundamental existential understanding as in Flora Courtois' case, it seemed nonetheless that Ellen was drawing from the same wellspring, and putting it to use in the service of untying personal knots. Reification of one such experience is not my aim—after all it was part and parcel of a complex therapeutic process—but perhaps Ellen and I, unawares, had been tilling and turning over the ground, enriching the soil, sharing and relinquishing ourselves and our understandings, enabling a liberating, enlivening experience such as this.

Mitchell (1993) writes of an incident from his own life that has some of the qualities discussed above:

> When my daughter was about two or so, I remember my excitement at the prospect of taking walks with her, given her new ambulatory skills and her intense interest in being outdoors. However I soon found these walks agonizingly slow. My idea of a walk entailed brisk movement along a road or path. Her idea was quite different. The implications of this difference hit me one day when we encountered a fallen tree on the side of the road, about twenty yards from our house. The rest of the "walk" was spent exploring the fungal and insect life on, under, and around the tree. I remember my sudden realization that these walks would be no fun for me, merely a parental duty, if I held onto my idea of walks. As I was able to give that up and surrender to my daughter's rythm and focus, a different type of experience opened up to me. I was able to find in that another way for me to be that took on great personal meaning for me [p. 147].

Again, while not identical to realization in Zen practice, Mitchell's experience did make real for him something that had not been so before, due to his constricted viewpoint. The tree, the fungi, the insects, his daughter, their relationship, and Mitchell himself came to life in ways previously inaccessible to him. Were he a Zen student, his teacher would ask him to present, not explain, how this relates to his practice and his essential nature. I could imagine a very direct, vivid, and humorous presentation.

We might say that new experiential possibilities (or structures) emerged from an experience of dissonance and letting go (no-structure). They became integrated through unintegration, and Mitchell's identificatory repertoire was broadened through a disidentificatory experience, though nonidentificatory might be a better word. Identity is an interesting notion. Something fell away and, out of that, something came forth, not quite in sequence, and with a direct immediacy. We might say that what emerged identified Mitchell as much if not more than his identifying with it. His self was enriched by a non-self experience.

Another analytic teacher of mine described a patient with whom, very slowly and with great difficulty, the analyst came to uncover, face, and give up the very thing that defined and anchored him most as an analyst: his hope and conviction that his patient could be helped and, further, would be helped by him. This internal shift, this radical relinquishment in the analyst, had a palpable impact on the emotional field between them. Paradoxically, only then did the impasse they were in untangle and new movement begin.

While the settings, aims, and methods are different in meditation and psychoanalysis, the qualitative nature of these experiences overlap. I am not alone in having encountered such moments with patients. In psycho-analytic or meditation practice (as in daily life), there are experiences that occur in the nondual dimension. These involve a falling away and a coming to life, not only sequentially, but simultaneously, in a dimension where time is not bound and where even "falling away" and "coming forth" are absent. One might say that Ellen touched the farther reaches of her subjec-tivity, were it not for the fact that subject and object were not present as such. I think that at the outer edge of one's subjectivity, even that falls away. What remains? If I say "nothing," that is still positing something. The philosopher Masao Abe, responding to a question about emptiness, said: "Nothing is not something called nothing." Ellen's experience was not the result of wish fulfillment. In fact, it is the very *absence* of wishing and related conflicts that enables such an experience to occur. Nor did it reflect a col-lapse of an internal space to think, reflect and to be—to the contrary.

Imagine a solid block of cheese. Slowly, it becomes porous like Swiss cheese. Lying on the grass in the park gazing up at the clouds one per-ceives this. Our experience becomes less opaque, there is a "break in the clouds." During a retreat a Zen practitioner had a dream in which she was playfully exploring a large house that had no exterior walls. She enjoyed gleefully the sun, the smells, and the sounds of the critters as her own home, her own body. As the chatter in the mind quiets of its own, as con-stricting and conflictual identifications slowly come to light and loosen, as the hard-packed dirt is turned over and aerated, as T.S. Eliot's "certain certainties" are questioned, things can grow, differently. In the course of this loosening up, there are moments when the continuously hard-working narrator, the commentator, the control-central, conceptual mean-ing-making grid through which experiences are taken in, classified, and understood—through which we literally construct our self—falls away. This falling away can be distinguished from falling apart. These are inef-fable moments, when we are not "making something," where what is immanent—closer to us than our own nose—can shine forth.

Melanie Klein writes of the epistemophilic instinct, the desire to know, embodied in the wish to enter the mother's body and apprehend its con-tents and mysteries from the inside out. This may be broadened to include the thirst for direct human knowledge of our own birth and death, the essential nature of our existence itself, and that of all beings. Getting to the heart of the matter, the body of knowledge, is fundamentally not a matter of inside or outside.

Relational and other analytic thinkers write of reviving collapsed symbolic capacity, expanding restricted narratives and experiential repertoires, and reconciling and balancing dialectical tensions. In the Zen view, however, it is the narrator *himself* who must be understood, to the bottom. We experience ourselves through our narrations of and reactions to, direct experience. We create running commentaries on our lives and then take them as real, as "me." This happens automatically, we forget it occurred, and we then mistakenly take the commentary for the play. This comedy (or perhaps tragedy) of errors continues and gets quite complicated as we then react in varied and conflicted ways to our identificatory constructions, taking them in turn—our reactions—as "me." In so doing, we come to lead second-hand lives. This is truly a case of mistaken identity! And what of our relationships with other beings, human and otherwise? We see others as in a dream, as if we were sleepwalking, through our socially conditioned and self-referencing perceptual filters. We do not see them at all, really, and so cannot relate with genuine compassion toward them (Fromm, 1960; Symington, 1994).

Meaning, structure, integration, subjectivity, aliveness are enriched and enlivened by direct experience in a domain of no-meaning, no-structure, unintegration, and the absence of sharply defined subject and object. A sense of self-identity was deepened as Ellen became less identified. She became more herself through an experience we might usually think of as not-much-like-self. Sartre (1981) wrote: "I am nearer to myself when I am far away." Wallace Stevens (1972) captures this quintessential human mystery in his poem "Tea at the Palace of Hoon":

> I was the world in which I walked, and what I saw
> Or heard or felt came not but from myself;
> And there I found myself more truly and more strange.

In both psychoanalysis and Zen practice—and the paths have important differences—the personal self develops out of, is transformed by, and finds its most authentic and satisfying expression and structure through encountering and exploring generative emptiness. This coming to life is a spiritual experience and represents touching down into what has been known through the ages as the dimension of the sacred. It is facilitated, or to use Erikson's (1966) term, "activated" by (though not limited to), a transformative relationship between analysand and analyst or meditator and spiritual teacher, in which they encounter each other, share and relinquish themselves and their understandings, and are transformed by and transform the other. There is no creation, no encounter with the new, no "spontaneous gesture" (Winnicott, 1958) without a falling away, usually not without significant anxiety and grief implicit in relinquishing versions of self-experience that are familiar.

There is a trans-formation, in a crucible as it were. In psychoanalysis the crucible is the therapeutic relationship in all its complexity, "real" and transferential, the process of free association, analytic listening, and the intimate, unhurried sharing of two subjectivities. The framework in Zen study is the practice of *zazen* on the cushion, mindfulness of daily life experience, and the student's relationship with his *sangha* and teacher. One's daily life interactions and experiences also provide, in both endeavors, a field of intensified experience and interaction. The container provided by the analyst allows the analysand to deepen and extend her realm of experience. Zen teacher Charlotte Joko Beck (1989) calls this process as it unfolds, albeit with a different intention, the "ABC's of Zen, A Bigger Container" (p. 50). We suffer more, perhaps, in the sense of allowing and bearing more deeply felt and more varied experience. As the container expands, it (along with the "sufferer") disappears and reconfigures—differently. Although we clearly *do not* become someone else, something new *is* created. Here is Ogden (1993) on the experience of reading:

> This book will not be "understood" by you; you will not simply receive it, incorporate it, digest it or the like. To the degree that you will have anything to do with it, you will transform it. (The word *transform* is too tepid a word to describe what you will do to it.) You will destroy it, and out of that destruction (in that destruction) will come a sound you will not fully recognize [pp. 2–3].

A vital, mature human life, with a psychological and spiritual dimension, involves the capacity to both fall away and to cohere, to let go and to come forth, to destroy and to create, to be something, somebody, and to be nothing at all. It involves the ability to move between the two, realizing moments where the two are identical, and moments where each appears as what it is, an organizing construct, and falls away completely. I think genuine transcendence, truly being *alive*, is in their differentiation, harmonizing, and ultimately in their falling away in fresh, unmediated experience.

THEORY

The interaction between psychoanalysis and meditative experience is not fundamentally a developmental, sequential, or what Ogden (1989) calls a diachronic matter. For example, he describes three modes of generating experience (the autistic-contiguous, the paranoid-schizoid, and the depressive). These dimensions do not exist in absolute, pure form. Rather they are synchronically related. Not only is each distinct, but each creates (makes possible), maintains, and negates the other. They are not simply sequential stages; there is always an interpenetration of the dimensions.

Mitchell (1993) also writes about analysis in a way that can be useful in beginning to develop a framework for thinking about the interaction of the domains of psychoanalysis and Zen:

Psychoanalysis at its best makes possible a more variegated experience of self. Past, present, fantasy, actuality interpenetrate each other. Not only are the intrapsychic and the interpersonal not incompatible, they are natural extensions of each other. In my view, the intrapsychic and the interpersonal are perpetually interpenetrating realms that continually fold back into one another [p. 143].

Engler (1986), in a seminal paper, suggests that we need to have and be a self *before* we can forget the self. However, while spiritual experience *does* occur in the context of qualitatively different levels of self-object relations and ego development, I do not think spiritual development is simply an end product of good-enough ego and self-object representational development. Neither does the notion of separate lines of development capture it. Rather, these two dimensions—letting go and coming forth-gathering together—common to both psychoanalytic and meditative experience and practice (though each privileged differently by the particular discipline), are fundamental capacities, potentialities, facets of our moment-to-moment lives; they are there from the beginning and create and give shape to our particular humanity. From the earliest moments, elements of each are present, and so it is throughout life. In developmental research we are learning more about how infant and parent navigate optimally in a reciprocal fashion through conjunctures and disjuctures. Both are needed and both parties to the interaction are capable of initiating either movement. Victoria Hamilton (1982) captures an important aspect of this interplay:

The experience of negation, or "the negative realisation," and the formulation of the simple negative are linked to separation, differentiation, to the perception of contrast and differences, to the making of distinctions, to the command "Don't," etc. However in my view these communications are *tolerated* in a context of togetherness, reciprocity, play, secure attachment and above all, predictable presence or reunion [p. 258].

Individuation and what is called healthy psychic structure develop through repeated good-enough navigation of such experiences. The process has its analogues in psychoanalysis and in Zen practice as well. The teacher-student relationship, the *sangha*, the forms, structure, schedule—*zazen* itself—these "hold" the student as he attends deeply, as the falling away and emerging unfolds.

Zen practice, like human development and psychoanalysis, is a journey with sequential steps and watersheds; at the same time, each step is precious, ineffable, complete in itself, sacred. A Zen teaching conveys this: "You may practice Zen upwards, but each step is of equal substance." The (in)famous Zen stick, the *kotsu*, says another teacher picking it up, is golden through and through. "If I cut it here (at one end), golden. If I cut it here (in the middle), golden. Here (at the other end), golden." We can enter the sacred dimension at any "point," any "position," any "stage"—in any moment. As in psychoanalysis, the sudden and immediate coexists with the gradual, the painstaking, and at times the imperceptible accretion of understanding.

The "mechanism" of this interaction, such as it is, functions quietly. When things are working there is no permanent disjuncture, paradoxes are no longer intractable hindrances, there is a free and playful to and fro. "Authenticity for the analyst, as well as for the patient," Mitchell (1993) writes, "is essentially ambiguous, more discernable in its absence than in its presence." It has often struck me that when we feel most alive we are least self-preoccupied. As with the notion of gravity, in such a context, ego, object, self, even integration are simply explanatory concepts—fingers pointing to the moon—which are more useful in helping describe and understand its absence, how such aliveness is compromised, than its presence. The simultaneity of letting go and coming alive becomes troublesomely paradoxical only when we attempt to catch its meaning in the net of either-or thinking.

It is when things are not working—when the gears are grinding, when there is calcification—that there has been a collapse of sorts into one of the modes. A meditator felt for some years that he had to extrude his sense of self as agent: "I sort of took myself out of the equation. There was no room for it in my Zen practice and with the group. We were to 'forget the self' and I took it literally. If I did this, then maybe there'd be the big payoff at the end." What a sense of betrayal and grief! In his case, self-denial did not translate into psychic collapse, although there have been such cases. Rather, collapse reflected an exclusive identification with experiences from the empty side of the spectrum, into which affectively charged experiences of aggression, sadness, loss, competition, and conflict were excluded, resulting in an impoverishment of self-experience, fulfillment, enjoyment, and a sense of competence and meaning.

Psychoanalysis has traditionally tended to privilege the side of structure, stability, adaptation, the development of personal agency, insight into the unconscious, and integration. Zen practice has tended to privilege the side of empty infinity, seeing into the nature of the self-structure and the identity of the experiencer himself or herself. "Forgetting the self" can be taken to mean a devaluation or extrusion of self as agent, but it does not necessarily imply that at all. Without good enough ego functioning it isn't easy to navigate our daily life. Permanent elimination of the ego is not the goal of Zen practice.

INTEGRATION

Looking comparatively at the paths of psychoanalysis and Zen practice reveals these two dimensions, relinquishing and bringing forth, each central to life; navigating and experientially integrating them, inexorable and impossible as it is, is the play, the joy, and the travail of a lifetime for each of us.

Loewald (1980) in a book review of the Freud-Jung letters, speaks of just such an integrative effort, and in quite a down to earth way:

> Psychoanalysis, I believe, shares with modern existentialism the tenet that suprapersonal and transcendental aspects of human existence and of the unconscious and instinctual life (so much stressed by Jung) can be experienced and integrated convincingly—without escapist embellishments, otherworldly consolations and going off into the clouds—only in the concreteness of one's own personal life, including the ugliness, trivialities, and sham that go with it [p. 416].

Loewald's words surprisingly echo the hard-won insights of many meditation practitioners and teachers, and a growing ideal in the field: the importance of exploring the relation between spiritual insight and character development. Although Loewald takes the Jungians to task for what he sees as their tendency to take refuge in escapist constructions, Jung and analytic psychology by no means have a monopoly on the tendency to jump from the ambiguity, complexity, unpredictability, conflict, and pain of our daily affective experience into other-worldly states. As Freud noted, this tendency is endemic to humankind, and represents a significant motivation for religion and spiritual practice. It is a not uncommon and mostly unconscious fantasy that, through diligent efforts, one will be rewarded with an exemption from the vicissitudes of life, one will magically leap from the groans and travails of everyday life and "arrive," fully enlightened and purified. "Build it and they will come," becomes the meditator's Field of Dreams; do it and it will come (and rescue you). Many meditators thus practice with one part of themselves and watch, expectantly awaiting, with another part.

In this fantasy, it is assumed that a direct osmotic transfer of benefit from the spiritual to the characterological and practical-life experience level occurs. But alas, this is not the case. Experience tells us that one can have insight into one's essential nature and still be a sociopath or an inveterate, self-deceiving alcoholic, exploitative of others in cruel ways. Robert Jay Lifton's concept of the human capacity for "doubling," which arose out of his study of torturers in Nazi Germany and elsewhere, is troubling but instructive. One can be an apparently loving parent, a cultured human being, and simultaneously, a practicing sadist.

The two dimensions, therefore, do not, of necessity, overlap. Progress in one domain does not automatically yield equivalent progress in the other. Integration is necessary. A respected Zen teacher, commenting on the shocking suicide of a respected leader of the Rinzai school (one of the two primary approaches to Zen, now less polarized then they once were) in Japan, explained it, and explained away, I am sure, his own despair and confusion as well, by saying that the person in question "must not have been fully enlightened." Another Zen teacher took a similar tack years ago when asked why those students who were progressing in their meditation practice and assuming leadership positions in the *zendo* (the Zen center or meditation hall) seemed, outside of the zendo, to behave in the same narrow, thoughtless, and arrogant ways they had at the outset of their practice. "They must not be truly doing *zazen*," he replied. The implication is that it couldn't be in the nature of the particular path itself; it must be in the student's application of the method. While this might be true in some cases, such a response simply props up the system status quo and delays its inevitable self-examination. (In psychoanalysis, a parallel myth might be the "fully analyzed" person.) But as Zen takes root in the West, the examination is in full swing, and there is keen interest of late in the relationship between meditation practice and the clarity of spiritual insight on the one hand, and the thick mix of our complex and often conflicted subjective and relational experience on the other. The teachings are there in Zen as this verse by Keizan Zenji conveys (Maezumi and Glassman, 1978b).

> Though clear waters range to the vast blue autumn sky
> How can they compare with the hazy moon on a spring night?
> Most people want to have it pure white,
> But sweep as you will, you cannot empty the mind.

However, their implications are only now being fully explored, as Zen practice encounters modern Western culture with its more developed psychological awareness.

Here is a story that conveys the interplay of the affective, relational dimension with the sacred:

> The congregation is gathered in an orthodox synagogue for the High Holy Days, and they are fervently davening (praying), rocking side to side. The religious climate is thick, alive with the devotional spirit. The rabbi is facing the Torah, chanting, praising the Almighty, "Lord, I am not worthy! In my heart I know that I am nothing." The cantor listens to the rabbi's words and joins him at the ark. He declares, "Lord, even though I have led your children today in fervent prayer, in beautiful sacred melody, I know that I am really nothing." Then a simple Jew who has been praying devotely all day stands up in the middle of the synagogue and cries out, "Lord, I just want you to know I am nothing!" The cantor leans over to the rabbi and whispers, "Look who thinks he's nothing."

Transcendence may be used as, but does not intrinsically equate with, self-inflation or escape. Some meditators mistake it for, or use it to avoid, transference. Others find unconscious affinity in ego-syntonic experiences of emptiness. For example, for someone with a personal history and unconscious self-representations significantly shaped by repeated loss, this can be a temporary way to protect oneself and keep from awareness residues of traumatic experience. Transcendence is not something one adds or patches on, something one achieves, attains or gains. Rather, it is a qualitatively different lived perspective on being human, arising out of an ongoing sloughing off. It involves a fundamental shift in one's relationship to the perceived obstacle, a new way of being with one's experience.

Dealing only with the content of the psyche has been compared to redecorating one's jail cell, or rearranging the deck chairs on the *Titanic*. The *structure* of how we relate to and construct the problem, how the obstacle's very existence is sustained by a dualistic subject-object split— there is me and there is my problem—is often ignored, assumed, taken for granted, part of the furniture of cultural and philosophical assumptions. Psychoanalysis and Zen share a commitment to making direct contact with one's experience and working with it. But whereas in contemporary psychoanalysis our self-structures themselves are explored and become more differentiated, pliable, and integrated, in Zen one inquires into the very nature of the structure in which the problem is embedded and through which it is maintained.

Erikson (1969) in his study of Gandhi, demonstrates a subtle understanding of the spiritual dimension in a human life:

> Each of us exists with a unique consciousness and a responsibility of his own which makes him at the same time zero and everything, a center of absolute silence, and the vortex of apocolyptic participation. Gandhi's actualism, then, first of all consisted in his knowledge of, and ability to gain strength from, the fact that nothing is more powerful in this world than conscious nothingness if it is paired with the gift of giving and accepting actuality. [He was able] to give meaning to what others must deny at all times but cannot really forget for a moment. Freud, in one of his "economic" moods, might well have said that, psychologically speaking, such men save others not so much from their sins (this Freud would not have claimed to know) but from the fantastic effort *not* to see the most obvious of facts: that life is bounded by not-life [pp. 396–397].

Not only is life bounded by not-life, it is *made up* of not-life elements. The mind in Zen is not enclosed by or defined solely as, the brain.

MIND

The notion of mind is evolving dramatically within psychoanalysis. Freud's early formulations, based on the thermodynamic model of the times, wherein there were determinate and determinable causes and quantifiable relations between particular, discrete elements that could be measured in quantifiable terms, have given way to several revisions. The impact of ego psychology, object relations, self-psychological theory, and infant developmental research has led to revised models of the mind. Intersubjectivist models now clearly do not view the mind as residing solely in the brain or the psyche of the patient or, for that matter, of the analyst. The analyst does not simply stand outside the situation, objectively observe the productions of the subject, and make uncontaminated clinical interventions that result in a change to the subject's mental condition. Changes in how the mind and the analytic situation are construed reflect a fundamental, perceptual paradigm shift that has occurred in fields as diverse as cognition, physics, and cosmology. Nowhere is this clearer than in the Zen view of mind.

The Japanese word for a Zen meditation retreat, *sesshin*, means "to touch the mind." It can also mean to receive the mind, to convey the mind. How do we do this? This mind, like the self, is empty. Wise teachers are everywhere, would we but recognize them. In *The Gateless Barrier* (Wu-men; trans. Aitken, 1990), Aitken relates a surprising encounter.

Te-shan was a well-established scholar who lectured frequently on the Diamond Sutra, an important Mahayana Buddhist text, in Western Szechuan province. He apparently felt threatened by the Zen teaching of realization that is not established on words and was wary of transmission outside tradition. So he traveled several hundred miles south to Hunan province with the avowed purpose of stamping out such heresy.

On the road to Li-chou with its many Zen monasteries, he stopped at a wayside refreshment stand. Here he met a great teacher of Zen who, like others of her sex, the Chinese recorders sadly fail to identify by name. Te-shan didn't pay any particular attention to her, but she discerned the potential of her new customer as he asked for *tien-hsin*. This Buddhist term means "refreshment," but the old woman played with its etymology: "punctuate the mind."

"Your reverence," this wise old woman politely asked, "what sort of literature do you have there in your cart?" This was her opening wedge in their dharma dialogue.

"Notes and commentaries on the Diamond Sutra," he replied shortly. He had no idea he was setting himself up. The old woman suggested a game: "I want to ask you a question. If you can answer, I will serve you without charge. If you cannot answer, then I won't serve you at all." Te-shan agreed, and she lowered the boom: "I hear the Diamond Sutra says, 'Past mind cannot be grasped, present mind cannot be grasped, future mind cannot be grasped.' Which mind does Your Reverence intend to refresh?"

Duh! For all his wisdom, Te-shan was confounded by the old woman. He recognized in a moment that he had been mistaken—not only in overlooking the virtue of the tea seller, but also in his "knowledge" of the sutra. He was ready to be taught [p. 180].

The mind contains nothing absolute, proprietary, or permanent, and is essentially insubstantial. "I am walking, I am loving, I am eating, I am imagining" are accurate statements. But is there really a mind separate from the activities? Enclosed by the skin? Perhaps pulling the strings: a driving, motivational, fundamental nexus? It is surprising and mysterious that although empty of permanent identity, this mind has boundless potential. It laughs, weeps, takes the children to school, goes to the bathroom, cooks dinner, makes love, gets lost, and finds its way.

The very insubstantiality of the mind implies and makes possible its complementary feature: interdependence. The image is the Jewel Net of Indra (Cook, 1977; Cleary, 1983). Each of us is a point in a net in which there are mirrors at each knot of a vast web, and each point reflects and contains every other point of the web. This is not unlike the hologram. It is precisely *because* the self and the mind have no absolute substance that we literally make up each other, we are composed by one another. We are all intimately connected, multicentered selves. Thich Nhat Hanh says we "interare" with all beings. This is in the same spirit as Winnicott: we cannot say infant without saying mother, we cannot say mother-baby unit without saying father (because father is part of mother's unconscious). We cannot say "paper" without saying tree, leaves, rain, sun, earth, lumberjack, storekeeper. They are all inherent in the piece of paper. *This* is because *that* is. Buddhists call this *paticca samuppada*," dependent co-arising." To come alive is to realize this interpenetration. Symington (1994) calls it "fertile mutuality" and unpacks the ways we narcissistically repudiate it in our deepest, unconscious emotional action toward ourselves and others.

The Buddha sat in meditation under the pippala tree until he saw into the nature of human suffering (and of course, his own). Legend has it that at dawn one day, he looked up and glimpsed the morning star. Everything fell away and he exclaimed, "I and all beings have at this moment attained the way" (Cleary, 1990). Enlightenment in Zen is simultaneously the enlightenment of bushes and grasses, tadpoles and quasars, ancestors and infants. In realizing our own essential nature, we realize the nature of all things. As we saw in the story of Mitchell and his young daughter, not only was he brought to life in a new way, so was his daughter, delighted I'm sure by the shift, and so were the many creatures in the fallen tree, including the fungi and insects.

Spezzano (1995) quotes Adam Phillips who referred to the psychological dimension of unconscious affective communication as a "hidden black market," the hidden exchange and mutual composition of our emotional lives. I think perhaps the "worldwide web" is already dynamically in place but we are unaware of its activity. In a lecture, Stoller once related a story Ralph Greenson told him about how Greenson "knew" a relative had been in an accident, although the two of them were thousands of miles apart. "The subject was quickly dropped," Stoller said. How do patients know when our silence is retributive, or when our attention has wandered and we are no longer with them in the same receptive way? We know that they know, even if they do not let themselves perceive it. Each of us also knows, each of us communicates affectively in such a way, yet we don't know how, and sometimes that, we are doing it. It is *as if* there were an actual web: touch here and the message gets across there, instantaneously. Though we often can't decode it, we experience its effects. An anecdotal account of a study group of the American Psychoanalytic Association, which has been meeting for some time to share experiences about the nature of related, nontraditional kinds of communication, ways of knowing and understanding each other, is quite illuminating in this regard (Mayer, 1996).

Neville Symington (1994) writes cogently in *Emotion and Spirit* of the "unseen emotional action" within and between people. Awareness and transformation in this field *is* the spiritual work of psychoanalysis, he writes. While this unconscious activity is not apparent, it is there, operative, and we can and must become aware of it. I don't think it is secret; in fact it takes shape and operates in our daily interpersonal activity. What is meant, after all, by the oft heard statement about parenting, "It's not what you say but who you are"? If we are unaware of its activity, as we commonly are, individually and culturally, we risk treating others as "not-me," dehumanizing them. As "enlightened," mature, helpful and insightful as we may be, we remain out of touch and fundamentally encapsulated. We value our freedom of thought, but unless we become privy to this "web," our freedom itself can function as a prison. The one who resists being confined and limited may not see his own self-limitation and confinement.

This interdependent field, the fundamental ground of Hua-Yen Buddhism as represented in the Avatamsaka Sutra and articulated over two thousand years ago (Cleary, 1983), bears an uncanny resemblance to the "intersubjective field" of contemporary psychoanalysis. Neither tradition, of course, has a monopoly, a patent on it. Whitman was familar with this web: "I am vast, I contain multitudes," he writes in "Song of Myself." So, in her own way, is a seriously troubled analytic patient of a colleague who said to her analyst: "If I don't have the experience of people in me and me in them, my life and my death have no meaning. My life is counting on being in you and you in me."

Autonomy and separateness were still terrifying and unintegrated for this woman. While we are insubstantial and interconnected creatures, there is something mysteriously unique and distinctive about our actions, about each point in the net, about each of us, the mark we leave in our wake, the way in which certain tendencies coalesce as our person. This absolute uniqueness, represented in infinitely rich variety, is one of the three "Bodies of the Buddha," or aspects of awakening, in Mahayana Buddhist philosophy; the other two are clarity-emptiness and interdependence-oneness.

BLIND SPOTS

It is a common misconception of meditative practitioners that spiritual practice and insight, bring, ipso facto, an exemption from life's emotional vicissitudes and imperfections—ultimate salvation. However, the fruits of either path—psychoanalytic or contemplative—can, at any point along the way, be highjacked, exploited for motives outside awareness, and turned into something else. We must ask "In the service of what?" Even one's insights themselves can become obstacles to awareness of our psychic activity. We become complacent and our understanding becomes like a frozen and stale intellectual object. Zen practice can be used to obscure awareness of what is happening internally and interpersonally, as in analysis too, analyst and analysand can collude, ignoring or supporting an obfuscating or deadening process.

A seasoned Buddhist teacher with deep insight into essential nature makes the point at a seminar that there is fundamentally "nothing to know." As he says it, however, he conveys precisely the opposite: that he does know and the others do not. He is not aware this is happening, but several group members are. A therapist has insight into corruption being a key element in the dynamics of perversion, yet she is totally unaware that her activities set in motion conditions which undermine the integrity of a clinic where she in on staff. A parent says his child is having too many sweets; within minutes, totally unaware of any connection to what just transpired, the parent fills up on the very same candies. A group of experienced, psychologically astute professionals meet for a week, with expert facilitation, to iron out interpersonal tensions. The meeting ends with unanimous agreement as to its efficacy. Within days, things explode and schisms are rampant.

Symington (1994) gives examples of a similar process as it develops in the analytic situation. Enlightenment or spiritual understanding is not an abstract event, detached from the emotional field between people. Rather, the analyst's experience in the field of the analytic relationship and his interpretive activity become the vehicle for bringing into consciousness such split-off psychic activity, much of which he sees as violent in nature, and for liberating integrity. Enlightenment and truth here begin with the awareness of this unconscious emotional activity. Insight, conscience, atonement, and compassion develop in concert.

None of us is exempted. Each new self-representational structure is both a discovery and may become the next blind spot, an obstacle to further learning. Language helps us to symbolize effectively and creatively as we live through a mode where "things in themselves" can be concrete and frightening. This developmental achievement itself, however, can be put at the service of avoiding a deeper encounter with ourselves and our fellows, as we actually are, and with a sacred yet surprisingly ordinary "things in themselves."

ANXIETY

Anxiety usually arises in the face of such a turning on its head of basic assumptions of who I am, what I do, and what my relationship with other beings is. Batchelor (1990) describes how Ernest Hemingway spoke of sitting at his desk each morning to face "the horror of a blank sheet of paper."

> He found himself (as any writer can confirm) having to produce by the end of the day a series of words arranged in a way that has never before been imagined. You sit there, alone, hovering on the cusp between nothing and something. This is not a blank, stale nothing; it is an awesome nothing charged with unrealized potential. And the hovering is the kind that can fill you with dread. Rearrangement of the items on your desk assumes an irresistible attraction [p. 70].

Not only in meditation and artistic creation does such anxiety arise, but also at the very outset of and during an analysis. An analytic patient described feeling adrift in a deep blue sea that was simultaneously inviting and frightening. Various specific and personal meanings of this sea emerged over time, but the analysand was also referring to her growing experience of enjoying and yet being terrified by, the freedom to explore and not be constrained by who she thought she was, by her limiting conceptualizations of self, other, and world. The dread of which Erikson and Batchelor speak is similar, but not reducible to, castration anxiety, separation anxiety, or even to annihilation anxiety. It is the dread implicit in the struggle to be really alive, to awaken, the dread of dying to what is known, of letting go of reassuring but limiting identifications and assuming one's place, coming to rest, in the mystery of each moment. It is knowing, as Kierkegaard wrote, that the dreadful has already happened, that it has already fallen away, and we are quite porous indeed! That we cannot possibly get there from here, that this is it. We are not invulnerable; things are not predictable, there is no ultimate control, we do not and cannot know everything, there is no permanent abode, no absolute meaning, or fantasied resting place. It is as we uncover and relinquish these notions and the matrix in which they are embedded that we can experience freedom and joy. This process can inspire not only anxiety, but also a powerful sense of betrayal and grief. Mourning is a passageway through which we can come to life.

KNOWING AND ILLUSION

For many, fear of death seems related not only to physical deterioration, the loss of capacities we've taken for granted, and their psychological impact. It also presents us with the sheer unpredictability, the seeming randomness of life, and the limits of our ability to know. Waiting for the results of medical tests for oneself or loved ones can evoke this kind of feeling. Helplessness indeed: magical thinking can return in the most "mature" of us; belief in a powerful, protective, or at least a knowing, deity can arise in the most hardened of atheists. Buddhism is known as the "Middle Way," originally a path distinct from both asceticism and blind sensual indulgence. Here the Middle Way might be the cultivation of a way to be with oneself (and others) that mitigates the rush either to all-knowing authority worship on the one hand, or mind-numbing hopelessness and its consequences on the other.

But death is not simply the passing of this body; we know the body wears out. Death is there in each lived moment, a gateway. In notes that were to become an autobiography, Winnicott (1978) wrote: "Oh God! May I be alive when I die." Perhaps learning to rest in the not knowing, in the mystery, is a springboard to wisdom and to the "peace which passeth understanding." I'm reminded of how Bion responded to Grotstein when the latter, in analysis with Bion, said that he thought he understood an interpretation Bion had made. "I was afraid of that," Bion replied (Grotstein, 1995).

It is not simply that spiritual experience (and particularly its cultivation or avoidance, as it were, in much organized religion) is intrinsically obsessive, as Freud thought, though it may be put by an individual or group at the service of obsessional defenses. Rather, obsessiveness and other "defenses," manic and otherwise, can arise in the wake of burgeoning awareness of the immediacy, the vividness, the empty, spacious playground of existence. A colleague was describing the experience of absorbed delight in the presence of the work of Manet. She worried that there might be some omnipotence attached to it. Omnipotence, however, couldn't be further from the experience itself; omnipotence would be the attempt to reproduce at will such an experience, to bring it under one's control.

The dual nature of the mind and the self is reflected in psychoanalysis in the debate about discontinuous versus continuous experience. Mitchell (1993) explores this issue cogently in his paper, originally entitled "On the Illusion of the Experience of a Separate Self," revised and now a chapter entitled "Multiple Selves, Singular Self." The original title captured a useful tension in the contrasting meanings of "illusion." Illusion, in the Winnicottian sense, is at the heart of play and freedom of mind. Yet the word is also used to describe self-deception, stories we tell ourselves which misrepresent what is so. One must have a discrete sense of self to function effectively and to live a fulfilling life, just as one must have, for example, a relatively differentiated body image and developed ego structure. For a sense of a personal self, with threads of continuity to its organizing story lines, a sense of its historicity is critical. However, upon examination (psychoanalytic or meditative), the structures of the mind, the constellations of me-you patterns through which we construct our experience of the world and ourselves, are far more fluid than we thought; in fact they can be found to be illusory.

Fisher (1992) examines the experience of the troubled adolescent and young adult. He suggests that "A sense of identity, defined as inner sameness and continuity, is like a snapshot of a system which is in constant motion. It captures features which are characteristic and familiar, but creates the illusion that we are organized in a more static way than we really are" [p. 454].

It is this very perception, and the experience that then arises, that can be the springboard for change, as it was for Ellen; and yet, says Mitchell, too much discontinuity may result in dread of fragmentation—"the discontuities are too discontinuous"—while too much continuity leads to paralysis and stagnation. The fundamental purpose in Zen lies not in the balancing of this dialectic tension but in facilitating direct experience in the realm where the distinctions themselves have fallen away and do not constrain perception. During the course of Zen practice, as in daily life itself, one can get caught up in, can collapse into, either the world of emptiness or the world of form.

ILLUMINATION AND THE ORDINARY

Self-knowledge in Zen is the *experience* that the two are not fundamentally separate: not two, not even "one." In the *Heart Sutra* (trans. in Aitken, 1993) we come to the heart of the matter: emptiness *is* form, form *is* emptiness.

The particular is itself the universal. The sacred, the fertile void itself is reflected in the personal, in each being, as it comes forth anew in each moment. Deep realization of this fact in one's daily life brings a change of heart. Hakuin Zenji in the *Song of Zazen* (Aitken, 1993) writes "All beings by nature are Buddha as ice by nature is water. Apart from water, there is no ice, apart from beings, no Buddha" [p. 179].

However, like unseen emotional action, this fact is obscured from ordinary consciousness. (Bandying around the concepts without integration through practice can lead to self-justificatory mischief: "It's all one, we're all empty, I am Buddha," and so on, can be used to rationalize all manner of narcissistic, ignorant, and cruel behavior.) Our most cherished views of self and other, of our very existence, must give way, must literally fall away. *This* is the "trans" of transformation, transformative experience, a much-used phrase these days.

The apparent paradox is that, only with this "forgetting the self" can we truly come to ourselves, can we come to *experience* the stuff of the self as the sacred. Self and object fall away. Yamada Roshi, at the time a middle-aged businessman and Zen student, was returning from work in Tokyo one day. While reading a book on the train, he came upon the phrase: "Mind is none other than the mountains and rivers and the great wide earth, the sun, the moon and the stars" (Dogen, in Kim, 1980, p. 148). He had read the words many times before, but they had not come alive for him. Everything fell away and there was only great laughter. What was so funny? Through an experience of empty infinity we can know *directly* (in contrast to *knowing about*) the personal and the sacred as identical. Meister Ekhart said: "The eye with which I see God is the very same eye with which he sees me." Soen Sa Nim, a Korean Zen teacher, used to say: "God is always calling but the phone is busy." I might add that she doesn't give a name when she calls. You can try to pick up the message later, but it is like reheating cold coffee.

Our personal experience is not extinguished, but returns in the realm of time and space, meaning, purpose, intention, choice, responsibility. We reinhabit the world of coming and going, shopping, getting to work, and feeding the baby. And we are the same, but not the same. "Singing and dancing are the voice of the Tao," writes Hakuin. And not only singing and dancing, but weeping and feeling angry. Suffering does not disappear forever. It is rather that *our relation to suffering is subverted.* There is not a permanent cessation, a permanent Nirvana that takes its place, as some see implied in the Buddha's teaching in the Four Noble Truths on suffering, the cause of suffering, the ending of suffering, and the path to liberation. Rather, just as I see, just as I hear, just as I feel, that's it! The fog has cleared, the internal mediatory dialogue has sloughed off, and the vividness can shine through, born of neither subject nor object, yet right in the midst of, and *as*, the very "obstruction" itself. Obstructions do not vanish permanently; it is simply that they no longer obstruct. Thought, imagery, affective and sensory experience, memory, personal history, and meaning do not evaporate forever. As Hakuin writes, "This very place is the Lotus land, this very body, the Buddha." Rather than being buffeted around, our lives become "Coming and going, never astray."

With understanding of emptiness, oneness, and uniqueness arises a sense of freedom and, simultaneously, compassion for all beings. Things have been turned on their axis, and each moment, each being—including the one right here, with this particular birthdate, birthplace, these particular parents, this particular gender, skin color, height, and weight—each one, just as it is, in its very ordinariness, its good, bad, and ugliness, is infinitely precious. We can see how this contrasts with the collapsed, concrete, "things in themselves" of the paranoid-schizoid position.

The other is none other than myself and yet, simultaneously, is completely other: distinct, unique, sacred. As meditation practitioners are discovering, such experiences do not—wishes to the contrary not withstanding—convey an exemption from the vicissitudes of human affective life and relationships. Indeed, they can become dissociated from affective life, compartmentalized and co-opted in the service of defending and protecting selected, identificatorily constructed versions of self. What about the person, the agent, and the agent's internal object world and its impact on relationships with other agents? The affective and relational realm is where many spiritual practitioners get hung up and come face-to-face with warded off, disowned parts of themselves, a protective "forgetting" that has sometimes been supported and abetted by the particular spiritual discipline, group, and teacher.

LIBERATION ON TWO (MUTUALLY POTENTIATING) TRACKS

Human experience cannot be captured by a theoretical formulation; by its nature it eludes final, definitive elaboration. Like a good response to a *koan*, a truly alive moment is beyond conceptual description. It must be embodied, lived. Discursive language cannot fundamentally convey it, though some language, like poetry, comes close. I fall prey to this most human of foibles, the attempt to capture in an image or a structure that which inevitably slips through such a net. I do so because I think there is value in expanding our view of what it means to grow as a human being, to cultivate and deepen the best of the perennial qualities that make us human, bearing in mind that the map is *not* the territory, and reading the blueprint is not the same as walking the land.

I have proposed that both paths, psychoanalysis and Zen, involve the activities of letting go and coming forth, though the two disciplines have tended traditionally to privilege one aspect more than the other. For purposes of comparison, the two approaches may be thought of as containing different "proportions" of each activity. The image of a double helix captures something of their dynamic relationship. Each strand is discrete, yet each intersects the other, and, in so doing, changes the other and is itself changed. Working in concert, the whole evolves in the direction of deeper aliveness, truth, integrated self-knowledge, and compassion for others.

Psychoanalysis affords the opportunity to develop experiential knowledge of self and other in (and out of) intimate relationship, and deepened, integrated awareness of personal and interpersonal activity in the realm of the unconscious emotional field. The analytic relationship and the heart-mind (Japanese: *kokoro*) of the analyst provides the experiential container, the ground in which the analysand brings himself to life as a separate and interdependent person. Zen practice offers the opportunity to see into the essential identity of the self-structure, of the experiencer himself.

The particular "wisdoms" of the psychoanalytic and meditative traditions can work hand in hand, enriching one another. For example, contrary
to expectations of unending bliss, as meditators access deeper dimensions
of unconflicted attentiveness, out of the unfolding spacious and nonjudgmental quality of attention, previously unintegrated, dissociated
and/or conflictual affective material may sometimes gradually emerge as
psychophysical experiences. McDonald (1996), a seasoned and gifted
meditation teacher with a personal history of serious trauma, vividly
describes her own confounding, harrowing, yet finally illuminating path
toward integrity which took her through both meditation practice and
intensive personal psychotherapy.

Regular meditation practice can help certain analytic or psychotherapy
patients contain and metabolize ambiguous, conflicted, or overwhelming
experience, and become more able to observe closely the interplay of
mental, emotional and somatic factors in the creation and maintenance
of certain painful psychic realities. Meditation practitioners often find
that psychotherapy or psychoanalysis can, in turn, free them up to continue and deepen their inquiry into existential matters, and to embody
and enjoy the fruits of their practice and discoveries in their daily lives
and activity.

During an initial session, a senior analyst asked a prospective
analysand whether the analysand's meditative experience might make it
difficult to benefit from analysis. This concern, while understandable, not
only proved unfounded but was in contrast to what other analysts and
analytic therapists have discovered about how meditation can broaden
and deepen their ability to practice their craft, to listen, connect, touch and
be touched, and understand their patients, themselves, and the process of
change (Coltart 1996; Deikman, 1982; Epstein, 1995).

As I began to realize that these two paths of inquiry, understanding,
and healing spoke to separate yet cross-fertilizing capacities and activities
of the psyche, integration became an interest. My sense however, is that
we can't really "get it together"; it *is* together. Articulating how this is so,
and not altogether so, is the enjoyable and perhaps impossible challenge.

Early on, a dream helped. I was preparing to return to Hawaii (where I
had studied Zen and founded a nursery school) after some years on the
East Coast, where I was finishing my graduate studies. I awoke one morning with a dream: "East, West, Center." My associations were first to the
East-West Center, a facility at the University of Hawaii which my Zen
teacher had helped direct earlier in his career. Then there was a temporal
association: first I had been in the West, then in the East, and now I was
going to stop off in San Francisco for my orals. Next, there was a spatial
one: East (Cambridge and New York), West (Hawaii), Center (San
Francisco). Then it occurred to me that I'd just finished my studies in
Western psychology and and was returning to complete studies in Eastern

meditative practice. These associations seemed interesting but incomplete. My attention drifted, and after a minute or so, it hit me: East, West (two streams), and center! But in this moment, the "center," such as it was, was no longer a theoretical integration of a dialectic but an experience curiously not identified with, while yet not apart from, myself. Further, the "East" and the "West" (as separate entities) seemed to have long since gone! Recently, nearly twenty years later, I realized something I had not been aware of at the time. During a class on dreams, it dawned on me all of a sudden, as if I had always known it, that the dream also represented my reworking of conception, birth, and differentiation from parents who had spent time separately on opposite coasts of the country. This may illustrate what I referred to earlier as the multidirectional continuum of curiosity about origins, in both its emotional-personal-historical and more broadly existential, aspect.

The clarifying and ongoing integration of the sacred with the personal, the ineffable with the affectively human, is a life-long task, as is, in its own way, the integration of insight and new experience into the human character in an analysis, and in our (often unaddressed but inevitable) postanalysis lives. "The challenge of course," writes Mitchell, "is to find a way to integrate the depths of self experience discovered in the 'unreal' analytic situation into the 'realities' of ordinary life" (p. 148). The parallel in Zen training is: How is insight into life and death, *gnosis*, the fruit of meditative practice on and off the cushion, lived in the hurly-burly of everyday life? Life assures there is no shortage of opportunities. While it is painful, unpredictable, and never how we imagined, neither is it just grim work. Both paths to relief of suffering and greater insight and love can be joyful, as implied in Freud's notion of the "playground" and Hakuin's "singing and dancing." It is like the play of shadows on the ocean, the "incredible lightness of being" alive and awake.

The ability to experience ourselves in novel ways is at the heart of successful negotiation, not only of adolescence and young adulthood, as Fisher writes, but of psychoanalysis and life itself, at every point along the developmental spectrum. In Zen, suffering is said to be caused by attachment, *not* attachment to each other, or the attachment of a baby to its parents. Zen scholar and teacher Katsuki Sekida once said, "Non-attachment, all I hear is non-attachment! If you weren't attached you'd be dead!" (Aitken, 1992).

Rather it is our unconscious predilection for protective, sometimes destructive, and always narrow, limiting, and fundamentally illusory views of self and other that lies at the source of our anguish. Becoming aware of how such views permeate our mind, by extension our bodies, our affective and relational experience, our very lives—how they literally constitute and constrain our "identity"—is the beginning of Zen practice.

Engler (1986) describes the apparent conflict inherent in the fact that what in psychoanalysis is a developmental achievement—that is, differentiating a separate self—is in Buddhism the very source of suffering. As Yasutani Roshi, one of the first Zen teachers to come and teach in America, said: "The core delusion is that I am here and you are there." But this, despite being axiomatic in most contemplative traditions, is not quite accurate. I don't think it is the *separate* self, illusory as it is, that is the problem—to the contrary—but rather the habitual, automatic, and tenacious attachment to constricting versions of such a self and its relations to others that informs and shapes our experience and behavior.

Engler concludes with the notion that "one must have a self before one loses it," a notion that has gained much popular currency. That is to say, from an expanded developmental perspective, both are achievements, but having a self precedes letting go of the self. I suggest, however, that the two are neither mutually exclusive nor are they simply sequentially related. Rather, we must *both* have (create) *and* not have (lose, destroy, see into) a self. Further, we must struggle with, ultimately accept, and hopefully come to enjoy their differentiation, their interpenetration, their necessary though incomplete integration, and their falling away in each moment of fresh, lived experience.

Rather than having to construct a self *before* we can discover no-self, as Engler suggests, I think it *takes* a (distinctive, personal) self to fully *embody* our essential (no-self) nature. And as one unravels, experiences, and realizes the empty, multicentered nature of all beings and of consciousness itself, the (particular, personal) self and its unique qualities are potentiated, brought to life and fruition. This seems closer to the experience of contemporary psychoanalysis, to the edge of current meditative practice, and to life itself.

REFERENCES

Aitken, R. (1978), *A Zen Wave*. New York: Weatherhill.
———— (1982), *Taking the Path of Zen*. San Francisco: North Point Press.
———— (1990), *The Gateless Barrier (Wu-men Kuan)*, transl. & with commentary by Robert Aitken. San Francisco: North Point Press.
———— (1992), *Zen Talks, Essays and Prefaces*. Honolulu HI: : Honolulu Diamond Sangha.
———— (1993), *Encouraging Words*. New York: Pantheon.
Batchelor, S. (1990), *The Faith to Doubt*. Berkeley: Parallax Press.
Beck, C. J. (1989), *Everyday Zen*. San Francisco: Harper and Row.
Blake, W. (n.d.), *Poems of William Blake*. Guernsey: Guernsey Press, 1995.
Cleary, T. (1990), *Transmission of Light (Denkoroku)*, transl. & Intro. by T. Cleary. San Francisco, CA: North Point Press.
———— (1983), *Entry into the Inconceivable*. Honolulu, HI: University of Hawaii Press.

————— & Cleary, J. C. (1977), *The Blue Cliff Record, Vol. 1.* Boulder, CO: Shambhala.

Coltart, N. (1996), Buddhism and psychoanalysis revisited. In: *The Baby and the Bathwater.* London: Karnac Books.

Cook, F. (1977), *Hua-yen Buddhism.* University Park, PA: University of Pennsylvania Press.

Courtois, F. (1971), *An American Woman's Experience of Enlightenment.* Los Angeles, CA: Zen Center Publications.

Deikman, A. (1982), *The Observing Self.* Boston, MA: Beacon Press.

Eliot, T. S. (1943), *Four Quartets.* New York: Harcourt Brace.

Engler, J. (1986), Therapeutic aims in psychotherapy and meditation: Developmental stages in the representation of the self. In: *Transformations in Consciousness,* ed. K. Wilber, J. Engler & D. Brown. Boston, MA: Shambhala.

Epstein, M. (1995), *Thoughts Without a Thinker.* New York: Basic Books.

Erikson, E. (1966), *Ghandi's Truth.* New York: Norton.

Fisher, C. (1992), Beyond identity: Invention, absorption and transcendence. *Adolesc. Psychiatr.,* 18: 448–460.

Fogel, G. (1991), Transcending the limits of revisionism and classicism. In: *The Work of Hans Loewald,* ed. G. Fogel. Northvale, NJ: Aronson.

Freud, S. (1907), Obsessive actions and religious practices. *Standard Edition,* 9:115–129. London: Hogarth Press, 1959.

Fromm, E. (1960), Psychoanalysis and Zen Buddhism. In: *Zen Buddhism and Psychoanalysis,* ed. E. Fromm, D. T. Suzuki & R. De Martino. New York: Harper.

Grotstein, J. (1995), From a seminar on psychoanalytic technique. Psychoanalytic Institute of Northern California, April.

Hamilton, V. (1982), *Narcissus and Oedipus.* London: Routledge & Kegan Paul.

Kim, H. J. (1980), *Dogen Kigen—Mystical Realist.* Tucson: University of Arizona Press.

Loewald, H. (1980), *Papers on Psychoanalysis.* New Haven, CT: Yale University Press.

Macy, J. (1995), Excerpt from an interview. *Inquiring Mind,* 11: Spring.

Maezumi, H. (1978), with Glassman, B. *The Hazy Moon of Enlightenment.* Los Angeles: Center Publications.

Mayer, E. L. (1996), Changes in science and changing ideas about knowledge and authority in psychoanalysis. *Psychoanal. Quart.,* 65: 158–200.

McDonald, M. (1995), Of mud and broken windows: Teaching the wounded soul. *Blind Donkey,* 15: Winter.

Mitchell, S. (1993), *Hope and Dread in Psychoanalysis.* New York: Basic Books.

Ogden, T. (1989), *The Primitive Edge of Experience.* Northvale, NJ: Aronson.

————— (1993), *Subjects of Analysis.* Northvale, NJ: Aronson.

Pagels, E. (1979), *The Gnostic Gospels.* New York: Random House.

Sartre, J. P. (1981), *The Family Idiot: Gustave Flaubert, Vol. 1.* Chicago, IL: University of Chicago Press.

Spezzano, C. (1995), How psychoanalysts learn. Paper delivered at a symposium at the Psychoanalytic Institute of Northern California entitled "What Is Contemporary about Contemporary Psychoanalysis?"

Stephens, W. (1972), *The Palm at the End of the Mind,* ed. H. Stevens. New York: Vintage.

Symington, N. (1994), *Emotion and Spirit.* New York: St. Martin's Press.

Winnicott, C. (1978), D.W.W.: A reflection. In: *Between Reality and Fantasy*, ed. S. Grolnick, L. Barkin & W. Muensterberger. Northvale, NJ: Aronson.

Winnicott, D. W. (1958), Mind and its relation to the psyche soma. In: *Collected Works*. New York: International Universities Press.

— 7 —

The Confluence of
Psychoanalysis and Religion

A Personal View

STEPHEN FRIEDLANDER

But he himself went a day's journey into the wilderness, and came and sat down under a broomtree; he requested for himself that he might die; and said: "It is enough; now, O Lord, take away my life; for I am not better than my fathers" [Kings, XIX:4].

We should read the Bible one more time. To interpret it, of course, but also to let it carve out a space for our own fantasies and interpretive delirium [Kristeva, 1993, p. 126].

Is commitment to a religious life consonant with the values of psychoanalysis? The founder of psychoanalysis, who unabashedly proclaimed himself "a godless Jew," disparaged religion because it conflicted with the ideals of science (as religion and science were generally understood at the time). Freud's view became the model for many psychoanalysts, not only in their practices, but in their personal lives as well. If psychoanalysis holds no respect for religion, why, I wondered, was I having a bar mitzvah at the age of 44?[1]

Given the bar mitzvah, it is already evident that I think religious commitment *is* consistent with psychoanalysis, and in this chapter I hope to explain how I formed this conviction. Having begun my essay with personal disclosure, I will go on to explore some of the questions that animate

---

[1]The bar mitzvah is an initiation ritual for Jewish male children that usually occurs when a boy reaches the age of 13. It consists of a course of study with a rabbi (and sometimes others) that culminates in the "bar mitzvah" (which literally means "son of the commandment") leading the congregation through the customary Sabbath service. A bar mitzvah ceremony betokens the assumption of adult responsibility for a religious life.

this anthology via the process of autobiographical reflection rather than attempt to maintain the distance associated with strictly academic investigation. The premise of my report is that the bar mitzvah ritual (and the preparations for it) profoundly changed my life in a manner comparable in scale and ameliorative potential to what psychoanalysis offers. Vivid emotional experience was crucial for this transformation, but new insights about myself and my position in the world were no less important. Both religious study and psychoanalysis contributed to the elaboration of insight and affect in my life, and both offered frameworks for integrating the two. The integration of insight and affect is, in the final analysis, precisely what is needed for any change to have lasting significance.

To say no more than this could suggest that "religious experience" might be a substitute for psychoanalysis, an idea that appeals only to nonanalysts. This is not my point at all. What I wish to discuss is how I passed beyond the conventional notion that psychoanalysis and religious life are congenial merely (or mainly) because they share a concerted interest in an authentically lived life. I want to focus instead on how I came to understand that whatever important benefits can be realized in their respective milieus—and the benefits do have a lot in common (see, for example, Fromm, 1950)—language has a determining effect on both the ends and means of the two disciplines. The conjunction, and, in fact, the confluence of psychoanalytic and theological interpretations of my experience in the course of the bar mitzvah suggested a synthesis of the two disciplines that had not been known to me previously.[2] Lacanian theory cast new light on the significance of communication, communion ("sharing or holding in common," *Oxford English Dictionary*), and reflection.[3] To put the matter succinctly, the analysand–religious practitioner's goal is, in both cases, to gain access to the Real via the Symbolic (technical terms in Lacanian theory which I define below). This, in brief, is what I set out in the following pages.

THE BAR MITZVAH AS A TURNING POINT

I was divorced in 1983, and exactly a year to the day after a separation from my wife, I had the first of two surgeries for cancer (Hodgkin's disease). The failure of my marriage seemed to be evidence of an emotional defect in myself and the cancer represented a sort of proof, a punishment for some

---

[2]I must emphasize that I mean synthesis—"the putting together of parts or elements so as to make up a complex whole" (*Oxford English Dictionary*)—not merger. Religious discourse and psychoanalysis are not interchangeable; the differences between the two remain important.

[3]It is no small irony that another atheistic psychoanalyst, Jacques Lacan, supplied the intellectual tools for integrating psychoanalysis and religion the way I have. Lacan's opposition to religion is discussed in Clément (1981) and Roudinesco (1990).

unarticulated fault (cf. Sontag, 1977–1978). Dick Felder, a psychiatrist with a strong interest in psychosomatic medicine and a longtime friend, came to visit me in the hospital. He told me that the one thing that stood out when he reviewed the literature on cancer and emotions was, "If you want to survive this, you better get connected to someone." A half-year later, I joined a Jewish congregation, something I had never done on my own, without realizing at the time that Dick's words had moved me in that direction. In retrospect, it is obvious that joining the temple was part of a strategy to reduce my loneliness and contend more successfully with guilt and despair, issues to which religious existentialists and psychoanalysts both devote themselves.

I decided to join the temple without expecting that religious activity would transform my life. It seemed perfunctory and pragmatic—perhaps joining a congregation would enhance my practice by increasing my visibility and normalizing my position in the community. However, the first time I attended High Holy Day services at the new temple, I was struck by the poetic beauty of the liturgy. This purely aesthetic appreciation was succeeded by a realization that the words of the liturgy, which derive mainly from the Torah (Genesis through Deuteronomy, i.e., the first five books of the Bible), embody the ethical ideals of Judaism. This realization led to a second shock: I had somehow allowed myself to think that I lived my life according to values that were uniquely my own. However, it was plain that the ethical ideals I considered to be my own were, in fact, *Jewish* ideals, conceived more than two millennia ago and passed down from one generation of Jews to the next. This discovery gave momentum to a gradually strengthening conscious desire to pursue Jewish knowledge and identity.

My exposure to Jewish culture and religion while growing up in a small town in the heart of the American Bible belt had been quite limited; I knew nothing, for instance, of how to read Hebrew prayers, of Jewish dietary law (*Kashrut*), or of standard Sabbath observance. My ignorance about these matters caused me no distress. First of all, I was unaware of what I was unaware of, and second, the importance of such things was drastically diminished in Reform Judaism.[4] With this background, it was easy to identify with the secular "Jewishness" of the first psychoanalyst. As Gresser (1994) explains:

> Freud [was] taught the humanist, German Enlightenment ethic of *Bildung*, namely, the "self-cultivation of one's intellectual and moral faculties through

---

[4]Reform Judaism, which originated in Germany in the early 1800s, emphasizes the ethical tradition of Judaism. One of its defining features is the rejection of *halakah* (the codification of traditional religious obligations). The philosophy of Reform Judaism was recently expressed as follows: "[The Jewish] tradition should interact with modern culture; . . . its forms ought to reflect a contemporary esthetic; . . . its scholarship needs to be conducted by modern, critical methods; . . . change has been and must continue to be a fundamental reality in Jewish life (Borowitz, 1983, p. xix).

a study of literature and philosophy, and the refinement of aesthetic sensibilities through the arts and music." Such an education would have prepared him to relinquish his attachment to Jewish tradition, considered to be "ill-suited to the cognitive and axiological requirements of the modern world," in order to make possible his "citizenship in the new era—a tolerant and humane era—envisioned by the Enlightenment" [p. 8].

Although I had little to relinquish as far as Judaism was concerned (unlike Freud), I wanted, just as he did, to hold "citizenship in the new era."

The Biblical Narrative

About two years after joining the temple, a strange question occurred to me: "If you're serious about being Jewish, why not have a bar mitzvah?" The essence of the bar mitzvah, as my rabbi explained at this time, is to learn enough Hebrew to be able to read a portion of the Torah and say the traditional blessings before and after the Torah is read. It is customary as well to give a short speech commenting on the significance of the passage for the week,[5] a *d'var Torah*.

The Torah portion for the week of my bar mitzvah, Genesis 27:1–13, tells the first part of the story of Isaac blessing his son Jacob. According to the text, G–d[6] planned for Jacob to be the third patriarch of the Jewish people (after Abraham and Abraham's son Isaac). For this to occur, Jacob had to receive his father's blessing. Traditionally, a father's blessing went to the firstborn son (who would be Jacob's older brother Esau, in this case). As a preparation for bestowing his blessing, Isaac told Esau to kill some game and prepare a meal for him. Rebeccah, the mother of the two sons, over-heard the conversation. Aware of the sacred destiny G–d intended for Jacob, she arranged for the prophesy to be fulfilled by having Jacob disguise himself as Esau and feed his father a meal she prepared for the occasion. Jacob followed her directions, although not without trepidation, and received the blessing from his father, as foreordained.

Interpreting the Text—First Thoughts

Modern readers are often inclined to look at Bible stories as psychological narratives.[7] I, myself, a psychologist-psychoanalyst, read the text at first as if it were about a contemporary family with whom I might become profes-

---

[5]A particular section of Torah is associated with each Saturday of the year, and the entire Torah is covered in the course of a year.

[6]Some devout Jews believe it is forbidden to write or say the holy name of the divinity. The written form G–d is a convention for honoring this restriction.

[7]In fact, some religious teachers use psychoanalytic thinking as a framework for interpreting Biblical texts (e.g., Cohen, 1995; Kushner, 1991).

sionally involved. What struck me initially was the unsavory quality of their dealings with each other: Jacob exploited his brother and duped his father under the influence of his mother, who conceived and managed the swindle. My reflection on the text was oriented to matters of this sort because, as previously mentioned, I wondered how psychoanalysis and religious commitment could be compatible when I began to involve myself with Jewish life.

The text has been translated into English many times. In one version, what Isaac said is rendered as "[P]repare a dish for me such as I like, and bring it to me to eat, so that I may give you my innermost blessing before I die" (Jewish Publication Society, 1988, p. 40). Another translation reads: "[M]ake me a delicacy, such as I love; bring it to me, and I will eat it, that I may give you my own blessing before I die" (Fox, 1983, p. 106). Whatever nuances various translations bring out, the invariant structure goes as follows: "Feed me that I might bless you (before I die)."

The most accessible idea in this phrase, in my reading of the text, is that an exchange will take place when a certain condition is met. My attention gradually turned to another level of exchange: the passage from concrete thinking to abstract reasoning. The foundation of ethical living, and the rise of culture depend on substitution and representation: a symbolic father for the living being who dominates others through brute force.

With the advent of psychoanalysis, a revision in our understanding of ethics per se became possible (and necessary!), since the existence of the unconscious casts doubt on how people assess their relations with others. In a psychoanalytically informed world, an aggrieved party cannot put all the blame on the antagonists. Even if there was some sort of deception, seduction, or coercion, we know people compromise their well-being for unconscious reasons. The psychoanalyst introduces the sufferer to a new method for learning about how the unconscious contributes to the problem.

Interpreting the Text—The Lacanian Perspective

Language was a crucial ingredient in Isaac's bargain with his son—the story is about *a blessing*—a fact that suddenly struck me one day as highly significant. Isaac demanded *something palpable* (food) and offered *something intangible* (words) in return. One could just as well say that he offered something impermanent (consumable) for something lasting (the memory of a father's blessing). This insight led me to consider the relationship between psychoanalysis and religion in a new light—that subjectivity is a function of the symbolic properties of language.

Jacob's future father-in-law, Laban, took the blessing as a "sign"[8] of material rewards that come to anyone who "possesses" the blessing:

---

[8]A linguistic sign is a particular type of language function in which a word simply means the "thing" immediately associated with it (Cassirer, 1955).

springs of pure water, herds of sheep, and other riches. Skeptical, modern readers may take the blessing as a sign that religious people cherish illusions, because the ostensible referent of the sign does not exist as an objectively demonstrable reality. Less skeptical readers know that the blessing is not a sign, but a symbol: Isaac meant to bestow, and Jacob meant to obtain, something symbolic, something corresponding to material wealth that is specifically *immaterial*—the personal fulfillment that comes with full participation in a religious (spiritual) culture.

At the moment that this association went streaming through me, I understood that the principle focus of Judaism had to do with symbolic functioning. The words "Feed me that I might bless you" succinctly convey a message about the importance of transformation in the medium of exchange: Matter must yield to metaphor. Anyone who regards all words as signs is at an impasse, for concreteness rules out all possibility of transcending the egotistic, materialistic, and acquisitive orientation typified by Laban. Religion awakens the subject to a nonmaterial reality; it organizes cultural life through its symbolic functions. The prohibition of idols, the emphatic insistence that G–d cannot be represented by material objects, declares the importance of symbolic functioning. Psychoanalysis awakens the person to an intrapsychic reality; it discloses the symbolic organization of the inner world, which develops in response to culture broadly conceived (society) and narrowly conceived (a specific family).

More on Words

Countless hours of practice reading the Torah and saying the accompanying blessings brought one lesson home to me—that the very words my Jewish forebears said for over two thousand years had become my own words. It did not matter that I read words in a book printed with modern technology rather than from a parchment scroll (during practice sessions), or that I voiced the words in a modern style rather than chanting them in the traditional manner. Experiencing the words of a text that originated with my ancient ancestors as *my* words, my text, had the uncanny effect of bringing me face-to-face with *the signifiers* that organize and support my own existence (Lacan, 1957).

In this context, a particular childhood memory acquired new importance. The *Shema*, Judaism's central prayer, was taught me by my great-uncle, Joshua Sprayregen, as we sat among family members in my grandparents' living room when I was four years old. My uncle did not bother telling me (as far as I can remember) what the words meant, or even that the words were significant for any special reason. Sharing the words—"*Shema Yisrael, Adonai eloheinu Adonai echad*"—was a form of play. As an adult, I saw that the prayer was not only a part of my personal history with family members. These words were the vital link with *the whole of Judaism*, that is, with "my family" in the widest conceivable sense. And, as I explain below, these words functioned as a kind of Ur-symbol, a symbol that Lacan calls *the name of the father*. The contours of this phenomenon were succinctly described by Thomas Mann (1934):

> Everybody has a father . . . nothing comes first and of itself, its own cause, but . . . is begotten and points backwards, deeper down into the depths of beginnings, the bottoms and the abysses of the well of the past . . . back to the beginning, the origin of the world and the heavens and the earthly universe out of confusion and chaos, by the might of the Word, which moved above the deep and was God [p. 9].

Condensing Mann's text thus, "Everybody . . . is begotten . . . by the might of the Word, which moved upon the deep and was God," the passage reads like a summary of the importance of language. The life of an individual is a function of the paternal prohibition, *the Word*, moving into "the deep," that is, the unconscious. Through praying and studying Torah I encountered "the father" that organized my life and my inner world—my actual father, Uncle Josh, Dick Felder, Sigmund Freud, Abraham, Isaac, and Jacob.

Further Reflections on Oedipal Dimensions of the Bar Mitzvah

My parents were nonplussed when I first told them I planned to have a bar mitzvah. They never disavowed their Jewish identity, but, as American Jews, they emphasized being "Americans" first. They assimilated to the culture around them and minimized their differences from everyone else. I imagine my plan disturbed them because it was "too Jewish" for their taste. I can also speculate that the idea of a middle-aged man having a bar mitzvah seemed too unconventional, a revival of the nonconformity I seemed to have left behind when I turned 30. In any event, I proceeded with my plans because I was doing it strictly for my own development.

Long after the deed was done, I could see oedipal triumph in what I accomplished. By doing something my father had never done, having a bar mitzvah, I had gone "beyond the father" (Martínez Luque, 1995). The significance of this particular going beyond the father might have gone unnoticed except for an unanticipated coupling of the Torah passage with life in the last years of the 20th century. After the bar mitzvah ceremony, my parents emerged from the crowd to greet me. "Tell him what you said to me," my mother told my father, and he said (with tears in his eyes), "I didn't know you could give a speech like that. It was like listening to Abba Eban[9] speak. That was the best speech I ever heard."

It is easy to think that the complimentary remarks from my father and mother[10] pleased me very much—they did! In the thoroughly psychologized culture we inhabit, it is tempting to read these exchanges as support for a popular idea that conveying love and admiration "builds good self-esteem." However, recasting Isaac's message into my own words—Feed me that I might bless you—helped me see it as a metaphor for structural (psychic) change. My destiny in no way compares to that of the Jewish patriarchs, but it is noble in its own way. I use knowledge that comes from the study of psychoanalysis and Judaism to help others penetrate, as Mann said, "the abysses of the well of the past" so that they, too, have an opportunity to experience the world emerging from "confusion and chaos, by the might of the Word." Given that I had just talked about the meaning of the Torah in terms of psychoanalysis, my father's blessing seemed to apply to my choice of both a profession and a religious life.

The Confluence of Psychoanalysis and Religion—First Recapitulation

From a strictly neutral point of view, a psychoanalyst should at least grant that religious involvement helped me by (1) furnishing a setting to explore the meaning of current experiences in the context of past relationships, (2) highlighting my unresolved narcissism by demonstrating that my ethical ideals had a source outside myself, and (3) developing my capacity for internalization. This last improvement was a function of the unique circumstance—for me—of making a major decision without discussing it with anybody. For six months after first hearing the question in my mind—Should I have a bar mitzvah?—*I considered the matter without discussing it*. There was no reason to keep it secret, but I took for granted that my involvement with this question would be diluted if I talked about it casually or repetitiously. All in all, I could say that the bar mitzvah enlivened me in a general way and helped me correct some distortions in my view of myself, take more responsibility for myself, and integrate neglected elements of my experience.

Such developments suggest that psychoanalysis and religious practice are not intrinsically antagonistic. The use of technical terms like the "unconscious," "narcissism," and "internalization" puts a psychoanalytic stamp on the discussion, but these changes could just as easily be

---

[9]Oxford-educated Abba Ebban, the first Israeli ambassador to the United Nations, is widely regarded as one of the greatest orators of this century.

[10]The following day, my mother said, "Yesterday was the best day in my whole life as a mother." And she repeated the message two weeks later.

discussed in a theological context. As Armstrong (1993) has said, "In all cultures, human beings have been driven by the same imperatives: to be intelligent, responsible, reasonable, loving and, if necessary, to change. The very nature of humanity, therefore, demands that we transcend ourselves and our current perceptions, and this principle indicates the presence of what has been called the divine in the very nature of serious human inquiry" (p. 385).

I came to recognize Jacob as my forefather through the bar mitzvah, and I eventually attained the same position as he: the position of being one who receives his father's blessing. A spontaneous enactment of this element of ancient Jewish history was not only unanticipated, it was absolutely unforseeable, as any discrete manifestation of G–d has to be.

Western religions are monotheistic; the names of G–d define this discourse. The potential for strain between psychoanalysis and religion is strongest precisely here. Before confronting this problem directly, I will give some perspective on how my relationship with G–d changed as a result of the bar mitzvah.

TORAH AND COVENANT

"Biblia, 'books' [in the plural] . . . is in truth one Book . . . united by the basic theme of the encounter between a group of people and the Nameless One, whom they dare to name as they are being addressed and in turn address Him—the encounter [i.e., the giving of the Torah to Moses on Sinai] between the two in history" (Buber, quoted in Fackenheim, 1987, p. 89). There is an ancient Jewish saying: "When is the Torah given? Whenever a person receives it!" I *received* the Torah when I experienced it as a personal communication, which is to say, when I *used* the text (cf. Winnicott, 1971). However, I follow Heschel (1955), who said that the existence of G–d is a prerequisite for an elevating experience of this sort to occur.

The Freudian sensibility and the religious sensibility appear intransigently incommensurate with respect to the idea of a covenant with G–d. The Freudian critique of religion implies that it would benefit me in some way to dispense, as Freud claimed to have done, with the idea of a covenant between G–d and the Jewish people. Would it not be more parsimonious—and, therefore, more plausible, more reasonable, and more mature—to say simply that I kept an implicit convenant with my ancestors? Fackenheim (1987) states,

> The modern reader may appreciate . . . [the Torah in its] historical setting . . . but can he accept in any sense whatsoever the traditional principle of *Torah min ha-shamayim*—that "the Torah is from heaven"? . . . the very possibility of a unique revelation to a unique Moses at a unique Sinai seems to have vanished with the advent of modernity. . . . It is a standard premodern

argument that an unbroken chain of reliable witnesses connects the present Jewish generation with that at Sinai, and that the revelatory event at Sinai was witnessed by no fewer than 600,000 Israelites—too many to be mistaken. . . . To the modern minded, this sort of argument conjures up theological debates as futile as they are wrongheaded—futile because each debater appeals to authorities rejected by the other, and wrongheaded because there are appeals to authority at all [pp. 23–24].

The transformation of my relation to my progenitors is an example of a multigenerational family romance. If I said that I was symbolically *incorporated* (or *re*-incorporated) into Jewish culture through the bar mitzvah, this would be a religious statement. A psychoanalytic statement would focus on the fact that I *incorporated Jewish culture in myself*. It may be useful to reiterate a crucial point: all of the texts (the Torah, my own autobiography) can be characterized in two ways. For instance, the story of Isaac and Jacob illustrates the function of substituting speech for action (a psychoanalytic context). On a theological axis, the fact that Isaac substitutes a symbol of G–d for a material object is the focus.

The alternatives are not mutually exclusive. How does it hurt me, psychoanalytically speaking, to say that I personally became a party to the Sinai covenant by participating in the multigenerational network that had preserved the Torah throughout the ages? It is not evident to me that a religious interpretation of this process interferes with my capacity to love and work, Freud's classic test of good functioning. The same holds true with respect to modern updates of psychoanalysis, such as the capacity to play (Winnicott) or to uphold my desire (Lacan). As far as I can see, psychoanalysis gives me no reason to forsake the religious claim.

Psychoanalysis can only be critical of immature religious practices. That is, an analyst has a responsibility to the analysand to facilitate awareness of the infantile sources of wishful thinking and the costs of defensive adherence to religious beliefs, but the concept of neutrality implies that analysts have no reason to oppose all religion a priori (Smith and Handelman, 1990). Religious reflection of a certain sophistication, on the other hand, reveals some of the limitations in conventional psychoanalytic thinking that persist today (e.g., Küng, 1979; Leavy, 1988). A well-developed religious attitude helps correct the ideological and reductive tendencies within psychoanalytic discourse that were markedly evident throughout much of this century.

THE IMAGINARY, REAL, AND SYMBOLIC

The distinction between sacred and profane is one of the earliest concepts in Western culture (Cassirer, 1955), and it typifies the process of dichotomous categorization that underpins so much of Western culture.

Psychoanalysis was originally erected upon an intellectual platform consisting of just such dualistic elements—self and other, active and passive, pleasure and pain, true and false, among others. In Lacanian theory, dualism itself takes on a new significance. All binary thinking is relegated to one category of mental process (the Imaginary) in a triad of three sorts of psychic process—Imaginary/Real/Symbolic (Lacan, 1988).

The Imaginary

Consciousness is largely constructed on the model of perception, where each perceptible point in the external field corresponds to one (and only one) point in the observer's image. Thinking that appears self-evidently true—that is, where object and idea correspond to each other on a one-to-one basis—belongs to "the imaginary order."

Most discourse, religious or otherwise, is permeated with the imaginary: unreflective notions of self, other, and the vicissitudes of their relationship. Religious discourse is particularly likely to include infantile elements of the sort that inspired Freud's hostile critique of religion because an individual's emotional economy influences which aspects of his/her patients' belief system (i.e., a previously organized discourse) get his/her attention. An exclusive reliance on second-hand language to represent what is potentially the most private, most important relationship in life—the relationship with G–d—seems inherently inauthentic to a modern, critical sensibility.

The Real

The real of psychoanalysis is, strictly speaking, all that is left over when every capacity we have to conceive and express ourselves is exhausted. The true agony of trauma and the ecstasy of orgasm are pure examples of "the real" because, whatever one says, their intrinsic reality is ineffable. The Hodgkin's disease precipitated an encounter with the ultimate real—death.[11] I also confronted the real during the Rosh Hashonah service (the moment when the question of a bar mitzvah first arose), the struggle with the meaning of the Torah, the giving of the speech itself, and the moment after that when the Rabbi put his hand on my head and formally blessed me as Isaac had blessed Jacob. Given that religious sages routinely deny that one can ever truly know the nature of G–d, a Lacanian analyst could be very comfortable saying, not that G–d is real, but that G–d is *"in the real."*

---

[11]In saying that I encountered the *real* qua death, I must emphasize that no matter how I struggle to put what I experienced during this encounter into words, all I can ever say about this experience (or any experience) is how I *imagined* it. The representation of my experience is always an expression of my experience *in the imaginary.*

The Symbolic

Lacan concluded that individual subjectivity is the product of an encounter between the child and the culture, and he utilized theoretical ideas from linguistics and anthropology to describe this process psychoanalytically. The culturally defined system of liberties and constraints called taboo rests on the idea of differences between one person and another. Lacan taught that distinctions in terms of gender, generation, and degree of kinship are *realized* as such within language. (See also Steiner, 1992, for an interesting discussion of this issue.) *Language* and *law* are conflated in this theory because they jointly represent the obligation on each person to renounce the pleasure of direct, wish fulfilling action in favor of relying upon words for the expression and partial gratification of wishes.

Language and Death

The shadow of death (the Hodgkin's disease) shaped this odyssey from the beginning, prompting me to align myself with a religious community, pursue a religious education, and open myself to self-transformation. In closing, I will highlight some more subtle ways that "death" figures in the story. One example comes from my personal analysis, where I realized that my postdivorce despair reflected an effort to kill myself, so to speak, for disappointing my mother. In discovering that my identity and subjective position were determined, not by myself alone, but by relationships with long (and not-so-long) dead ancestors, I ran into another example of death at work.

Social life depends on taming the instincts. Freud (1913) said that effective restraining factors (ethical ideas) emerge only in the aftermath of patricide. Lacan, virtually alone among post-Freudian theorists, treated the death drive as a primary element of psychoanalysis. In his reading of the Freudian fable, Lacan (1993) stressed that the father's death has an influence on the survivors by means of the *father*. (Compare this with my remarks on the oedipal dimensions of the bar mitzvah.) The crux of the matter is that the encounter with language is a form of death. This idea was implied in the text I read, since Isaac linked the transmission of the blessing (i.e., the transformation of the son through enfolding him in the word of G–d) to his own impending death. He said, "Do this . . . before I die."

Recently, I chanced upon an old Jewish teaching (Steiner, 1992) that gave a rich resonance to the idea that language and death are related "According to the medieval Kabbalah, G–d created Adam with the word *'emeth,'* meaning 'truth,' writ on his forehead . . . Erase the initial *aleph* which, according to certain Kabbalists, contains the entire mystery of G–d's hidden Name and of the speech-act whereby He called the universe into being, and what is left is *meth*, 'he is dead' " (p. 130).

SUMMARY

Life is woven from many streams of discourse. If the two discourses called "psychoanalysis" and "theology" flow together in contemporary life, it is because both have evolved considerably since Freud argued the issue. Subjectivity is a central concern for practitioners in both fields, even though they may focus on different manifestations of the subject-object relation. Some analysts treat religion and psychoanalysis alike as equivalent, in that both foster humanistic values: "an attitude in which [one's] life is devoted to the realization of the highest principles of life, those of love and reason, to the aim of becoming what [one] potentially is, a being made in the likeness of G–d" (Fromm, 1950, p. 118).

The bar mitzvah marked a turning point in my life. Spiritually exhausted from a "journey into the wilderness" (see the epigraph to this chapter), "deadlocked" with problems of intimacy and alienation, the decision to join a religious congregation was very propitious (although I had no intuition of this at the time). The process of preparing for the bar mitzvah ceremony allowed me to recast the issues into terms susceptible of more creative solutions, and the completion of the bar mitzvah ritual yielded a new freedom to think about what I needed to do, and wanted to do, with my life. This was no simple matter of arriving at a special insight at one specific time. I became eager to participate in Jewish ritual and ongoing study of religious texts. The process of learning to *read* the Bible— that is, read it in a personal way—and of opening myself emotionally to the resonance of ancient ritual showed me how richly compatible the resources of Jewish tradition are with the psychoanalytic mission. I was reminded of this again when I chanced to encounter the passage from Kings (see the epigraph) where, as Elijah testified, one's symbolic position with respect to his "fathers" stands out as fundamental.

It is surely ironical, in view of Freud's perspective, that the bar mitzvah also enabled me to extend my understanding of psychoanalytic theory and solidify my commitment to psychoanalysis as a vocation. So, I remain simultaneously engaged in these two quests, finding a charming irony in certain words said in every Jewish service: "Behold, a good doctrine has been given unto you; forsake it not. It is a tree of life to them that hold fast to it, and its supporters are happy. Its ways are ways of pleasantness, and all its paths are peace." Postmodernists in psychoanalysis (Barratt, 1993) and theology (Borowitz, 1991) accept the need for relentless engagement with an intractable problem, an idea expressed in the words of Kristeva (1993):

> Let us say, then, that everything ends up as fire—the fire of Heraclitus, the fire of the burning bush, the fire that burned Isaiah's tongue, or the fire that bedazzled heads with Pentacostal tongues. The truth of the matter is that I envisage the fate of meaning during an analytic session in a similar fashion—

as a meaning that is multifaceted, indefinable, set ablaze, yet One Meaning that exerts its influence everywhere. We can admit that this meaning requires the analyst to cling to the Bible's rigor, logic, and love, so that this fire might be and not die down right away. All the same, it must not blind us into thinking that this fire is the only thing that exists, for it need only state the truth at one point or another [p. 125].

Psychoanalysis and Jewish study effectively coincided in disclosing to me the ambivalent relationship we all have with "the father": hatred for being obliged to renounce wishes, gratitude for the opening of so many possibilities for loving relations with others as a result of internalizing "his" prohibitions. Today, the word doctrine evokes the very same ambivalence. A reliance on dogma in either religion or psychoanalysis betrays the critical spirit that must support our project in these times, but an open-minded critique of doctrine drives us to recognize our enormous debt to the fathers (e.g., Freud, the patriarchs) who gave us the project of interpreting their words.

CODA

Kristeva (1993) writes:

The Bible is a text that thrusts its words into my losses. By enabling me to speak about my disappointments, though, it lets me stand in full awareness of them.

This awareness is unconscious—so be it. Nevertheless, it causes me, as a reader of the Bible, to resemble someone who lives on the fringe, on the lines of demarcation within which my security and fragility are separated and merged. Perhaps that is where we might discover what is known as the sacred value of the text: a place that gives meaning to these crises of subjectivity, during which meaning, disturbed as it is by the object-abject of desire, eludes me and "I" run the risk of falling into the indifference of a narcissistic, lethal fusion [p. 119].

Narcissism puts us in danger of an impoverished existence. I feel that nothing protects one from this threat as well as an ongoing investment in the unique forms of discourse that are associated with authentic religious and psychoanalytic questioning.

REFERENCES

Armstrong, K. (1993), *A History of God*. New York: Ballantine Books.
Barratt, B. B. (1993), *Psychoanalysis and the Postmodern Impulse*. Baltimore, MD: The Johns Hopkins University Press.

Borowitz, E. B. (1983), *Reform Judaism Today*. New York: Behrman House.
———— (1991), *Renewing the Covenant*. Philadelphia, PA: The Jewish Publication Society.
Cassirer, E. (1955), *The Philosophy of Symbolic Forms*. New Haven, CT: Yale University Press.
Clément, C. (1981), *The Lives and Legends of Jacques Lacan*, trans. A. Goldhammer. New York: Columbia University Press, 1983.
Cohen, N. (1995), *Self, Struggle and Change*. Woodstock, VT: Jewish Lights Publishing.
Fackenheim, E. L. (1987), *What Is Judaism?* New York: Summit Books.
Fox, E., trans. (1983), *In the Beginning*, comment. & notes, E. Fox. New York: Schocken Books.
Freud S. (1913), Totem and taboo. *Standard Edition*, 13:1–161. London: Hogarth Press, 1955.
Fromm, E. (1950), *Psychoanalysis and Religion*. New Haven, CT: Yale University Press.
Gresser, M. (1994), *Dual Allegiance*. Albany, NY: State University of New York Press.
Heschel, A. J. (1955), *God in Search of Man*. New York: Farrar, Straus & Giroux.
Jewish Publication Society (1988), Tanakh. *The Holy Scriptures*. New York: The Jewish Publication Society.
Kristeva, J. (1993), *Reading the Bible*, trans. R. Guberman. New York: Columbia University Press.
Küng, H. (1979), *Freud and the Problem of God*, trans. E. Quinn. New Haven, CT: Yale University Press.
Kushner, L. (1991), *GOD was in this PLACE & I, I did not know*. Woodstock, VT: Jewish Lights Publishing.
Lacan, J. (1953), The function and field of speech and language in psychoanalysis. In: *Écrits: A Selection*, trans. A. Sheridan. New York: Norton, 1977, pp. 30–113.
———— (1957), The insistence of the letter in the unconscious. In: *Écrits: A Selection*, trans. A. Sheridan. New York: Norton, 1977, pp. 146–78.
———— (1977), *Écrits: A Selection*, trans. A. Sheridan. New York: Norton.
———— (1988), *The Seminar of Jacques Lacan, Book I*, ed. J.-A. Miller (trans., notes J. Forrester). New York: Norton.
———— (1993), *The Seminar of Jacques Lacan, Book III*, ed. J.-A. Miller (trans., notes R. Grigg). New York: Norton.
Leavy, S. (1988), *In the Image of God*. New Haven, CT: Yale University Press.
Mann, T. (1934), *Joseph and His Brothers*, trans. H. T. Lowe-Porter. New York: Knopf, 1948.
Martínez Luque, E. (1995), *Intrinsecus* psychoanalysis. In: *Confronting the Challenges to Psychoanalysis*, ed. S. Friedlander. Knoxville, TN: International Federation for Psychoanalytic Education, pp. 23–28.
Roudinesco, E. (1990), *Jacques Lacan & Co.*, trans. J. Mehlman. Chicago, IL: University of Chicago Press.
Smith, J. H., ed. & Handelman, S. A., assoc. ed. (1990), *Psychoanalysis and Religion*. Baltimore, MD: The Johns Hopkins University Press.
Sontag, S. (1977–78), *Illness as Metaphor*. New York: Farrar, Straus & Giroux.
Steiner, G. (1992), *After Babel*. Oxford: Oxford University Press.
Winnicott, D. W. (1971), *Playing and Reality*. New York: Basic Books.

— 8 —

Transcendence and Intersubjectivity

The Patient's Experience of the Analyst's Spirituality

RANDALL LEHMANN SORENSON

W hen working with patients who are religious, does it make any difference if the analyst has some openness to the possibility of transcendence or experience of the sacred? Or, to put it in terms more narrow and stark, does it make any difference if the analyst believes in God?[1] These are odd questions for psychoanalysis. Their oddity emanates from multiple sources. Beyond the traditional antipathy between psychoanalysis and religion, which stems from the more circumstantial element of Freud's confession of atheism personally, there are three more substantial objections: one philosophical, another clinical, and the third pedagogical.

The confluence of all three objections makes it deceptively odd to recognize that the questions I am posing are not merely rhetorical, but are also empirical and, therefore, amenable to imaginative quantitative investigation. Through a process of curiosity and wondering, I specifically explored the idea that therapist-analysands' experience with how religious issues were addressed in their own personal therapy as patient might, for these persons, shape both how they describe their developmental God representations, and how they handle religious issues with their patients.

---

[1] Some analysts might treat these ways of posing the question as not at all synonymous, and reject the status of the second as a subset of the first. That is, participation in religious life is viewed as something totally separate from, if not actually inimical to, openness to the possibility of transcendence or experience of the sacred—and there seems to be no shortage of religious adherents who serve as evidence for this perception. In what follows, I argue that the emergence of such evidence within the scope of psychoanalytic practice, however, is rarely the unearthing of preexisting facts, and is more commonly the co-construction of a particular analyst-patient dyad. I present empirical evidence that suggests the apparent foreclosure of mystery prevalent among religious analysands may itself be a co-construction of these patients' experience of analysts who view this essay's first two questions as orthogonal.

Before presenting what I found, however, I think it useful to discuss the three objections I mentioned. If not, I fear my project—no matter how significant the results statistically—might strike some analysts as completely unintelligible, or even absurd. It still may. By addressing these objections, however, I hope my original questions may strike other analysts as intriguing and, perhaps, even worth exploring. Other than in my own previous study (Sorenson, 1994e; see also Cohen, 1994, and Sorenson, 1994b), the notion of analysts' countertransference to religious issues in psychotherapy is something of a taboo, and thus there is no possibility here to review other research. None exists.

A Philosophical Objection

Despite Freud's claims of ignorance about philosophy—or perhaps because of it—rank-and-file psychoanalytic clinicians, from Freud's day until recently, have been able to persevere in psychoanalytic practice in a manner largely uninformed by pertinent philosophical developments. This perseveration has yielded a double irony: not only could psychoanalysis be on the intellectual vanguard in some aspects of 20th-century thought, while at the same time remaining on the trailing edge of other cultural developments, but also the discrepancy itself could occur through processes that function outside conscious awareness, the very domain to which analysts had lain special claim.

One such generally unexplicit philosophical strand in Freud's thought was a commitment to a positivistic epistemology, an orientation that was prevalent and convincing to many in early 20th-century Vienna, but which by now has been generally discredited for more than half a century. Despite having fallen into disfavor in most other circles intellectually, Freud's legacy of positivism shows amazing persistence to this day in the practice of virtually all of us as psychoanalytic clinicians. Even in contemporary psychoanalytic discourse, it is not uncommon to hear appeals to "clinical facts" we are said to have in common and by which we are to adjudicate competing theories (Wallerstein, 1990), or, in psychoanalytic case conferences, to hear references made to the "clinical material," as though this was some kind of uninterpreted raw data or brute fact (Meehl, 1973). Another remnant of positivism in psychoanalysis is our continuing penchant for inanimate, impersonal metaphor which de-emphasizes a process of necessarily inextricable, highly personal, and intersubjective mutual influence. Whereas Freud spoke originally of a blank screen, fascination in subsequent decades has continued with notions of a container (Bion), a frame (Langs), and more recently still, a mirror (Kohut).

According to their Principle of Verification, positivists assigned all propositions to one of three categories: those that were empirically true, those that were empirically false, and the rest that were deemed "cognitively meaningless." A statement like "It is raining outside" fell into category one or two, whereas all reference to transcendence, such as "God is love," was relegated to category three. Although positivism didn't last long as an intellectually viable position (some wag once impudently pointed out that the positivists' Verification Principle was itself empirically unverifiable, and thus, by its own criteria, cognitively meaningless!), its vestiges in psychoanalysis may lead some contemporary analysts to believe that analysis of transcendent experience is necessarily wrongheaded and unscientific. By contrast, contemporary philosophers of science, to whom I suspect most of us practicing clinicians have not had much exposure, would warn us that criteria for demarcation of science versus nonscience is more elusive than our positivistic heritage would lead us to believe (Laudan, 1983).

Given positivism's relatively brief flowering earlier this century, its long-term significance in the context of several millennia of intellectual history is uncertain and too soon to judge. There is another movement of thought that has stood the test of time, however, and it makes a point somewhat similar to positivism with regard to transcendence. This much more substantial objection to the legitimacy of analysts addressing religious experience has its origins in the work, two centuries earlier, of Immanuel Kant. The genius of the philosopher from Konigsberg was his creative synthesis between the earlier quest for certainty in Cartesian rationalism and the challenge of epistemological nihilism in Humean empiricism. In contrast to both, Kant argued that we could have true knowledge, but only through the sensory pathways by which our minds organize experience. We thus can never know a thing-in-itself (which he termed the "noumenal" realm); all our knowing is constrained by the imposition of our human mental channels of spatial-temporal organization (which he termed the "phenomenal" realm). On this point Kant (1963) was emphatically clear: "[T]he domain that lies out beyond the sphere of appearances is for us empty. That is to say, we have an understanding which *problematically* extends further, but we have no intuition, indeed not even the concept of a possible intuition, through which the objects outside the field of sensibility can be given" (p. 272).

Once we accept Kant's bifurcation as a satisfactory solution to the presumed dichotomy between objects-known and subjects-who-do-the-knowing, the conclusion is ineluctable: analysis of the noumenous is inherently out of the question. The sole legitimate purview for analysts cannot extend beyond the phenomenal realm. Gil Noam and Maryanne Wolf (1993), who teach at Harvard and Tufts Universities, respectively, describe an experience in New England that illustrates this Kantian approach to spirituality in psychoanalysis, an experience, I believe, that is indicative of a common psychoanalytic perspective on religion, regardless of geographic region.

At a recent meeting of psychoanalysts in Boston, a seasoned teacher reviewed the clinical work of a candidate whose patient was a deeply religious Catholic woman. The patient's psychological language incorporated many spiritual metaphors about the relationship between God and guilt. Picking up on the insecurity of the analyst who mentioned that she had difficulties dealing with the religious experience of her patient, the consultant said with authority and conviction: "Why should you treat her religious concerns differently than you deal with any associations that emerge in psychoanalysis?" He meant his remarks to encourage the young analyst to enter all experiences of her patient and to try not to remain aloof from the religious ones. Although he sounded convincing, and had a positive impact on the treatment, the remark is troubling. Are spiritual associations really the same as any other associations? Should they be treated in the same way as other associations? [pp. 201–202].

John McDargh (1993), a theologian at Boston College who is involved in both clinical practice and the interdisciplinary conversation between psychology and religion, has raised a related question that, for psychoanalysts who endorse a Kantian epistemology, will also seem exceedingly odd. McDargh asks: "Is it *therapeutically* sufficient for a clinician to appreciate the psychological value of an individual's religion, or may it also be necessary for a clinician to take a position on the *ontological* status of the client's religious inner world?" (p. 173).

How we answer the questions by Noam, Wolf, and McDargh depends on the alternatives we perceive available to us. If we endorse Kant's presentation of our options, then we have no other choice: we must say that spiritual associations are functionally the same as any others, and that it is indeed therapeutically sufficient to appreciate nothing beyond the psychological value of an individual's religion. For Kant, the idea of God can extend problematically beyond the phenomena; it's just that our knowledge is limited by the a priori categories. Or again: We *can* know things, including "God," but only through the categories. From this it follows that it simply will not do to try to smuggle transcendence through the portal of Kantian phenomena, if this invokes some sort of direct apprehension or unmediated access. Related to this impossibility, I find compelling the critique by philosopher and psychoanalyst Victoria Hamilton (1982) of Wilfred Bion, when she argues, in essence, that he misunderstands Kant.

Bion blurs Kant's distinction between *a priori* and sensible knowledge when he proposes equivalence between the "things-in-themselves" and the "beta-elements"—that is, the raw, pure, discrete sense-impressions. Because both are ultimately unknowable, Bion states an incorrect equivalence. The chief characteristic of the "beta-element" is its corporeality and concreteness. It is "undigested"—that is, unworked over by mental functions. Inadvertently, Bion subsumes the noumenon under a corporeal conception. An elision occurs in his theory of thinking between the transcendental "thing-in-itself" and the psychotic "beta-element." In my view, this confusion arises because of Bion's misunderstanding of the *problematical* use of the concept of the noumenon. He fills up a concept which is "empty" (Kant) and gives it a *positive* employment [p. 251].

I understand Hamilton's point to be that there is no way to employ Kant's noumenal realm transcendentally, either by means of the ineffability of mysticism or the unspecifiability of intuition.

If Kant's thought is commonly regarded as the zenith of critical philosophy during the Enlightenment, ongoing intellectual history has continued to change in the centuries since, often in ways profoundly different from what those in the Enlightenment ever could have imagined. Even so, radical change often occurs in the name of nonchange, through familiar and existing terms that disguise or simply do not convey the full extent of the revolution-in-process. Radio, in succeeding the telegraph, for example, was introduced as the "wireless"; the automobile was initially understood as a "horseless carriage." In neither case could anyone have envisioned the economic, ecological, and familial impact of the automobile on industrialized society, or the significance of radio signals in geosynchronous satellite transmission for an electronic global village. Kant's is termed "critical" philosophy; that a developing new constellation of thought is termed "postcritical" is similarly deceptive—much like the "wireless" or the "horseless carriage"—because this new term only describes what it comes *after*, and underemphasizes the radical transformation of epistemology it portends.

Throughout the 20th century there have been multiple contributors to this emerging new "postcritical" paradigm, and although these authors certainly would not all agree with each other on every point, one vital thinker is physicist and philosopher Michael Polanyi, whose 1958 book, *Personal Knowledge*, had as its apt subtitle, *Towards a Post-Critical Philosophy*. In a recent essay, philosopher Ronald Hall (1993) contrasts critical and postcritical epistemology, arguing that for all that critical philosophy sought to oppose speculative ideals of objectivity, Kant's critique was not radical enough, and falls short of what Polanyi offers. Hall explains:

As I am reading it, objectivism presumes an ideal of objectivity according to which reality is defined as that which is completely independent of a knowing subject. As objectivism has it, the embodied, situated, human knower inevitably contaminates this pure reality with subjective elements, that is, with evaluations, commitments, perspective, passion, and so forth. Consequently, the objectivist thinks that the ideal knower would be a disembodied god who passively comprehends, *sub specie aeternitatis*, the whole of reality as it is in and of itself.

Although critical philosophy objected to this ideal of objectivity, this objection by the Kantian critical philosophic tradition is less than radical because it fails to see that the ideal it opposes (and subtly accepts) is not only not attainable, either in fact or in principle, but rather is demonstrably self-defeating. The speculative ideal defines the limits of critical epistemology; only from the speculative ideal would one think to call human knowing inherently *limited* by the fact that it is human [p. 73].

In Polanyi's work, Hall sees a new ideal of what comprises objectivity.

On this radically new ideal, we will not be inclined to say that as long as there is a subjective component in knowing, objectivity is an impossible dream. Rather, we will say that objectivity is obtainable *because* there is a subjective component in knowing. Post critical philosophy offers us the prospect of an access—a human access—to things-in-themselves; it tells us that we do not have to be gods to be objective knowers; it tells us, moreover, that human beings are not only not obstacles to objectivity, but the enabling means of its pursuit [p. 77].

From a slightly different vantage point, I view the work of Daniel Stern (1985) in infant observational research as also offering something like a neo-Kantian or even postcritical epistemology, especially in his work on affect attunement in infants. Like Kant, Stern posits modal sensory pathways through which infants (and all humans) know the world, including vision, audition, gustation, olfaction, and kinesthetic awareness, among others. Unlike Kant, however, Stern also posits an underlying capacity for amodal signal processing that is partially independent of, while also common to, all sensory input pathways. Also unlike Kant, for Stern the capacity for interaffectivity, rather than posing the skeptic's problem of how ever to know the existence of other minds, is what *permits* the psychological birth of human selfhood in the first place. Stern gives multiple examples of this phenomenon, of which I will mention just three.

A nine-month-old girl becomes very excited about a toy and reaches for it. As she grabs it, she lets out an exuberant "aaaah!" and looks at her mother. Her mother looks back, scrunches up her shoulders, and performs a terrific shimmy with her upper body, like a go-go dancer. The shimmy lasts only about as long as her daughter's "aaaah!" but is equally excited, joyful, and intense.

A nine-month-old boy bangs his hand on a soft toy, at first in some anger but gradually with pleasure, exuberance, and humor. He sets up a steady rhythm. Mother falls into his rhythm and says, "kaaaaa-*bam*, kaaaaa-*bam*," the "*bam*" falling on the stroke and the "kaaaaa" riding with the preparatory upswing and the suspenseful holding of his arm aloft before it falls.

An eight-and-one-half-month-old boy reaches for a toy just beyond reach. Silently he stretches toward it, leaning and extending arms and fingers out fully. Still short of the toy, he tenses his body to squeeze out the extra inch he needs to reach it. At that moment, his mother says, "uuuuuh . . . uuuuuh!" with a crescendo of vocal effort, the expiration of air pushing against her

tensed torso. The mother's accelerating vocal-respiratory effort matches the
infant's accelerating physical effort [p. 140].

In each of these episodes, *mere mimicry is not enough*. If the infant's voice
rises and lowers in pitch, for example, and the mother merely does the
same with hers, the infant experiences the mother as robotic, mechanical,
and a less-than-fully human other, an outcome which engenders a similarly less vital sense of self in the baby. If, by contrast, the mother raises
and lowers her eyebrows and facial expression, matched in time with the
infant's vocalization, the baby has a sense of affective attunement, and
self-enhancement ensues. It's as though the baby were saying, "I can see
you *get* it—your response back to me shows me you aren't just mimicking
me, you've taken it in, processed it, and sent it back to me in a way that
shows you really understand!"

Stern's work on cross-modal perception and Polanyi's contributions
toward a postcritical epistemology are but two instances among many
that pose new possibilities for how psychoanalysts may think to work
with all aspects of patients' experiences, including patients' religious
experience—and these ways are very different from earlier perspectives
steeped in critical philosophy and positivism. The point here is not that
postcritical philosophers have supposedly had the final word and that no
future conversations in philosophy will supervene; this is most certainly
not the case. Besides, the unfolding trend-in-formation of what's been
termed postcritical philosophy is a loosely organized, ramshackle structure at best, with no single spokesperson, no unified agenda, and an indeterminate future. The point, rather, is that intellectual history has
continued to move on, not only from the positivism of Freud's day at the
turn of this century, but also from the critical philosophy of the 18th-
century Enlightenment. We psychoanalysts, however, to the degree that
we imitate Freud's claim to ignorance about pertinent philosophical
concerns, are at risk to persist in outmoded forms of empathic exploration of our patients' religious experience (Sorenson, 1994a, 1994c,
1994d; Spezzano, 1994).

A Clinical Objection

My question originally was, When working with patients who are religious, does it make any difference if the analyst has some openness to the
possibility of transcendence or experience of the sacred? Or, more narrowly, does it make any difference if the analyst believes in God? Another
objection is the clinical concern that it is the *patient's* reality alone that matters, and not the analyst's. Advocates of this perspective would express
concern that it is the patient who is in analysis, not the analyst, and that
ideally the analyst's contribution should be negligible, or at least so

unobtrusive that the patient's experience is central and the analyst's idio-
syncrasies and personal beliefs—regarding God or anything else, for that
matter—are of no practical relevance.

Evelyne Schwaber (1986, 1990) is sometimes cited in this sense, as
though her goal were total immersion in the patient's affective field so as
to minimize the analyst's distinct presence. The way I read Schwaber,
however, her interest is not that the analyst should try to disappear from
the two-person intersubjective field, but rather the opposite. It is precisely because the goal of an invisible or noninteractive analyst is as
impossible as it is misguided that it is essential to pay attention to the
myriad ways in which the analyst impacts the patient—often without
direct awareness of either analyst or patient. Lacking this awareness, the
analyst then attributes the patient's motivation solely to intrapsychic
processes within the patient.

Lewis Aron (1991) addresses this topic from a related and very creative
perspective. The more customary approach for a psychoanalytic paper
would be with a title something like "The Analyst's Experience of the
Patient's Subjectivity," but Aron offers an insightful inversion. He writes
on "The Patient's Experience of the Analyst's Subjectivity." Aron avers:
"Patients seek to connect to their analysts, to know them, to probe beneath
their professional facade, and to reach their psychic centers much the
same way that children seek to connect to and penetrate their parents'
inner worlds" (p. 29). When thwarted in this regard, an experience of frustration may be mistaken as evidence of patients' innate aggression or
endogenous envy. As Aron allows, when pondering "the rich Kleinian
imagery of the infant's attempts in unconscious phantasy to enter into the
mother's body, we may wonder whether the violent, destructive phantasies encountered are due only to innate greed and envy or whether they
are not also the result of the frustration of being denied access to the core
of their parents. Could these phantasies be an accurate reflection of the
child's perceptions of the parents' fears of being intimately penetrated and
known?" (p. 39).

If Aron's question is a fair one, might there be similar implication for
analysts' work with patients who are religious? Certain religious patients
might be especially difficult for some analysts to treat, due not so much to
these patients' inherent "unanalyzability" as to their perceptions of the
analyst's fears of being intimately known along what is often highly personal terrain, the analyst's own relations to mystery and transcendence.

In the spirit of Aron's reversal, I could also turn around my original
questions by countering, How could it *not* make a difference what the analyst's experience was with respect to transcendence? And why *shouldn't* it
matter? Once we shift our analysis from a one- to a two-person psychology, how could anything about either of the participants not matter?
Indeed, the wish to not matter, and the guilt about making a difference in

the relational field just by the very act of the observer observing, is itself a by-now anachronistic feature of a largely outmoded positivistic ideal for science. Moreover, because this shift to a two-person psychology entails not only a shift from a drive to a relational model, but also from a positivistic to a social constructivist epistemology (Hoffman, 1991), our understanding of everything, including notions of transcendence (our own and how we view our patients', theirs of themselves, and their perceptions of ours), is necessarily incomplete and perspectivally situated. It thus becomes a misplaced question to ask whether the analyst believes in God, because the question must be asked, Whose God? And which God? There is evidence that "God" is an object that is, or can be, continually constructed and revised throughout life (Sorenson, 1990; Key, 1994). From this it follows that no two persons' Gods are alike, nor is one's God necessarily identical across one's lifetime—and this is true even of the Gods we reject or the Gods in which we don't believe (Rizzuto, 1979).

The question then becomes, Must religious patients only be treated by religious analysts? I think not, any more than holocaust survivors, for example, must only be seen by analysts who are the same. A recent Roper poll, however, reported that over one-third of the American population believes the holocaust never happened. Although the polling methodology has been questioned, and a subsequent Gallup study found that the number of Americans who think Nazi genocide may be fictional is only one in ten, not one in three (Kifner, 1994), the question for psychoanalysis still remains: What if the analyst were among this ten percent? What difference would it make to the analysand as a holocaust survivor to have an analyst who was technically skilled in empathic listening, but who did not believe the patient? This analogy is especially apropos to religiously committed patients, since, as with holocaust survivors, the relevant experience in question obviously has central significance to the person's psychological organization and representational world. Perhaps if the analyst were a fellow survivor, he or she might be too close to the experience, and be at risk to understand the patient through the analyst's experience rather than the patient's. But to varying degrees, fortunately or unfortunately (depending on your epistemology), isn't that what always happens in all forms of empathic knowing? Is direct apprehension of another person's subjective state—unmediated by our own organizing principles of subjectivity—possible or desirable? And besides, at issue in the holocaust illustration is not whether analyst and patient experience could be too proximal, but rather if it ever could be too distal, and what impact the analyst's private disagreement with what the patient counts as real might have on the treatment, even if cloaked in technical neutrality or skilled empathic listening.

Take childhood sexual abuse as another example. Once again, we may ask the question, Would it make any difference if the therapist didn't believe the patient? This change in illustrations complicates matters because there are, in fact, some therapists who manufacture false memories of abuse in their clientele, whereas most all therapists would acknowledge the horrible historicity of the holocaust and would view it as tantamount to an obscenity to pretend the atrocity never happened. The historicity of divine intervention in human affairs is more ambiguous than evidence for the incidence of genocide or incest. Even so, the point here is that divination of notions such as "reality orientation" or "mental health" are necessarily perspectival and value-laden enterprises in which the contribution of moral and political judgment is typically and subtly disowned by proponents.

Martin Frommer (1994) made a similar argument about the role of technical considerations when analyzing homosexual men. Point for point, the tensions Frommer outlined for psychoanalytic perspectives toward homosexuality are the same for religion: a history of pathologizing the orientation, with little if any attention to helping patients develop a positive sense of this aspect of their identity; earlier techniques that tried to encourage patients' renunciation of their commitments and convictions; and more modern approaches that seek to avoid taking sides on the issue and instead seek a pattern of neutral inquiry. As much as the more modern approaches are an advance and an improvement, Frommer is suspicious of analytic claims to "neutrality," a term that psychoanalyst and professor of German Axel Hoffer (1985) has argued should more faithfully be translated "indifference." Frommer (1994) explains the basis for his suspicions.

> One might think that a depathologized view of homosexuality would naturally result in a neutral stance, but it is a mistake to assume that the analyst operates from a position of neutrality regarding the patient's homosexuality merely because he or she adopts a technically neutral stance toward it.
>
> Recent concepts of intersubjectivity that have reshaped traditional thinking about transference and countertransference suggest that whether or not the analyst behaves as if he were neutral, the patient is nonetheless influenced by the subjectivity of all the analyst's feelings, whether or not they enter treatment through overt verbal communication [p. 217].

Because indifference about sexual orientation in one's own personal life is an unlikely state of subjectivity, Frommer argues for the advantage of homosexual analysts being better suited to treat homosexual patients, by virtue both of being more directly empathic via similar experience themselves, and by being a source for positive role modeling for the struggling analysand.

While I am open to Frommer's arguments regarding psychoanalysis and homosexuality in general, and find many parallels with regard to religious patients in particular, I find myself less enthusiastic to recommend analyst-patient matching on the basis of religion as an unequivocally good thing. My reservations, to be sure, are not based on some positivistic lauding of "neutrality," or a disavowal of passion and a pretense of indifference. My reasons have more to do with what, at core, may be the therapeutic action of psychoanalysis. Freud's answer to this question, on more than one occasion, was that in psychoanalysis "the cure is effected by love" (McGuire, 1974, pp. 12–13), or again, "our cures are cures of love" (Nunberg and Federn, 1962, p. 101)—and by this he meant *transference* love. The differences between this type of love and its romantic and infantile precursors for Freud were negligible, a point made especially well by Joan Riviere's translation of Freud's essay "On Transference Love" (Freud, 1915).

> [I]t is true that the love consists of new editions of old traces and that it repeats infantile reactions. *But this is the essential character of every love. . . .* The transference-love has perhaps a degree less of freedom than the love which appears in ordinary life and is called normal; it displays its dependence on the infantile pattern more clearly, is less adaptable and capable of modification, *but that is all and that is nothing essential* [p. 167; italics added].

For Freud, transference was an error, "a *false connection*" (Breuer and Freud, 1893–1895, p. 302), and there are those analysts today who remain faithful to Freud's epistemology.

> The great importance of the transference in psychoanalysis lies in its unique epistemological role. When a patient reports past or present experiences with a spouse, sibling, or parent, the analyst, who is not omniscient, can only defer to the patient's long experience with people the analyst has perhaps never even met. When the patient's experience of the analyst himself is at issue, the analyst is in a position to make an independent assessment, since he has himself had the opportunity to observe first hand *all* the events that have gone into forming the patient's experience of him. Or rather, he has observed all the relevant events external to the patient. This enables him to infer with a relatively high degree of certainty the contribution that internal events have made to the patient's overall experience of the analyst. The sense of conviction about these internal events that both analyst and patient may thus arrive at is unparalleled in any other type of interpretation [Caper, 1988, pp. 62–63].

For Freud, as for contemporary analysts who followed Freud's positivism, the claim to authoritative certainty was the axis on which successful analyses turned. The value of transference love was that it provided the necessary motivation for the patient to submit to Freud's interpretative explanations— "when it is lacking, the patient does not make the effort or does not listen when we submit our translation to him" (McGuire, 1974, p. 12).

Other contemporary analysts are less sanguine about the prospect of finding refuge in certitude. Jay Greenberg (1991), for example, argues that even when patient and analyst alike share the conviction that an episode in treatment should be labeled as transference, this may serve a defensive function to protect both participants from uncomfortable observations patients make about their doctors. About her critical appraisal of her analyst, for example, a patient declared, "If I didn't know it was all projection, I couldn't have said a word of it" (p. 52). Stephen Mitchell (1993) likewise notes how an appeal for compliance and deference on the part of the patient toward the doctor, while congenial to Freud and his era, strikes late 20th-century sensibilities as strangely discordant and anachronistic. And from the various perspectives of intersubjectivity theory (Stolorow and Atwood, 1992; Stolorow, Brandchaft, and Atwood, 1987) and social constructivism (Hoffman, 1991, 1992) still other modern psychoanalytic theorists would question the possibility and value of any person's claim to epistemic hegemony.

André Haynal (1993), psychoanalyst and main editor of the Freud-Ferenczi correspondence, has noted that if for Freud love meant *transference* love, for Sándor Ferenczi it meant *counter*transference love, much as Leopold Szondi, a student of Ferenczi from Zurich, "often spoke of the therapist as a 'soul donor'—an analogy with 'blood donor' " (p. 202). If this characterization of Ferenczi's view is fair, then there are potentially profound and fertile connections between the early Hungarian theorists in psychoanalysis (including Ferenczi and his student Michael Balint) and later Hungarian theorists in epistemology and philosophy of science (such as Michael Polanyi). What Ferenczi was struggling to articulate was an epistemology that required frank and candid human involvement in the human sciences—an inclination that was in many ways ahead of his time and is today decidedly more contemporary than aspects of Freud's positivism.

This brings me full circle to my hesitation about the supposed benefit of analyst-patient matching on the basis of religious (or nonreligious) status. If the question is reframed in contemporary terms of the vitality and centrality of what Ferenczi referred to as countertransference love, then adjudication of "fact" and "fantasy" or "accurate" versus "distorted" reality perceptions becomes misguided and beside the point. In the sense of postcritical epistemology, transference and countertransference become the fundament by which we know anything at all; rather than being embarrassing sources of error, they are the means by which we organize personal meaning and significance. Projection, rather than being a distortion of reality, becomes the precursor for empathy (Grotstein, 1981). And empathy, even with all these ongoing changes in psychoanalytic theory, invokes no epistemological circumvention of hermeneutics. Rather than being an unmediated channel to another's mental state, empathy is always interpretive (Stern, 1994).

In Ferenczi's sense of countertransference love, empathic knowing takes more than just humoring the patient. It requires authentic participation, and the same must surely apply to psychoanalytic explorations of spirituality. What matters more than the particular religious status of either participant is a willingness and openness for authentic personal involvement, which conceivably could include a disjunction of subjectivities between analyst and patient. Ferenczi's complaint in his personal analysis with Freud, after all, was that the latter was too reluctant to take up the *negative* transference (DuPont, 1988). Perhaps even Ferenczi's term "countertransference" is an expression of the language available to him at the time, whereas today we have other options that presume less unidirectionality, as Aron (1991) indicates:

> In my view, referring to the analyst's total responsiveness with the term *countertransference* is a serious mistake because it perpetuates defining the analyst's experience in terms of the subjectivity of the patient. Thinking of the analyst's experience as "counter" or responsive to the patient's transference encourages the belief that the analyst's experience is reactive rather than subjective, [when it is actually] emanating from the center of the analyst's psychic self. . . . It is not that analysts are never responsive to the pressures that the patients put on them; of course, the analyst does counterrespond to the impact of the patient's behavior. The term countertransference, though, obscures the recognition that the analyst is often the initiator of the interactional sequences, and therefore the term minimizes the impact of the analyst's behavior on the transference [p. 33].

In previous work (Sorenson, 1994e), I found no support for the notion that a particular religious orientation on the part of the analyst was necessarily boon or bane: What seemed to matter was

> not the co-religionist status of the participants per se nor the noetic content of specific beliefs, but the manner in which religious issues are approached. Creedal parallelism and doctrinal twinship between patient and therapist was neither a necessary liability, as some theorists have suggested, nor a necessary asset, as others have proposed. Instead, a stance of respectfully curious, sustained empathic inquiry into the subjective meanings of the religious person's world of experience seemed to have the most transformative effect on these patients' subsequent practice as therapists. Picking a therapist of the same religious denomination was no guarantee of securing this most precious quality, any more than was a therapist from a different religious orientation— or nonreligious orientation—a warrant for its absence [p. 341].

If the therapeutic action of psychoanalysis is indeed love—not only in Freud's sense of transference love but also in Ferenczi's sense of countertransference love—and if even the word *countertransference* is as Aron (1991) argues "a serious mistake because it perpetuates defining the analyst's experience in terms of the subjectivity of the patient" (p. 33), how can it be any different when it comes to our patients' experience of our own spirituality? The clinical objection that such exploration has no place in psychoanalytic technique strikes me as tenuous.

A Pedagogical Objection

The third objection to examining empirically the patient's experience of the analyst's spirituality is pedagogical. It is well known by now that psychoanalysis is one of the few intellectual disciplines in the 20th century to develop outside the environment of the university. Also well known is that in North America, contrary to Freud's wishes and consonant with his fears, so-called lay analysts, such as clinical psychologists—arguably the ones with the best university training for empirical research—have historically been denied full access to psychoanalytic education. The result is a psychoanalytic pedagogy that systematically excludes, and even devalues, research. Allan Compton (1994) develops precisely this point with prose that is at once eloquent and stark:

> The structure of psychoanalytic education has mitigated strongly against the development of research. The "tripartite model" of psychoanalytic education—seminars, supervised case work, and training analysis—is built upon the idea that psychoanalysis in its essence is a method of scientific investigation—that is, the erroneous idea that work in the context of discovery on single cases only is sufficient for scientific advance. Nowhere is the absence of the dimension of research more strikingly clear than in the comparison to that of a graduate department in a university, where the keystone is research.
>
> The tripartite model of psychoanalytic education is, in addition, hierarchical rather than three legged: classes are less important than supervision which is less important than the training analysis. Institutes function mainly as referral clubs and devices to support financially those who have attained training analyst status, a forum where masters can attract apprentices, not as centers of graduate education. Training analyst status is the career goal; and the rewards of that status are an enhancement of one's practice. This is very clearly a self-perpetuating situation [pp. 16–17].

Compton's argument is that the structure of institutes, the structure of curriculum, and the structure of psychoanalytic practice all stand in opposition to psychoanalytic research. When institutes are typically structured to serve the faculty, rather than the other way around, for example, research programs are seen to "impinge on the hegemony of the faculty-training analysts, and consequently tend to be short-lived" (p. 18). And the typical psychoanalytic curriculum, while it emphasizes diagnosis and clinical technique, virtually ignores the contributions of research to both these areas. Most challenging of all Compton's critiques, in my view, is how the structure of psychoanalytic practice has profound financial ramification for the prospect of psychoanalytic research:

> The structure of psychoanalytic practice also discourages research. All money generated by psychoanalytic practice goes into the pocket of the practitioner—not unlike the results of other forms of professional service. But,

because of the free-standing, university-unaffiliated status of almost all psychoanalytic training programs, there is no tradition of a career track in empirical research in psychoanalysis. Academic departments in universities tend
to be unfriendly towards members of their faculties who "waste time" with
psychoanalysis, rather than "real research." Psychoanalytic institutes tend to
see academicians as "not real analysts." Grant awarding bodies are readily
put off by the loose science and grand claims of psychoanalysts [pp. 18–19].

As an analyst in private practice who also teaches both at an APA-
approved doctoral program in clinical psychology and at a psychoanalytic
institute, Compton's assertions ring true. The recently formed APA
Division 12 (Clinical) Task Force for the Promotion and Dissemination of
Psychological Procedures, for example, has as its mission "to formally
identify treatments with demonstrated efficacy and to disseminate these
empirically validated treatments to practitioners," and to date has identified 25 such approaches (Sanderson, 1995, p. 4). Needless to say, psychoanalysis is not among them. My sense is that psychology is moving toward
a future that increasingly recognizes only those treatment modalities with
empirically proven efficacy. If this proves so, and if current models prevail
in institute training, the day may come when psychoanalytic approaches to
clinical practice—irrespective of other considerations regarding third-
party reimbursement and managed care—will not be able to be a part of
any psychology graduate school doctoral program that seeks APA
approval. That is, quite apart from questions of whether practitioners will
find patients who would receive any insurance compensation for psychoanalysis, students in psychology (and presumably other mental health pro-
fessions) could not even be taught psychoanalysis in university graduate
schools. Given the previously mentioned separation between psychoanalytic institutes and university graduate schools, this might seem to pose no
real loss. To those of us who believe the future of psychoanalysis depends
in part on vigorous participation in the world of ideas that is university life,
however, forfeiture of this opportunity could well result in a corrosive
marginalization of psychoanalysis in North America.

There are similar tensions within institute life. During my term as
Director of Doctoral Programs at my own psychoanalytic institute, for
example, my task was to coordinate curricular and staff resources for
candidates who seek a Ph.D. in Psychoanalysis, which the state has
accredited our institute to award. I found some reluctance on the part of
prospective faculty to be associated with courses having to do with
research. Some analysts are reluctant to be exclusively pegged as
"researchers"—a position they feel has diminished status—thereby limiting their access to potential referrals for candidate-analysands' training
analyses or supervision of control cases. Others have no interest in, or are
intimidated by, the world of research. By at least one measure, the pattern of analysts' dearth of interest in psychoanalytic research seems to

apply beyond my own local institute to the national level, too: I counted the number of APA Division 39 Section I members (Psychologist-Psychoanalyst Practitioners) who also chose to join Section VI (Psychoanalytic Research), and found that the number was less than 15 percent. This was so even though the sections have roughly the same number of members, and the tuition to join Section VI is extremely modest ($10 per year).

The upshot of all this is that, compared to the number of service hours performed annually by all practitioners, very little research is done in psychoanalysis. As further evidence of this, perhaps the most indicting sentence for psychoanalysts in the 864-page fourth edition of *Psychotherapy and Behavior Change* is the following, taken from a chapter that summarizes psychodynamic approaches: "When all the published articles on transference are considered, the ratio of theoretical to empirical articles is roughly 500 to one" (Henry, Strupp, Schacht, and Gaston, 1994, p. 479)! When it comes to research, analysts seem inclined to engage in all-or-nothing thinking. Either it's what we're *always* doing all day long in our offices just by seeing patients,[2] or it's what we should *never* be doing because it's injurious to or incompatible with the process of psychoanalytic inquiry.[3]

This means that any essay on psychoanalysis which employs some combination of clinical, philosophical, and empirical sophistication may well stand out like a sore thumb, or seem incompatible with other contributions. The submission I am offering here is a university essay by a psychologist, and, for the reasons I have detailed, may seem to some analysts triply odd. When it comes to the viability of the analyst's taking a position with regard to issues of transcendence, the philosophical objection is "it's impossible," the clinical objection is "it's unhelpful," and the pedagogical objection is "it's unnecessary." Modern epistemologies suggest it's none of these. Instead, it may be indeed possible, helpful, and necessary—particularly for patients who consider themselves religious, and perhaps

---

[2]"Like every other scientist, a psychoanalyst is an empiricist who imaginatively infers functional and causal relations among his data" (Brenner, 1982, p. 5).

[3]A variant of this perspective is one in which research, while not injurious or incompatible, is instead deemed on par with interesting clinical vignettes: "In my view, the findings of 'empirical research,' when addressed to clinically relevant questions pertaining to the psychoanalytic process, should not carry any more weight than case studies or compelling clinical vignettes that bear on the same issues. Each source of understanding affords particular analysts and analytic therapists possibilities to take into consideration as they encounter unique moments in their work with particular patients, nothing more and nothing less" (Hoffman, 1995, p. 110). Donald Spence (1994) laments this equivalence of what he terms Galilean versus Aristotelian methods of science: the former studying multiple occurrences of an event, no one of which takes precedence over others; the latter valuing study of a single occurrence or specimen for its quintessential or archetypal significance.

for all patients regardless of their conventional religious involvement—to work with analysts who welcome their patients' exploration of the analyst's spirituality. This possibility I tested empirically.

WHAT I DID

I teach doctoral seminars on psychoanalysis and psychotherapy at an APA-approved clinical psychology program, which has as part of its specific charter to examine points of commonalty and tension between Christianity and the behavioral sciences. In the course of my teaching, I thought to ask students to write autobiographical accounts of (a) their own developmental representations of God that arose from their family of origin, (b) their experience with how religious issues were addressed in their own personal therapy as the patient, and (c) their ways of working as therapists with religious issues in other persons who sought treatment. I viewed the assignments as personal rather than the standard academic fare, so I offered students the option of writing on different topics of their choosing for full course credit if they so elected. Because I also wanted to avoid as much as I could any interpersonal circumstance that pulled for a confessional tone of mandatory or compulsive self-disclosure on students' parts, out of regard for their privacy, I suggested that if there were something particularly personal or sensitive that they would prefer I not know, they could exercise their right by not including it in their papers. Most students elected to write these essays, and their efforts struck me as both honest and courageous.

As I read the different assignments across a semester, I had the unintended experience of imagining that I could match the essays by author despite the months that separated the assignments, and even if all identifying and stylistic information were thoroughly removed or controlled. How students worked on religious issues in their own therapy as the patient seemed to shape both how they came to experience their developmentally evolving conceptions of God, and how they themselves worked as therapists when interpreting religious issues in others as their patients. I decided to put my hunch to the test empirically. Using excerpts from 12 students' essays, I found in an earlier study that other expert judges could make these matches, too (Sorenson, 1994e). I could not infer any causal relations from the research design, however, which merely counted the frequency of successful versus unsuccessful matches via a chi-square contingency analysis.

In the present study I extended my previous research by submitting data from 60 student essays to linear structural equation modeling. With this, I could specifically test a model of directional causality that my previous study suggested. The model I proposed is also a test of the contemporary theory of narrative psychology (Howard, 1991; Sarbin, 1986; Spence, 1982, 1987), which argues that putatively historical accounts by patients in clinical work can be viewed to be as much co-created constructions in the present as archeological uncoverings from the past.

What I Measured

In the interest of parsimony and comprehensiveness, for the present study I rated therapist essays according to adjectives from Gorsuch's (1968) higher-order factor of a "Companionable/Benign Deity" (in which God is experienced as comforting, warm, real, powerful, approachable, and gracious), and an orthogonal, first-order factor Gorsuch labeled "Wrathfulness" (which depicted God as avenging, blunt, critical, cruel, jealous, and damning).[4] Because therapists wrote about both their current God concepts during ongoing therapy, and retrospective accounts of their notions of God prior to therapy, I made an assessment of each. I wanted to make my criteria as objectively reliable as possible, in order to increase the chances of agreement between how I and an independent person rated the essays. Protocols were scored dichotomously as credit/no-credit (1 or 0) for the presence in students' essays of the two Gorsuch factors for God adjectives I used, with scales ranging from 0 to 2 for God-Representation-without-Therapy (1 point for Benign Deity, and 1 point for Wrathfulness), and the same for God-Representation-with-Therapy.[5]

---

[4]Because a conservative subject-to-variable ratio for multivariate statistical methods is approximately 10 to 1, and my sample was 60 subjects, I wanted to select a total of six scales that were as representative as possible of the three domains: God concept, experience in personal therapy, and clinical practice. For parsimonious assessment of God concepts, one possibility was Osgood, Suci, and Tannenbaum's (1957) classic Semantic Differential, which seeks to account for all human construction of meaning along just three dimensions: evaluation (for example, good versus bad), potency (strong versus weak), and activity (active versus passive). While reviewing the literature on assessment of God concepts, Carrie Doehring (1993) noted, however, that two weaknesses of the Semantic Differential are that it forces judgments to be bipolar and dichotomous (good or bad, but never both), and that some of the core adjective pairs, when applied to representations of God, seem peculiar (such as "sharp versus dull") (p. 33).

A more comprehensive and useful instrument according to Doehring's review was Richard Gorsuch's (1968) Adjective Ratings of God Scale, which involved a factor analysis of 100 adjectives, including ones from the Semantic Differential. Gorsuch found eight oblique primary factors, five of which were represented by just two second-order factors, which in turn loaded on a single third-order factor, which assessed a Benign-Companionable Deity. An orthogonal first-order factor measured persons' conceptions of God along a dimension of Wrathfulness. A recent study confirmed many of Gorsuch's original findings, including the third-order and Wrathfulness factors (Schaefer and Gorsuch, 1992).

[5]Ten percent of the protocols were selected at random and scored independently by a second rater, which yielded good interrater reliability for both scales (.82 and .87, respectively).

For the variables on therapists' experience with how religious issues were handled in their own therapies as the patient, plus how they worked as the therapist with religious issues in others, I created two scales based on my knowledge of what student therapists had written in their essays. I termed these scales "Therapist Analysis of the Transcendent" and "Therapist Orientation toward the Transcendent." The former (which I'm abbreviating here with the label "Analysis") involved three items. First, the analyst made interpretations that conveyed a sense of the transcendent as "real," as opposed to interpreting references to transcendence in terms of human tradition only, or as transference only. Second, the analyst approached issues of transcendence in an open and comfortable fashion, as opposed to an approach that was more conflicted, less open or comfortable, and inhibited exploration. Third, the analyst made interpretive connections regarding the patient's representational experience of God, parents, and the analyst. These connections occurred at the analyst's own initiative, in which the analyst was respectfully curious, broached the topic, and made a detailed inquiry into the patient's world of experience. A contrasting analyst made comments infrequently, if at all, about the patient's organizing themes vis-à-vis the patient's experience of the sacred, and did so only if the patient initiated the topic. Analysts with this style remained passively receptive if patients wanted to broach the topic, but viewed analysis of this material as especially precarious—something requiring extraordinary sensitivity.

Regarding "Therapist Orientation toward the Transcendent" (which I'm abbreviating as "Orientation"), there also were three items. First, analysts viewed patients' experience of the sacred as something positive, as a potential resource for strength and healing, as opposed to viewing it negatively and emphasizing only its pathological functions. Second, analysts viewed religion as something primary or central in life for many people, for whom it would be a natural topic of exploration in psychotherapy, as opposed to viewing it as a foreign or peripheral topic that had no legitimate place in psychoanalytic inquiry. Third, patients made comments about evidence of the analyst's intimacy or familiarity with the transcendent in a way that fit the patient's aspirations. It was not that the analyst pontificated on these matters, but the patient would make comments about the analyst's personal openness to mystery, and lack of foreclosure to mutual exploration of not only the patient's hope, faith, and ultimate meaning, but also the patient's experience of the *analyst's* spirituality. Other analysts were characterized, by contrast, as having antipathy toward spirituality, or an orientation toward transcendence which the patient did not admire.

I did the same thing for therapists' work in clinical practice with religious issues *in others* using the Analysis and Orientation scales. The three items were scored dichotomously, as with the God Concept assessment, thus yielding a possible range of scores from 0 to 3 for each scale.[6]

Latent Variables

Until fairly recently in the history of psychology, it was not possible to compare multivariate models with measures of statistical significance. Solutions to multiple regression, canonical correlation, or factor analysis, unlike their univariate counterparts, offered no basis by which to compare results from different samples. With multivariate research, the best that anyone could do was perform exploratory analyses endlessly, and hope that the factors that surfaced were similar to those of previous studies. This wish was rarely fulfilled, however, because all exploratory analyses capitalize on chance associations in a given data set, and thus conflate spurious sources of variance with the model being generated. A further limitation is that repeated, exploratory multivariate studies were usually atheoretical, functioning primarily via computer algorithms rather than a particular scientific hypothesis or theory. This approach obviously impedes both development of better theories in science and the utility of scientific findings for clinical theory and practice.

Karl Jörskog (Jörskog, 1969; Jörskog and Sörbom, 1979) pioneered the development of causal modeling with latent variables. This strategy has increasingly entered the mainstream of contemporary psychological research, providing the benefit of multivariate hypothesis testing, without assuming the absence of error in hypothesized models, and without requiring contrasting control groups in order to establish the efficacy of a given intervention (Bentler, 1980). These developments are especially useful for clinical research, in which no-treatment control groups are often not practical (if not potentially unethical), and in which the clinical variables in question neither operate in isolation nor are necessarily synonymous with paper-and-pencil measurements.

In the present study, I used Peter Bentler's (1992) program for linear structural equation modeling to test the causal paradigm suggested by results from a previous study (Sorenson, 1994e). In that study, psychologists could match the therapist's work with religious issues in clinical practice with that therapist's personal God representation. This made intuitive sense from my reading of the students' essays. If, for example, persons had a representation of God as a distant and cold figure, they seemed to be much less comfortable hearing about religious issues from their clients. Furthermore, data from the previous study indicated that

---

[6]The scales for Analysis and Orientation in therapists' experience in personal therapy, and in their own clinical practice as therapists themselves, produced satisfactory interrater reliabilities (.80, .76, .84, and .79, respectively).

when it came to how therapists worked with religious issues in treatment, even more powerful a determinant than the therapists' God concepts was these therapists' experience with how religious issues were handled in their own therapy as the patient. If therapists' God concepts influenced how they worked with their own patients' religious issues in treatment, these God concepts seemed themselves to be a product of how, for these therapists, *their* therapist worked with them. The following causal model was thus submitted for analysis in the present study:

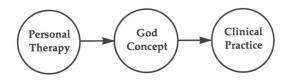

An Empirical Test of Narrative Truth

Because the latent factor for God concept, which includes *retrospectively narrative* elements on God representations prior to therapy, is placed in the causal sequence *after* the influence of the experience in personal therapy, the above model provides a possible test empirically of the debate on whether clinical truths are found or made. Freud favored the former. For all his dedication to the power of the unconscious in coloring all human perception, Freud's epistemology was what contemporary philosophers of science would call "Naive Realism," and one of his favorite metaphors was the psychoanalyst as archeologist (Freud, 1937).

> But just as the archeologist builds up the walls of the building from the foundations that have remained standing, determines the number and position of the columns from depressions in the floor and reconstructs the mural decorations and paintings from the remains found in the debris, so does the analyst proceed when he draws his inferences from the fragments of memories, from the associations and from the behavior of the subject of the analysis [p. 259].

Donald Spence (1982) argues that the archeological metaphor is misleading, and that analysts' interpretations are usually unwitting *narratives* that would benefit from empirical process and outcome studies to determine the *historical* truth of what really happened, although others call for a hermeneuticism untethered to external "verification" (see Bruner, 1993). Another author who articulates with consistency and clarity a thoroughgoing constructivist epistemology that truth is as much constructed as discovered is Donnel Stern (1994). He reminds us that "to assume that the patient's experience is already "there" makes it difficult to appreciate how fully the analyst and the patient participate moment-to-moment in the construction of one another's experience, how they co-create everything that takes place in the analysis—not only the transference–countertransference, but even the patient's memories and reports of concurrent events outside the treatment (p. 443).

I think a position somewhere between historical truth and narrative truth—one that clearly rejects positivism but stops short of social constructivism—is that of intersubjectivity theory developed by Robert Stolorow and his colleagues (Stolorow, Brandchaft, and Atwood, 1987), who stress that

> the reality that crystallizes in the course of psychoanalytic treatment is an *intersubjective reality*. This reality is not "discovered" or "recovered," as implied in Freud's (1913) archeological metaphor for the analytic process. Nor, however, would it be entirely accurate to say that it is "created" or "constructed," as some authors have claimed (Hartmann, 1939; Schafer, 1990; Spence, 1982). Rather, subjective reality becomes *articulated* through a process of empathic resonance. The patient comes to analysis with a system of developmentally preformed meanings and organizing principles, but the patterning and thematizing of his subjective life is prereflectively unconscious (Atwood and Stolorow, 1984, ch. 1). This unconscious organizing activity is lifted into awareness through an intersubjective dialogue to which the analyst contributes his empathic understanding. To say that subjective reality is articulated, rather than discovered or created, not only acknowledges the contribution of the analyst's empathic attunement and interpretations in bringing these prereflective structures of experience into awareness. It also takes into account the shaping of this reality by the analyst's organizing activity, because it is the analyst's psychological structures that delimit and circumscribe his capacity for specific empathic resonance. Thus analytic reality is "old" in the sense that it existed before as an unarticulated potential, but it is also "new" in the sense that, prior to its entrance into an empathic dialogue, it had never been experienced in the particular articulated form that comes into being through the analytic process [pp. 7–8].

From the perspective of contemporary interpersonal psychoanalysis, I understand Paul Wachtel's (1977) "woolly mammoths" analogy as getting at a point similar to Stolorow's intersubjectivity theory. Wachtel writes about how impressed Freud was by the seeming freshness of repressed memories, as though these were kept in an amnestic deep freeze from the Jurassic era. "Freud's description of the persisting influence of the past is reminiscent of the tales of woolly mammoths found frozen in the Arctic ice, so perfectly preserved after thousands of years that their meat could be eaten by anyone with a taste for such regressive fare" (p. 28). For Freud, the mystery was how early beliefs could persist despite the myriad disconfirmations throughout subsequent life. For Wachtel, early beliefs persist not *despite* subsequent life experiences but *because* of them: "the early pattern persists, not in spite of changing conditions but because the person's pattern of experiencing and interacting with others tends continually to recreate the old conditions again and again" (pp. 552–553). Wachtel concludes: "Rather than having been locked in, in the past, by an intrapsychic structuring, the pattern seems from this perspective to be continually being formed, but generally in a way that keeps it quite consistent through the years. It may appear inappropriate because it is not well correlated with the adult's "average expectable environment," but it is quite a bit more closely attuned to the person's idiosyncratically skewed version of that environment [p. 53].

WHAT I FOUND

At precisely the point of theoretical controversy mentioned above regarding historical truth versus narrative truth, the model I had initially proposed did not fit the data; amendment of this one offending component, however, resulted in a model that fit the data extremely well. That is, if subjects' retrospective accounts of developmental God representations were forced to be causal products of individuals' experience in personal therapy, the multivariate model failed to converge.[7] When data on the God concepts *before* therapy were dropped as causal products *of* therapy, leaving only the Wrathfulness-With-Therapy and Benign-Deity-With-Therapy, the resulting model fit the data extremely well.[8]

Two questions ensue: (1) Where then in the model to put the pretherapy God concept? and (2) Is this outcome a disconfirmation of the narrative theory of historical construction? Regarding the first question, I tried placing the pretherapy God concepts causally prior to therapist behavior, because many would say that analysts' options are determined by the nature of the religious patient's God representation. For example, if the patient's God representation prior to treatment is too punitive or rigid,

---

[7] As many as 60 iterative attempts failed to yield a solution. Examination of standardized residuals, which reveal points of potential model misspecification, showed that the failure of convergence involved the God concept items Wrathfulness-Prior-to-Therapy and Benign-Deity-Prior-to-Therapy.

[8] $\chi^2 = 3.304$, 7 df, $p = .856$, Bentler–Bonett Normed Fit Index $= 0.960$

many clinicians would say this greatly limits or affects the analyst. Data from the present study, however, do not support this hypothesis. Placing as a latent variable subjects' "God-Concept-Without-Psychotherapy" causally prior to these persons' experience with religious issues as the patient in their own personal therapy, produced another model that could not be solved through repeated iterations, and thus the following model had to be rejected as a poor fit with the data:

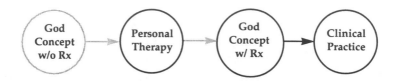

From the data, what is most salient is the finding that persons' God concepts prior to experience in personal psychotherapy were generally unrelated to (1) how their therapist worked with religious issues in them as the patient, (2) how these persons as mental health practitioners worked with religious issues in others, and even to (3) how their God concepts emerged during or subsequent to therapy.[9] By contrast, God concepts that arose during or subsequent to therapy not only shaped how therapists worked with religious issues in others, but also were themselves a function of how the therapists' analysts addressed issues of transcendence in the training analyses. Whether this therefore entails refutation of

---

[9]The one exception was Wrathfulness with and without therapy, .327, which means about 10% of the variance is accounted for and 90% is indeterminate. Why God concepts prior to therapy did not fit into the causal model is apparent by examining the correlation matrix of the measured variables:

1	Benign Deity With Therapy	1.000						
2	Wrathfulness With Therapy	−.086	1.000					
3	Personal Therapy Orientation	.273*	−.304*	1.000				
4	Personal Therapy Analysis	.212*	−.397*	.703*	1.000			
5	Clinical Practice Orientation	.231*	−.209	.306*	.271*	1.000		
6	Clinical Practice Analysis	.215*	−.240*	.441*	.369*	.392*	1.000	
7	Benign Deity Without Therapy	.198	−.035	.064	.062	−.031	.047	1.000
8	Wrathfulness Without Therapy	−.177	.327*	−.007	−.048	−.215*	−.036	.027	1.000

Notions of a Benign Deity that emerged for subjects during psychotherapy correlated positively both with these subjects' experience of their therapists' orientation toward, and analysis of, transcendence, and also with the subjects' own clinical practice regarding religious issues when they were the therapist for others ($p < .05$). The same was true, only with a negative correlation, for Wrathfulness ($p < .05$). Consistent with Gorsuch's previous studies, Wrathfulness was orthogonal to notions of a Benign Deity, whether for God representations with therapy ($r = −.086, p > .05$) or without ($r = .027, p > .05$).

narrative psychology, which was my second question, I take up in the following section.

WHAT I THINK THIS MEANS

The notion that these data contradict narrative clinical theory is something I address first, followed by six vignettes that illustrate the results clinically. I conclude with what I think are implications for analysis of transcendent experience in psychoanalytic process.

An Orthogonal Narrative?

Do the present study's outcomes constitute a refutation of narrative psychology? What are the alternatives? One possibility is that subjects did, in fact, create retrospective God stories that just didn't happen to fit persons' current narrative constructions of God, but this is a weak argument. It's not just that they created comedies or tragedies (Gergen and Gergen, 1983; White, 1973); it's not that God was once bad and then became good, once harsh and now friendly, or the reverse. If this were the case, then there would have been significant negative correlations, when in fact there was none. Moreover, if the subjects were indeed creating revisionist history, it was apparently in a fashion that was largely stochastic, an outcome which, to the best of my knowledge, hermeneutic theory would not predict. Even so, we cannot say that pretherapy God concepts are brute facts in history either, because these conceptions did not fit a causal model in which they determined the therapist's behavior in personal therapy. The larger point from the present study is this: *it was difficult to predict how a religious patient's God concept would turn out, given its pretherapy status; much more determinative was the orientation toward and analysis of the transcendent by the patient's analyst.* These data also failed to provide evidence for the necessary superiority of religious matching between patient and analyst. To conclude from the present data that religious patients should only see religious analysts is unwarranted—indeed, many who did have such matches experienced alienation from their God, and many who did not had opposite outcomes.

I doubt that the outcomes from the present study "refute" narrative psychology. The whole notion of the so-called decisive experiment is part of the larger myth of positivism in scientific lore; in real life, progress in science rarely works that way (Kuhn, 1962). I likewise make no claims that this study "proves" anything definitively for psychoanalysis merely because my presentation of an unconventional topic for psychoanalytic inquiry is articulated in the methodological terms of conventional science. Indeed there are those who would argue that psychoanalysis, as a clinical practice, is a convention of language in its own right, one which neither permits nor requires experimental "correspondence" (Spezzano, 1993). Even if we grant this position, I believe results of studies such as the present one nonetheless add an interesting voice to the conversation, and it seems myopic to disregard their contribution merely because they are scientific in the conventional sense.

Some analysts might also take issue with the legitimacy of asking questions about patients' religious experience. The old view was that the analyst should never make inquiries, and should instead let patients bring up whatever they want, for fear of otherwise "contaminating" the transference with the analyst's agenda. To this I reply that if it were anything else we valued—a significant developmental relationship, for example, or the possibility of childhood sexual abuse, or a potential transference manifestation—we'd find a way at some point, tactfully and sensitively, to ask. To not value exploration of something the patient views as central is not a neutral intervention.

Six Clinical Illustrations

One implication is how much influence we have as analysts on religious patients' God representations. Even more poignant, depending on our analysis of transcendent experience, our effect is not necessarily benign. Given the quantitative presentations I have offered thus far, I thought one other way to supplement and to convey a feel for this differential effect was with three brief vignettes in each direction (benign-malignant, malignant-benign), which illustrate the creation of various God representations in patients as a function of therapists' interventions.

Impact of low orientation and analysis scales

Vignettes 1 through 3 illustrate the influence of psychoanalytic therapists who, while otherwise helpful, managed to avoid exploring religious patients' God concepts altogether, or who did so in a manner that was experience-distant for the patient. Patients' God representations shifted from being warm and emotionally available to disengaged or punitive, and work with other patients took on the qualities of how issues of transcendence were handled in the student therapists' own personal therapy. As mentioned earlier, students come to this clinical doctoral program with backgrounds in Protestantism or Catholicism, and their expressions of faith in what follows reflect these religious traditions; it remains for future research to address persons from other backgrounds of faith.

Vignette 1. Therapist A grew up with a God with whom he felt an emotionally engaged relationship, and from whom he experienced friendly interest. In beginning personal therapy, he knew his therapist by reputation to be a Christian, and chose him partly for that reason. Mr. A wanted to know that there was, in his words, "a common thread and commitment to a similar God present in our relationship." He also hoped to not have to discuss his own representations of God: "I wanted someone where there would be little chance of being challenged in my belief system." His therapist went along with Mr. A's unspoken directive, and faith issues were never addressed by either his therapist or himself in treatment. In terms of Mr. A's experience of his therapist's spirituality, Mr. A summarized, "As far as my therapist is concerned, I probably know more about his theoretical orientation than I do about his religious orientation."

About his present God concept, Mr. A reports, "Currently I am fairly disengaged with God emotionally." He is not affiliated with a religious denomination, nor does he attend church on a regular basis. In Mr. A's own clinical practice, he sees parallels with his view of God and his own therapy: "As with my own therapy, religious issues have not been a significant concern of many of my clients thus far." In his experience, all the clinical populations with whom he has worked so far have not yet been ready or able to explore dynamic formulations of God representations. Mr. A is very honest and insightful, and the parallel with his own circumstances troubles him:

> Of course, this brings up questions in my own mind. Does my own lack of exploration of spiritual issues in therapy translate into the lack of it in my work with clients? Does my own ambivalence about the subject impact the way in which I listen to and interpret possible religious struggles or questions? Do I actually keep the client's religious issues at bay because of a process that is occurring in me? These are not only difficult questions to answer, but, now that I see them in relationship to my own effectiveness at truly addressing client issues, it concerns me.
>
> I would, of course, like to say I am willing to discuss any issue that a client may bring up. However, quite honestly, this exploration has made it apparent to me that I have a long way to go in understanding who I am, not only personally, but professionally.

Vignette 2. "To me, being a Christian and having Christian parents symbolized security in a frightening, unpredictable world. I believed that we were protected from evil, or anything threatening, as though we transcended it." In her early childhood, God was Ms. B's magical protector. He failed. In adolescence she was diagnosed with a chronic, degenerative medical disorder, and some years later she found herself involved in a physically abusive relationship. She priced a gun and contemplated suicide. To Ms. B, "God and my family were good and I was bad." She has found her own intensive psychoanalytic psychotherapy during the past seven years very helpful. "Only in the last few years have we even discussed God in therapy. But the whole time I have been learning about Him. Throughout my life I had been told never to rely on people—only God. I never relied on either. Over time I have been learning what it means to trust, to be respected, to be known." Her therapist's acceptance of Ms. B, whom Ms. B knew to be Christian, translated into a sense of God's acceptance, although she also has some misgivings about his analysis of her faith:

> I think my therapist was very comfortable exploring religious material, but he never brought it up, and I think I needed permission to talk about it. I had no idea what therapy was supposed to look like, so I talked about whatever I imagined might be important. It was like the blind leading the mute. I kept thinking, "As soon as he gets enough data, he'll figure out what the hell is going on with me and he'll tell me." He never did. I finally realized I wasn't getting answers, but I was getting a lot of love, acceptance, and containment.
>
> To me, God is a real person, but neither one of us acted as if He was an important object to deal with in treatment. Instead, we operated as though my feelings about Him were merely residual from parental objects. I wish we would have talked about my feelings toward God more. I wish he would have asked, thereby acknowledging the importance of my relationship with God, and my God concept. I wish that I would have known that talking about my thoughts and feelings toward God and making sense out of them was acceptable and not just avoidance of deeper issues. Interestingly, even though we both believe in God, we reduced my religious beliefs to psychological issues inadvertently.

Her current conception of God is of a devouring and intrusive figure whom she respects from a distance. "Lately I have noticed a shift in my relationship with God. Instead of feeling abandonment, I fear intrusiveness and loss of myself as a separate person. I respect and love God, but have unconsciously chosen to do so at a distance." Her clinical practice with others as their therapist has similarities with her own current God representation and experience in her personal therapy.

> Looking back, as I naively created an impression of what therapy "should" look like, I have passed this on to my patients. Also, as I have desired distance from God, my reluctance to enter their relationship with God has probably been noticed. Even when I have felt very comfortable with God, I did not openly query their religious thoughts or feelings. At best, it has been my clients who take the lead in exploring their relationship to God, and it is I who have followed. They were probably wondering where I was, as I did with my own therapist.

Vignette 3. For Mr. C, "God was never talked about relationally. We never talked about Him as if He were another Person among us. He was Someone we believed in and Someone we were committed to, but, above all, He was an uncomfortable subject." Even so, he always felt close to God, adding that "describing Him 'out there' feels almost irreverent in some way." In his own therapy, Mr. C has brought up the issue of God "only very rarely." He sought a Christian therapist because, as he says, "I wanted someone who would understand and support my faith." He said he was afraid he would be "led astray" by a non-Christian therapist, and felt that his own faith in God was fragile. "I think I chose a Christian therapist because I wanted to be with someone who would make sure I did not experience any jolts." In the first year and half of treatment, God was mentioned only once, at his therapist's initiative, when she asked: "Do you see God as similar to your father in that way?" Mr. C said he "quickly denied any connection, and was vaguely irritated that she was getting 'tangential.' " The therapist dropped the matter at that, although he continued to feel a benefit from her presence in the room.

> I would feel like I could barely make it between sessions. In the midst of that pain, the key thing I remember (and this is going to sound pretty vague) was how the room *felt* with my therapist in it. That feeling, that ambiance, is the thing I remember most. It felt like, in the midst of the pain and turmoil, I could go there and have a haven. It was warm and safe there. More than all the interpretations and insights, somehow the feel of that room was most healing to my spirit.

In his current God representation, following his initial experience in therapy, he strives to segment his God representation from dialogue with others.

> I think I have this fear that to relate about God with other people, to have a "shared God," somehow runs the risk that He may become different than the God I know. . . . As long as I can remember, I have had this drive to segment my experiencing of God off from others' experiencing of Him. It is as if conversing about Him, hearing all the unique perceptions and distortions others have of Him, renders Him some stranger to me.
>   At the most basic level, though, the key issue is probably that I am a guarded person about revealing my own world of thoughts that I keep to myself because I fear that, in sharing them, they will lose some of their value. The best metaphor for this is the way I struggle getting my film developed. I very carefully choose my setups and my subjects, and take real joy in taking pictures. When it comes to getting the film developed, though, I have a mini-crisis. My view is that as long as that film is in my camera, it is safe. It is hard for me to take it out and pass it to the film developer, who might somehow damage or destroy my film. To hold on to God in private, then, somehow keeps Him safe. He is the one who shares my inner world, and I protect my view of Him there.

Mr. C has yet to have a client who discussed religious issues in his own clinical practice, even though he would welcome that event were it to surface. He volunteered a possible connection between his own personal therapy and God representation, and between those elements and his work with his own patients.

I grapple with wondering if my difficulty in revealing my own intimate walk with God in my own therapy has been somehow felt by my clients and has inhibited their exploration of spiritual issues (which even formally nonreligious people still have). Perhaps it has not. Yet I am still aware of this dynamic in other areas of my work. For instance, I am personally much more able to accept my feelings of sadness and have a more difficult time with anger. I realize that I draw my clients out more and feel more able to be giving when they express sadness than when they express anger. Yet, I find that in my own therapy and in my own growth, as I become more able to embrace all parts of myself, I am more able to embrace others in their totality. As all parts of myself become more open and have been "brought to light" by God in my relationship with Him, the more my clients will feel at home with me in their own struggles in this regard.

Mr. C has recently begun seeing a second therapist, and although Mr. C still has ambivalence about discussing God, he delights in how his therapist interacts.

I have been slowly revealing my thoughts about God. When I do so, although I have some ambivalence, I typically find a real joy in it. The more I share, the more I find that I have a hunger to talk about Him and to share how meaningful He has been in my life. It feels so rich to talk about Him throughout my life, to see in my therapist's eyes a respect and shared reverence for Him. She has also helped me in applying biblical metaphors to other areas of my life. In that way, it has helped to unify my experiencing and allowed me to more fully see how God is applicable to all areas of life.

Impact of high orientation and analysis scales

In vignettes 4 through 6, the therapist analyzed the patient's God representations in a way that yielded high scores on the Analysis and Orientation scales. Patients' God concepts shifted from a harsh or impersonal deity to a more resilient and accepting presence. Work with other patients for these student therapists took on qualities of their own personal therapists' active yet respectfully curious analysis of transcendence.

Vignette 4. Ms. D grew up with a fairly distant and impersonal God, whom she equated with her relationship with her father.

I remember my dad reading his Bible every morning over a bowl of corn flakes, but he never said a word about God and I apparently knew enough not to ask. God was a very private thing that you did not talk about at home. It's interesting that as I was just writing I slipped and called God a "thing" instead of a person. I suppose that about sums it up. God was a thing you did at church. He was not very personal and certainly was not someone to be close to. My early impressions of God were that he was important, powerful, distant, and demanded obedience, which was basically how I experienced both my parents.

Although Ms. D considered her relationship to God to be very important during her growing-up years, it was "primarily motivated by guilt and fear." In her personal therapy, she sensed that it was acceptable to address issues regarding her faith and her concept of God, and when she did so, these issues were actively explored and related to developmental issues. Through the therapeutic process, Ms. D developed an increased ability to trust and be intimate with others, which she reports has transferred to her view of God as well. Ms. D believes this growth was facilitated not only by her therapist's accepting attitude, but also by his "relentless" exploration of her repressed anger toward others and toward God. Her stance that she had no right to be angry at God was interpreted as a defense against actually experiencing her rage.

> As a result of finally acknowledging and experiencing my anger at God, particularly for allowing my childhood traumas to occur, I experienced some changes in my relationship with God. My image of Him as punitive and withholding was altered, and I began to believe that He accepted me, even with feelings and behaviors that had always been labeled "bad." There was less need to hide who I was, and I was able to be more intimate with God. I think much of my ability to finally be able to express these feelings to God was due to my therapist first accepting the "badness" in me.

In her current practice, Ms. D finds that her clientele "frequently discuss their religious concerns in therapy and appear to feel comfortable in doing so." Ms. D explores these concerns in a fashion similar to her own therapist, and relates them to developmental issues when there appears to be a connection.

Vignette 5. Ms. D saw her military father as "a person to be revered, feared, respected, obeyed, appreciated, loved, and one not to provoke to anger." She continues: "These attributions translated easily into a 'heavenly Father.' I found it effortless to assume that God would demand the best, be intolerant of any imperfection, and punish whatever He felt necessary in order to 'whip me into shape.' " Her mother and other figures in her extended family of origin, if more flexible, were also easily overwhelmed, so Ms. D concluded that "God could be nurturing, caring, compassionate, but these qualities were only accessible to the degree that I cared for others, could be depended upon, and relinquished 'selfish' desires in the service of others." Parochial education also contributed to her God representations.

> God was mysterious, unknowable though omnipresent, and distant despite His omniscience. Church, with its multiple icons, cathedral ceiling, confessional booths, and stained-glass windows was a place of reverence, worship, and stilted silence. Mass was an unquestionable obligation, First Holy Communion a rite of passage, and Confirmation—well—the bishop had not

visited in eight years and there were 200 of us to be confirmed; I spent the majority of "class time" rehearsing the processional.

Ms. D began therapy with someone she hoped would understand her because of the therapist's coreligionist status, although the therapist's metaphysical commitments seemed discordant with Ms. D's. " 'I can feel that you are a healer' was one of her reflections to me in my first session. I recall feeling that I had just been swept into a Star Wars film without my permission; it was extremely uncomfortable." Ms. D reported, "I was afraid of having my religion dismantled without having a worthy substitute being offered as a replacement." At a holiday break that came after 12 sessions, Ms. D broke off treatment and never came back. She later resumed treatment in multiple sessions per week of psychodynamic psychotherapy for five years. This therapist welcomed analysis of Ms. D's representations of God, which had a disquieting yet transformative effect:

> The containment of therapy allowed me to venture into newer, less fundamental arenas of church communities, as well as to examine more of the feminine characteristics of God's nature. I no longer see God as strictly a male patriarch as I had before. Somehow, God has expanded beyond any categories—almost to the point where I have no categories any longer. I recognize that I am still in process of releasing what does not feel internally congruent along spiritual lines, yet I have little to replace the old. At times, this is the most uncomfortable space to stand. It does not feel peaceful, though I experience it as honest and hopeful.

In Ms. D's clinical practice, she sees herself as much more open to address religious issues in therapy, although she has the most difficulty doing so with patients who come out of backgrounds most similar to her own:

> Compared to where I was five years ago, I can recognize much progress in the ongoing pursuit of spiritual development. Still, I find myself reticent to actively pursue extremely religious patients, especially those of fundamental Evangelical backgrounds. I wince internally at every proclamation of tenets that mandate universal conformity to a conservative Western interpretation of the Gospel, the Bible, and strategies for ministry; this is exacerbated by ideology that places things in black and white categories of systematic theology. My hope is that one day I will be able to effectively work with patients who present their religion in this manner. Right now, I think it most ethical to acknowledge my limitations and defer to others more competent to traverse those themes.

Vignette 6. For Mr. E, God was "someone to be served, sacrificed for, and feared." As he affirms, "Enough praying could grant a person absolution from sins or time off from purgatory after death." Or again: "The God of my childhood was a harsh God. He was not very friendly or relational. Concepts of intimacy, love, and caring were foreign, not to be found with God or others. Of course God loved us, that was something to be believed not experienced." At different points over a four-year period Mr. E saw a psychoanalytic clinician from two- to four-times per week, and his analyst, while "not pushy" about religious issues, "really processed these beliefs with me and, consequently, I came to a different understanding of God." He continues:

> I have learned that God is a lot tougher than people give him credit for being. He is not the stoic military office who wants obedience without question but who says, "Come, let us reason together." He is not the harsh task master who requires sacrifice of personhood, but the one who says, "My yoke is easy and my burden is light." Furthermore, God is not put off by my anger or questions. If I cannot wrangle over the tough issues with God, what's the point?

In his current clinical practice Mr. E feels comfortable analyzing religious patients' conceptions of God, and does so with sensitivity. "It has been a fascinating experience for me to explore and understand who patients believe their God to be and how they relate to him." Some of his patients address their representations of God quite actively, and with others Mr. E waits for what seems like an appropriate opportunity to broach the issue with tact.

The Faint, Sweet Smell of Apologetics—But Whose?

From the previous vignettes the question arises, Aren't the changes in God concepts largely introjection of the therapy experience? To this I answer, Yes, of course, but—and this is the point—what exactly is introjected depends on *what* the analyst does and *how* he or she does it. Moreover, for patients who happen to be religious and who are themselves clinicians, the analyst's personal orientation towards, and analysis of, transcendence not only has a big effect on these patients' God concepts, but also impacts their subsequent clinical work with all the other religious patients who see these therapists across their professional careers. The scale of influence is multiplicative.

Nonetheless, some psychoanalysts will question the possibility of useful interdisciplinary dialogue between psychoanalysis and religion on the basis of either positivism and a commitment to classical psychoanalytic theory (Rice, 1994), or the claim that all such conversation is contaminated by "the faint, sweet smell of apologetics that hangs over the writings" (Beit-Hallahmi, 1992, p. 121). All ad hominem arguments entail omnidirectional olfaction, however, and prove little: they can always be used with equal effect to detect the apologetical aroma of the critic's commitments as well. For example, if one's motivation for imagining fruitful dialogue between psychoanalysis and religion were dismissed as an expression of ideology, then reluctance to adopt newer psychoanalytic epistemologies would be presumably no less motivated by other ideological commitments. Besides, as I have argued elsewhere (Sorenson, 1994a), ideology per se is no culprit; openness presupposes prejudice (Gadamer, 1975).

What, then, might be the proper import of this study? While only 5 percent of the American public does not believe in God or a higher power (Gallup Organization, 1985), one survey found as many as 56 percent of mental health practitioners to be agnostic or atheistic (American Psychiatric Association, 1975). In terms of not emotional equivalence but statistical incidence, analysands who are religious may find themselves facing odds equivalent to those of holocaust survivors who encounter the obscene claim that Nazi genocide is fiction. If we analysts tend to be less religious (or at least less conventionally religious) than the typical American public who seeks our services, how we behave with regard to patients' experience of transcendence—welcoming not only analysis of our patients' spirituality, but also analysis of our patients' experience of our own spirituality—can often be, for these patients, something like a divine gift.

REFERENCES

American Psychiatric Association (1975), *Psychiatrists' Viewpoints on Religion and Their Services to Religious Institutions and the Ministry: A Report of a Survey Conducted by the Task Force on Religion and Psychiatry*. Washington, DC.

Aron, L. (1991), The patient's experience of the analyst's subjectivity. *Psychoanal. Dial.*, 1:29–51.

Atwood, G. & Stolorow, R. (1984), *Structures of Subjectivity: Explorations in Psychoanalytic Phenomenology*. Hillsdale, NJ: The Analytic Press.

Beit-Hallahmi, B. (1992), Between psychology and religion. In: *Object Relations Theory and Religion*, ed. M. Finn & J. Gartner. Westport, CT: Praeger, pp. 119–128.

Bentler, P. (1980), Multivariate analysis with latent variables: Causal modeling. *Ann. Rev. Psychol.*, 31:419–456.

——— (1992), *EQS Structural Equations Program Manual*. Los Angeles: BMDP Statistical Software.

Brenner, C. (1982), *The Mind in Conflict*. New York: International Universities Press.

Breuer, J. & Freud, S. (1893–1895), Studies on hysteria. *Standard Edition*, 2:1–309. London: Hogarth Press, 1955.

Bruner, J. (1993), Loyal opposition and the clarity of dissent: Commentary on Donald P. Spence's "The hermeneutic turn." *Psychoanal. Dial.*, 3:11–19.

Caper, R. (1988), *Immaterial Facts*. New York: Aronson.

Cohen, P. (1994), Considering the interplay of patients' and therapists' God representations. *J. Psychol. & Theol.*, 22:345–347.

Compton, A. (1994), Research: The missing dimension. Paper presented April 16 at the Spring Meeting of APA Division 39 (Psychoanalysis), Washington, DC.

Doehring, C. (1993), *Internal Desecration*. Lanham, MD: University Press of America.

DuPont, J., ed. (1988), *The Clinical Diary of Sándor Ferenczi*, trans. M. Balint & N. Z. Jackson. Cambridge, MA: Harvard University Press.

Freud, S. (1913), The claims of psychoanalysis to scientific interest. *Standard Edition*, 13:165–190. London: Hogarth Press, 1955.

———— (1915), Further recommendations in the technique of psychoanalysis: Observations on transference-love. In: *Freud*; trans. J. Riviere. New York: Collier Books; 1963, pp. 167–179.

———— (1937), Constructions in analysis. *Standard Edition*, 23:255–269. London: Hogarth Press, 1964.

Frommer, M. (1994), Homosexuality and psychoanalysis: Technical considerations revisited. *Psychoanal. Dial.*, 4:215–233.

Gadamer, H-G. (1960), *Truth and Method*, 2nd rev. ed., trans. G. Barden & J. Cumming. New York: Seabury Press, 1975.

Gallup Organization (1985), *Religion in America: Gallup Report 236*. Princeton, NJ.

Gergen, K. J. & Gergen, M. (1983), Narratives of the self. In: *Studies in Social Identity*, ed. T. R. Sarbin & K. E. Scheibe. New York: Praeger.

Gorsuch, R. (1968), The conception of God as seen in adjective ratings. *J. Sci. Study Religion*, 7:56–64.

Greenberg, J. (1991), Countertransference and reality. *Psychoanal. Dial.*, 1:52–73.

Grotstein, J. (1981), *Splitting and Projective Identification*. New York: Aronson.

Hall, R. (1993), Critical and postcritical objectivity. *Personalist Forum*, 9:67–80.

Hamilton, V. (1982), *Narcissus and Oedipus*. London: Karnac.

Hartmann, H. (1939), *Ego Psychology and the Problem of Adaptation*. New York: International Universities Press, 1958.

Haynal, A. (1993), *Psychoanalysis and the Sciences*. Berkeley, CA: University of California Press.

Henry, W., Strupp, H., Schacht, T. & Gaston, L. (1994), Psychodynamic approaches. In: *Handbook of Psychotherapy and Behavior Change*, 4th ed., ed A. Bergin & S. Garfield. New York: Wiley, pp. 467–508.

Hoffer, A. (1985), Toward a definition of psychoanalytic neutrality. *J. Amer. Psychoanal. Assn.*, 33:771–795.

Hoffman, I. (1991), Discussion: Toward a social-constructivist view of the psychoanalytic situation. *Psychoanal. Dial.*, 1:74–105.

———— (1992), Some practical implications of a social-constructivist view of the psychoanalytic situation. *Psychoanal. Dial.*, 2:287–304.

———— (1995), Review Essay. *Psychoanal. Dial.*, 5:93–112.

Howard, G. S. (1991), Culture tales: A narrative approach to thinking, cross-cultural psychology. *Amer. Psychol.*, 46:187–197.

Jörskog, K. (1969), A general approach to confirmatory maximum likelihood factor analysis. *Psychometrika*, 34:183–202.

———— & Sörbom, D. (1979), *Advances in Factor Analysis and Structural Equation Models*. Cambridge, MA: Abt Books.

Kant, I. (1963), *Critique of Pure Reason*, trans. N. K. Smith. London: Macmillan.

Key, T. (1994), Impact of inpatient psychiatric treatment on self-esteem, object relations maturity and God image. Unpublished doctoral dissertation, Rosemead
School of Psychology.

Kifner, J. (1994), Pollster finds error on Holocaust doubts. *The New York Times*,
143:A12, May 20.

Kuhn, T. S. (1962), *The Structure of Scientific Revolutions, 2nd ed.* Chicago, IL:
University of Chicago Press.

Laudan, L. (1983), The demise of the demarcation problem. In: *Physics, Philosophy,
and Psychoanalysis,* ed. R. S. Cohen and L. Laudan. Dordrecht, Holland: Reidel
Publishing Co., pp. 111–127.

McDargh, J. (1993), Concluding clinical postscript: On developing a psychotheo-
logical perspective. In: *Exploring Sacred Landscapes,* ed. M. Randour. New
York: Columbia University Press, pp. 172–193.

McGuire, W., ed. (1974), *The Freud/Jung letters,* trans. R. Manheim & R. F. C. Hull.
Princeton, NJ: Princeton University Press.

Meehl, P. (1973), Why I do not attend case conferences. In: *Psychodiagnosis.*
Kingsport, TN: Kingsport Press, pp. 225–323.

Mitchell, S. (1993), *Hope and Dread in Psychoanalysis.* New York: Basic Books.

Noam, G. & Wolf, M. (1993), Psychology and spirituality: Forging a new relationship. In: *Exploring Sacred Landscapes,* ed. M. Randour. New York: Columbia
University Press, pp. 194–207.

Nunberg, H. & Federn, E., eds. (1962), *Minutes of the Vienna Psychoanalytic Society,
Vol. 1, 1906–1908.* New York: International Universities Press.

Osgood, C., Suci, G. & Tannenbaum, P. (1957), *The Measurement of Meaning.*
Urbana, IL: University of Illinois Press.

Polanyi, M. (1958), *Personal Knowledge.* New York: Harper & Row.

Rice, E. (1994), Reply to Randour. *Psychoanal. Books,* 5:481–484.

Rizzuto, A. (1979), *The Birth of the Living God.* Chicago, IL: University of Chicago Press.

Sanderson, W. (1995), Which therapies are proven effective? *APA Monitor,* 26:4.

Sarbin, T. (1986), *Narrative Psychology.* New York: Praeger.

Schaefer, C. & Gorsuch, R. (1992), Dimensionality of religion: Belief and motivation as predictors of behavior. *J. Psychol. & Christianity,* 11:244–254.

Schafer, R. (1990), Narration in the psychoanalytic dialogue. *Critical Inq.,* 7:29–53.

Schwaber, E. (1986), Reconstruction and perceptual experience: Further thoughts
on psychoanalytic listening. *J. Amer. Psychoanal. Assn.,* 34:911–932.

—————— (1990), Interpretation and the therapeutic action of psychoanalysis.
Internat. J. Psycho-Anal., 71:229–240.

Sorenson, A. (1990), Psychoanalytic perspectives on religion: The illusion has a
future. *J. Psychol. & Theology,* 18:209–217.

Sorenson, R. (1994a), Ongoing change in psychoanalytic theory: Implications for
analysis of religious experience. *Psychoanal. Dial.,* 4:631–660.

—————— (1994b), Reply to Cohen. *J. Psychol. & Theology,* 22:348–351.

—————— (1994c), Reply to Spezzano. *Psychoanal. Dial.,* 4:666–672.

—————— (1994d), Sea changes, interesting complements, and tormented souls.
J. Psychol. & Theology, 22:319–321.

—————— (1994e), Therapists' (and their therapists') God representations in clinical
practice. *J. Psychol. & Theology,* 22:325–344.

Spence, D. P. (1982), *Narrative Truth and Historical Truth*. New York: Norton.
—— (1987), *The Freudian Metaphor*. New York: Norton.
—— (1994), *The Rhetorical Voice of Psychoanalysis*. Cambridge, MA: Harvard University Press.
Spezzano, C. (1993), A relational model for inquiry and truth: The place of psychoanalysis in the human condition. *Psychoanal. Dial.*, 3:177–208.
—— (1994), Illusion, faith, and knowledge: Commentary on Sorenson's "Ongoing change in psychoanalytic theory." *Psychoanal. Dial.*, 4:661–665.
Stern, D. B. (1994), Empathy is interpretation (and whoever said it wasn't?). *Psychoanal. Dial.*, 4:441–471.
Stern, D. N. (1985), *The Interpersonal World of the Infant*. New York: Basic Books.
Stolorow, R. & Atwood, G. (1992), *Contexts of Being*. Hillsdale, NJ: The Analytic Press.
—— Brandchaft, B. & Atwood, G. (1987), *Psychoanalytic Treatment*. Hillsdale, NJ: The Analytic Press.
Wachtel, P. (1977), *Psychoanalysis and Behavior Therapy*. New York: Basic Books.
Wallerstein, R. (1990), Psychoanalysis: The common ground. *Internat. J. Psycho-Anal.*, 71:3–20.
White, H. (1973), *Metahistory*. Baltimore, MD: Johns Hopkins University Press.

— 9 —

On the Horizon of Authenticity

Toward a Moral Account of Psychoanalytic Therapy

JOEL GREIFINGER

In the heyday of psychoanalytic hegemony in American psychiatry and "mental health," psychoanalytic therapy was the sanctioned prescription for a significant range of ills attributed to the mind. In those bygone days, even sufferers who were neither terrifically wealthy nor themselves therapists often entered psychoanalysis. They shared the widespread cultural belief that this procedure could cure them of the neurosis that their complaints were diagnosed as expressing. For the most part, both analysts and analysands saw themselves as participants in a therapeutics that was based upon the application of a complex set of technical procedures to this end.[1] Even health insurers, increasingly the "third party" to many analytic transactions, bought this picture.

Today, almost no one buys it without reservations. Cultural faith in truth-claims generally, and particularly those dealing with the explanation of human behavior, has shifted significantly. Evolving fashions in psychopathology and its etiologies have reshaped the presumed object of any cure, talking or otherwise (Hacking, 1995). Whatever else it represents, the era of Prozac and managed care has disrupted those presuppositions that have previously discouraged the examination of psychoanalytic therapy[2] for what it is and always has been—a moral conversation. It is moral conversation in the double sense that it is a conversation about

I wish to thank Cheryl Klausner, Lynne Layton, Mitchell Silver, Carmen Sirianni, Andrea Walsh, and Dan Willbach for their help with this essay.

[1]For a helpful study tracing distinctions between "technical" and "practical" reason from Aristotle to Gadamer, Habermas, and others, see Dunne (1993).

[2]In this essay, I am using the term "psychoanalytic therapy" to refer to all psychoanalytically oriented therapies, including psychoanalyis. I use the term "analysand" to refer to the subject of such therapy, as it is the most specific term and avoids the medical, commercial, and paternalist connotations of patient or client. The terms "analyst" and "therapist" are used interchangeably to refer to a psychoanalytically oriented clinician.

questions of the "good life," and a procedure with particular moral aims. So much seems to be self-evident and uncontroversial but, as we know, it is not.

In recent years, the critique of "positivist" epistemology, which saw its beginnings in phenomenology and ordinary language philosophy, has worked its way to the heart of the human sciences. The social-constructivist "turn" in psychoanalysis represents a clinically driven attempt to explore the ramifications of this shift in our understanding of the possibility and character of knowledge. While contributors to this expanding tradition have reformulated a number of our long-held assumptions, little attention has been focused on the historically and culturally situated moral context and content of the psychoanalytic enterprise. In what follows, I hope to make a contribution to the development of such a focus.

In a collection of essays devoted to "the moral disposition of psychoanalysis," Joseph H. Smith (1986) writes, "Many elements of the conventional vocabulary of moral deliberations are largely alien to the psychoanalytic lexicon. *Moral, ethical, virtuous, righteous*, and their opposites are words that seldom appear in the theory or the clinical dialogue" (p. 52). He elaborates, "The analysand may present a moral dilemma, but the analyst's interpretation is either correct or incorrect, even though, if correct, the interpretation may be a significant step in clarifying the moral dilemma" (p. 52). Further, "One consequence of analytic neutrality is that the analyst's concept of health does not occupy center stage" (p. 53). In sum, "the impact of psychoanalysis on the vocabulary of moral deliberation is more a measure of its stance and the clinical theory of technique that justifies that stance than it is of its specific interpretations or its general theory. . . . Interpretations are responsive to particular analysands. In content, they are morally neutral, as is the general theory. One cannot look to psychoanalysis for answers to the question of what the good life would be" (p. 54).

NEUTRALITY: FROM EPISTEMOLOGY
TO THE "GOOD LIFE"

To those psychoanalytic therapists who have come to see the stance of technical neutrality as an epistemologically inadequate account of the psychoanalytic dialogue, Smith's positions may smack of naivete, raising a "here-we-go-again" irritation. In his account, the analyst's certainty has been vouchsafed by a vantage point outside of a fully interpersonal encounter. Once again, the analyst is able to parse facts from values due to the Archimedean view thus granted over a specifically psychoanalytic object domain. Neutrality is meant to bestow its epistemic benefits on the analyst in a twofold manner. It grants a privileged purchase on "what is really going on" and, by extension, allows the analyst to interpret from a morally neutral, disembedded position. As has become increasingly clear to many within psychoanalysis, this "stance and the clinical theory of technique that justifies that stance" have served to maintain the illusion that the analyst's interventions can lay claim to a measure of "objectivity."

Much of this clinical theory has been concerned with convincing analysands that, despite their "transference" expectations, the analyst really only wants for them what they find they want for themselves, stripped of the distorting irrationalities of their neurotic patterns. In this view, interpreting the transference has meant refuting the analysand's suspicion that the analyst wanted something from them or wanted them to be a certain way. The analyst's "neutral" reply was meant to signify that this belief of the analysand's was, indeed, part and parcel of her "problem." The analyst's only moral goal was the analysand's "autonomy." Neutrality was meant to guarantee not only the analyst's privileged observational position, but his ethical detachment as well.

There is increasing agreement in relational psychoanalytic quarters about what has been termed the analyst's "participation." From the Freudian tradition, Gill's (1982, 1983, 1984) work played a decisive role in arguing for the necessity of understanding the psychoanalytic dialogue as fully interpersonal. In the process of acknowledging and attempting to account for the analyst's "participation," however, Gill sought a method that would preserve the analyst's moral neutrality under the revised epistemological premises of a "two-person psychology." The thoroughgoing analysis of transference in the "here and now" was counterposed to the unanalyzed suggestion that inhered in the traditional model by virtue of its incomprehension of the analyst's interpersonal impact. This led to a set of technical recommendations for the almost compulsive interpretation of transference allusions as a sort of damage control in the attempt to purify the psychoanalytic situation of suggestion. Although the analyst's sense of certainty might have been shaken, the hope and belief that technique could keep the "pure gold" of analysis relatively unalloyed with suggestion were still alive.

This "anxiety of influence" (to misappropriate Bloom's, 1973, phrase) has always been the central pillar of psychoanalysis' moral self-understanding. It is therefore not surprising that there would be attempts, even among relational theorists, to salvage an account of the psychoanalytic dialogue in which the analyst is still not participating as a moral agent: an account, for example, where she can maneuver herself into an "impartial" position in response to the analysand's needs, while accepting her limited clairvoyance as to "what is going on." This is what Greenberg (1991) hopes to supply with a model that "suggests both the inevitability of the analyst's participation in the clinical process and the therapeutic value of his impartiality" (p. 215). Such "therapeutic value" is linked to avoiding the reenactment of impingements upon the analysand that occurred with dangerous "old objects." The analyst must be careful not to "use her influence" because this may produce just the sort of inauthentic compliance (and disavowal of the unacceptable) that has brought the analysand to therapy to begin with. Giving up on the possibility of neutrality altogether can be experienced as a profound disorientation to a therapeutics that, as I will explore below, draws its conceptual legitimacy and therapeutic power from an ideal of authenticity.

Much recent work in what has become known as the "social-constructivist" approach to psychoanalytic practice has challenged any account of the psychoanalytic situation which fails to acknowledge that the psychoanalytic dialogue occurs between two participants interacting on all levels. In this view, the analyst must accept both uncertainty as to the meaning of any and all aspects of the ongoing transaction "in the moment" and the largely unfathomable flow of unattended and unformulated experience retrospectively. In the context of such a view, I argue that any remaining remnants of the belief that the analyst, by training, technique, or structural position, holds a privileged epistemological purchase on a uniquely psychoanalytic object domain should be abandoned.

The work of Hoffman, Mitchell, and D. B. Stern, in particular, has come a long way toward fleshing out a description of a psychoanalytic situation which self-consciously assumes the always already functioning "mutuality" (Aron, 1992) of the participants. Their phenomenologically rich explorations along constructivist and hermeneutic lines have helped us to fundamentally rethink our ways of doing psychoanalytic therapy. Nonetheless, I want to suggest that we are just beginning to draw the implications of our rejection of the "objectivist" account of psychoanalytic therapy. In particular, we have not looked seriously at what is implied for the moral position of psychoanalysis.

In the oft-quoted passage from *New Introductory Lectures*, Freud (1933) wrote that psychoanalysis "is incapable of creating a *Weltanschauung* of its own. It does not need one; it is a part of science and can adhere to the scientific *Weltanschauung*" (p. 225). This has been the backdrop for all objectivist accounts of psychoanalytic therapy, including Smith's. Beyond what is taken to be a "morally neutral" valuation of individual autonomy, the only moral point of view the analyst contributes to the analytic dialogue is a commitment to "uncovering the truth." If we no longer believe that the scientific worldview, in the sense in which Freud meant it, provides an adequate description of what transpires in psychoanalytic therapy (or in any other interpersonal situation, for that matter), then the putatively value-neutral objectivity of science no longer serves. It might seem that once we have adopted a nonobjectivist position, the analyst would be free to cease chasing the tail of suggestion. Hoffman (1992) states as much when he writes that, "Suggestion, that bugaboo of the process in a positivist framework, becomes an intrinsic aspect of any interpretation in the alternative framework." (p. 290). Yet, the work of Gill and Greenberg, among others, suggests that the ramifications of the "mutuality" position for the moral character of psychoanalytic therapy remains controversial, even within that framework. So we must ask anew from inside our social-constructivist understanding: does psychoanalytic therapy embody and thus engender a particular worldview or, as I prefer to call it, moral ideal? And if it does, should our explicit acknowledgment of this ideal lead to changes in the way we think about and act within the psychoanalytic situation? My answer to both questions is "yes." In the remainder of this essay I explicate this by putting my answers into the context of current debates within the budding tradition of social-constructivist psychoanalysis as well as raising relevant concerns from contemporary hermeneutic and moral philosophy.

THE SELF IN MORAL SPACE

In an introduction to a symposium titled "What Does the Analyst Know?" Mitchell (1992) aptly concludes, "Psychoanalysts can no longer offer themselves in good faith as purveyors of wisdom or experts in the structure of the human mind, but rather as experts in the creative exploration of the contours and textures of individual subjectivity and the struggle for personal meaning" (p. 285). This represents a decisive break from any remnants of objectivistically derived authority. It also allows us to raise more sharply than heretofore the question of psychoanalysis' moral ideal. We are led to ponder: What gives psychoanalysts (or any one else, for that matter) a purchase on what we are able to recognize as "contours and textures"? From where do we derive the felt experience that something like "individual subjectivity" is real, for us? Why is it important to us that the meaning that we are struggling for is *personal*, and what is the terrain upon which it is played out? It is clear that what is at stake here for the analysand is preeminently what is felt to be "individual" and "personal," and that this is what, in our peculiarly modern usage, we refer to as "the self." It is equally clear that this project of self-exploration, in which the analyst has some nontechnical expert role to play, is motivated by a necessarily powerful sense that the nature and extent of that self are somehow problematic. In order to begin to understand this we need to look at what it means to "have" or "be" a self, and especially one that feels propelled to "find" and "fulfill" itself through self-exploration.

In his recent work, Charles Taylor (1988) has elegantly drawn the historical illustration of his contention that "the self only exists in a space of moral questions, that moral topography is not an external addition, an optional extra, but that the question of being or failing to be a self could not arise outside of this space" (p. 317). There can be no sense of self without a sense of moral orientation. "To know who you are is to be oriented in moral space, a space in which questions arise about what is good or bad, what is worth doing and what not, what has meaning and importance for you, and what is trivial and secondary" (Taylor, 1989, p. 28). However they are couched and whatever their particular historically and culturally defined content, such questions appear to fall along three axes: our sense of respect for and obligations to others; our understandings of what makes a full life; and the range of notions concerned with dignity in the sense of ourselves as commanding respect (1989). These make up what I will call "questions about a good life." Our frameworks for approaching these questions form the horizon for our sense of meaning. It is within the frameworks, which have both fostered and been a consequence of modernity, that the quest for *personal* meaning, in the sense that such meaning leads one to feel that one is being "true to oneself," is experienced as a superordinate "good" in living one's life.

There is a debate raging over what kinds of "selves" we are and what kind we should be. Some argue that, while flawed, the modern world provides unprecedented opportunities for pluralism and individual self-fulfillment (Habermas, 1986; Benhabib, 1992). Others point to just this emphasis on the individual, to the detriment of a sense of solidarity and community, as an impoverishment of the "self" that masquerades as progress (MacIntyre, 1981, Bellah et al., 1985). Still others radically question the very concept of the "self," and scrutinize how we ever come to believe that we are unitary, coherent selves or that, if we conduct a proper search, we can find our "true self" (Foucault, 1978; Rorty, 1986).

In an essay aimed at recontextualizing the debates between "rooters" and "knockers" of modern individualism, Taylor (1991) suggests neither side truly appreciates that "a powerful moral ideal is at work here, however debased and travestied its expression might be. The moral ideal behind self-fulfillment is that of being true to oneself, in a specifically modern understanding of that term" (p. 15). By moral ideal, he is referring to "a picture of what a better or higher mode of life would be, where 'better' or 'higher' are defined not in terms of what we happen to desire or need, but offer a standard of what we ought to desire" (p. 16). It is what he has elsewhere referred to as a "framework" within which the "web of questions" that define the self are given content and contour (Taylor, 1988, 1989). And although in the modern world no framework is shared by everyone (or exists unalloyed in any individual), and none can "sink to the phenomenological status of unquestioned fact," the particular moral ideal of self-fulfillment in its modern sense holds a great deal of moral force in defining our understanding of what makes one's life worthwhile. Taylor (1991) uses the term "authenticity" for this contemporary ideal.

The emphasis on relationally wrested authenticity represents a shift in the moral orientation of psychoanalytic discourse. In the drive model and its ego-psychological offshoots, the emphasis was squarely on fostering the ego's expansion in order to substantially reverse its servitude to the "masters" of id, superego, and reality. Reading the psychoanalytic literature in the "era" of drive theory (which I believe is waning) one knows which "side" the analyst is *really* on in his supposed neutrality. Such an orientation drew its sense of self-evident "rightness" from an ideal represented by the disengaged self of Enlightenment reason. Taylor (1989) links the genesis of this ideal to the establishment of modern individualism and its embodiment in the control over nature aspired to by modern science.

The ideal of authenticity, while a form of individualism, departs from placing special value on disengagement. The disengaged self aspires to a kind of neutrality in relation to itself for the purpose of self-control analogous to the control over external nature. "Where id was, there ego shall be" could be its motto. In contrast, the ideal of authenticity values self-exploration not so much to foster self-control, but rather because the question of being or having a self has become "visible," as it had not been previously. The achievement of an "authentic" sense of self only becomes a figure when the ground has shifted to make such an achievement problematic. It is just such a context, generalized in modern societies, that has made this the characteristic moral dilemma of modern "selves." This dilemma has been narrativized as a key theme in relational psychoanalytic theories of development. We value self-exploration because we feel we must come to understand the extent and limits of our condition if we are to feel "true to ourselves" and reach a fulfilled level of self-acceptance.

This question of being or failing to be a self, of the authenticity of this self, of its "trueness" to itself, and particularly how this both presupposes and is constrained by other people, that is, its dialogical nature, is the defining kernel of all relational psychoanalytic narratives of development. It is also the background or horizon in and through which relational psychoanalytic therapy takes place. It "always already" gives shape to the exploration and articulation of the questions that bear upon the realization of a "good life" for the analysand. These presuppositions or prejudgments structure our investigations into the genesis, conflicts, constraints, and ongoing reproduction of the patterns of striving towards largely unarticulated and often conflicting or contradictory "goods."

The theory and practice of psychoanalysis from all relational perspectives is grounded in this ideal of authenticity. The moral legitimacy of its particular understanding of self-fulfillment as a superordinate good forms the basis for both the explanatory power of the theories and the therapeutic "bite" of the practice. It is only in and through the largely implicit appeal to this shared moral "horizon" that our developmental descriptions and therapeutic interventions can make any claims to validity or effectiveness (assuming that these are not synonymous). If the terms in which we live our lives derive their meanings in significant part from a moral ideal of authenticity, then our best account of those lives will inevitably make use of those terms. If this is so and if, as I am suggesting, relational approaches to psychoanalysis are procedures whose purpose is the realization of a historically powerful variant of this ideal, self-fulfillment through self-exploration, then the way in which we go about this realization is best described in terms of the "web of questions" concerning authenticity implicitly at the center of contemporary psychoanalytic theory and practice.

DEVELOPMENTAL THEORY AND THE "DIALECTIC OF AUTHENTICITY"

What are some of these questions, and how are they unique to our modern sensibility? Questions that underlie our sense of self are preeminently about being true to ourselves. This, in turn, is inextricably intertwined with our awareness that we are selves at all only in and through our relations with others. The growth of modern individualism both creates this awareness and makes it problematic. It creates the possibility of being an individual with one's "own self" in this modern sense and simultaneously creates its characteristic dilemma: "what is truly me?" Thus, these questions hang in the air of the psychoanalytic dialogue: "If I come from you, which part is me?" "How can I be for you and still be for me?" "If I am me only as I internalize you and make it me, *is* there a real me?" "What do *I* really want?" What do I *really* want?" "In what ways can I be true to myself and still feel deserving and loved and esteemed by you?" It is precisely a self defined in and through such questions that our theories set out to explain. This is why all of our relational psychoanalytic developmental theories are centrally concerned with and presuppose what I will call the "dialectic of authenticity."

While the details vary, the main drama is the same. The sense of self arises from a set of generalized expectations derived from our experiences with important others. One moment of the process, seen as the child's pregiven maturational dispositions, opens onto the spontaneous unfolding of her developing abilities. The other moment is the facilitating and constraining role of the other. The other's responses to the child shape the contours and boundaries of experiences which are permissible to show others, and even to acknowledge to oneself, as oneself. In less than optimal circumstances, some types of experience may remain unintegrated. Terms for the interpersonal processes leading to such inauthentic disclaiming vary between the major theorists: Mahler's (Mahler, Pine, and Bergman, 1975) enmeshment during separation-individuation, Kohut's

(1977) failures in mirroring, Fairbairn's (1952) bad object, Winnicott's (1965) impingements leading to a compliant false self, D. N. Stern's (1985) affective misattunements. The latest is Greenberg's (1991) duality of effectance and safety drives, where our desires for competence and autonomy come into conflict with our need to maintain object ties based in our experience of what the other will recognize, tolerate, and esteem. All of these are stories about how we may fail to negotiate a satisfying sense that the range of our experience is truly ours without suffering dire interpersonal consequences. They are all premised on the belief that such a question of our authenticity is one we should and do care deeply about, deeply enough so that our sense of personal being depends upon it. It is both a product of and our attempt to explain our need for our lives to be "our own" lives. This is what gives these theories their narrative power for us. Criticism that Daniel N. Stern universalizes the construction of a historically and culturally specific sense of self is accurate (Cushman, 1991). Nevertheless, Stern provides us with the most satisfying and nuanced constructivist account thus far of how we become the kinds of selves we are. That is, how we become selves morally driven to know where they begin and end.

While all relational psychoanalytic developmental theories thematize the "dialectic of authenticity," they are by no means morally univocal. Some have persuasively argued that Kohut's theory, for example, tends to exalt the lone artist who "finds himself" in his work. In his self-psychological tales there is a devaluation of love as against work, and of "object-love" as against "narcissism" (Eagle, 1984; Layton, 1990).

Some might suggest that this should alert us to the "narcissistic" moral premises of the ideal of authenticity itself. Certainly, a narrowly self-centered view of fulfillment is possible within this moral framework. But it can be argued (though not within the confines of this essay) that such a limited view of what it means to be "true to oneself" is not an inevitable consequence of the tenets of this ideal, and can even be shown to be an inadequate account of its potentials, by its own lights.

PSYCHOANALYTIC THERAPY AS "GENUINE CONVERSATION"

A recognition of the cultural and historical rootedness of the psychoanalytic situation is critical to a full appreciation of Donnel B. Stern's (1991) analogy between the practice of social-constructivist psychoanalysis and the neo-Aristotelian hermeneutics of Hans-Georg Gadamer. In a remarkable series of essays, D. B. Stern (1983, 1985, 1989) has attempted to elaborate an account of psychoanalytic practice without any objectivist presuppositions. No longer a quasi-scientific set of technical procedures grounded in a uniquely appropriate theoretical discourse, psychoanalytic therapy is recast as a dialogue geared to coming to an agreement. Such agreement, synonymous with the "truth" about the subject of the discussion, is arrived at through "genuine conversation" to which both participants bring their prejudices or prejudgments as the ground against which communications from the other are understood. Based on these prejudices, each projects a complete interpretation of the other's "text." Over time, the sum total of such interactions forms a "tradition." This is what we would commonly refer to as a "transference–countertransference configuration." What makes the psychoanalytic situation analogous to Gadamer's "genuine conversation" is the possibility of the participants finding their way to a "fusion of horizons." Here, the mutual interrogation and elucidation of previously unarticulated prejudices allows the creation of a "truth" about the subject matter which in no sense pre-existed the dialogue for either party. Such a conception makes a number of claims that are radically at odds with assumptions long thought basic to psychoanalysis.

Most crucially, it disavows the efficacy of a concept of a dynamic unconscious. As Stern succinctly says, "lack of awareness now means the absence of explicit reflection, not the inaccessibility of a hidden reality." Much rests on this turn, because the adequacy of a practical, hermeneutic account, as opposed to a quasi-objectivist theoretical one, is premised on the participants' ability in principle to identify and explicate in dialogue what has heretofore habitually remained out of the analysand's awareness. If aspects of the analysand's experience are, in principle, inaccessible through hermeneutic reflection but amenable to epistemologically adequate theoretical formulation, the analyst must once again supplement her role as "conversant" with the quite different (and I suggest morally corrosive) role of scientist, with the analysand herself as the object. In the former role, the analyst's interventions are always from a first-person perspective, and are thus open to an elucidation of their constitutive prejudices. In the latter, they are viewed as derived from theoretical knowledge of lawlike regularities. In this case, while the application to the particular instance may be challenged, the validity claims of the theory itself cannot be discursively redeemed within the context of hermeneutic conversation. The analyst must once again be viewed as an "expert in the structure of the human mind." In his debate with Habermas, Gadamer (1976) mordantly questioned just such a claim. Isn't the analyst's status as expert itself a product of tradition? "How does the psychoanalyst's special knowledge relate to his own position within the societal reality (to which, after all, he does belong)? . . . What happens when he uses the same kind of reflection in a situation in which he is not the doctor but a partner in the game? Then he will fall out of his social role! A game partner who is always 'seeing through' his game partner, who does not take seriously what they are standing for, is a spoil sport whom one shuns" (p. 41). If "genuine conversation" is our aim, such a characterization must be applied to the psychoanalytic situation where it is apposite, as well.

In an uncharacteristically cavalier explication of this debate between Gadamer and Habermas, D. B. Stern (1991) asserts that for Habermas, "objectivity comes before hermeneutics," "social science is . . . capable of objectivity and psychoanalysis is the prime example" (p. 73). As I believe it is both unnecessary and unhelpful to portray Habermas's position as a caricature of the positivist ones he has spent his intellectual life critiquing in order to side with Gadamer, I would like briefly to survey the issues at stake. The debates marked a conceptual parting between thinkers whose work shared a common thrust: that the subject of knowledge and action was inherently social, historical, and embodied, and that belief in the possibility of a transcendental subject was illusory. Habermas holds a consensus theory of truth wherein validity claims are redeemable through discourses whose normative features resemble Gadamer's vision of "genuine conversation." He disavows any normative notion of "objectivity," in our everyday understanding of the word in the sphere of social knowledge, as inappropriate.

The crux of their disagreement centers on Habermas's (1979) argument that there are domains of social phenomena where the radical context-dependency of dialogic understanding can and must be lessened through the application of theoretical discourses that draw upon systematically generalized empirical knowledge. Such knowledge would be drawn preeminently from the "rational reconstruction" of species-wide competences. The results would be fallible and hypothetical, and would allow for quasi-causal explanation and a vantage point for critique. Examples of such reconstructions are Chomsky's generative grammar, Piaget's stages of cognitive development, Kohlberg's theory of moral development, and Habermas's own attempt to reconstruct communicative competence through a universal pragmatics. Habermas argues that validity claims about the structure underlying such competences go beyond the competence of the native speaker. A native speaker need not be aware of the grammar underlying his ability to generate meaningful sentences. Dialogic explication alone cannot produce an adequate account of this phenomenon. While all explanation ultimately has recourse to natural language, and is therefore hermeneutic, such hermeneutic agreement is a necessary but not sufficient condition for establishing the "truth" of, for example, a generative grammar. Such truth calls upon a theoretical discourse whose validity claims presuppose the possibility of a trans-historical and cross-cultural (i.e., quasi-transcendental) consensus. Gadamer's reply is that theoretical discourses themselves are the product of traditions, and thus no theoretical knowledge can trump the context-dependent understanding reached in hermeneutic dialogue. We understand from a point of view that is on the same level as what is understood. (See McCarthy, 1982, for an illuminating account.)

Habermas's most pressing concern is moral.[3] How can we recognize and critique what is oppressive in tradition if it always represents our unattended horizon? We'll return to this question later, but for now let me state what is most immediately relevant to this context. Whatever can be said of the adequacy and universality of Kohlberg's stages of moral development or Habermas's universal pragmatics (and much has been said, e.g., Flanagan, 1991; Cooke, 1994), psychoanalysis has failed to meet any of the criteria necessary to be taken seriously as a theoretical discourse based upon systematically generalized empirical knowledge, in Habermas's sense. Reviews of its lack of accomplishment in this area, both by those who bemoan this as failure (e.g., Grunbaum, 1984; Eagle, 1984) and those who disclaim it as an appropriate aim, are legion in recent psychoanalytic literature. Habermas himself seems to have given up trying to fit psychoanalysis to this mold; mention of it as an example of "rational reconstruction" has disappeared from the extensive justification program for his theory, which he has carried on since the end of his debate with Gadamer in the early 1970s. This implies no criticism of psychoanalysis, just a clarification of the sort of discipline it is. It is not a theoretical description of the development of species-wide competences or the pathologies of such.[4] Rather, it is a practical discourse whose explanatory power and efficacy is highly context-dependent to the rootedness of a particular moral ideal.

---

[3]In the sense in which I am using the term. Habermas (1990), following Kant, distinguishes types of practical reasoning, separating "ethical" questions concerning the good life from questions of justice, which are understood to form the proper domain of moral theory.

[4]One possible counter is that psychoanalytic developmental theory represents a reconstruction of the pretheoretical knowledge and intuitions underlying what Habermas terms "authentic self-presentations." It chronicles the developing competence in making valid claims to truthfulness of the form, "I really believe what I'm saying when I tell you that p (as when, for example p = My mother was a saintly woman who could do no harm"). Even when not explicit, such claims to truthfulness are raised in all communicative action and are an ineliminable component in the social interaction of any conceivable form of life. Bracketing the question of whether such intuitions can be rationally reconstructed in any case (a possibility Habermas, 1990, raises), let me sketch why psychoanalytic theory makes such a poor candidate.

In everyday communicative interaction, when we question a truthfulness claim ("Do you really believe that?"), what we are asking is whether one's conversation partner is *aware* of having beliefs (or desires, feelings, etc.) which contradict the stated or implicit claim. One can thus have an authentic self-presentation in the sense of allowing for the relatively smooth coordination of action through discourse without bringing to awareness previously unattended beliefs, in all but the most extreme instances. Such unattended beliefs, desires, and feelings are the starting point for psychoanalytic theorizing. Most of psychoanalytic theory is dedicated to thematizing the occlusions of awareness, assuming that many of the subject's beliefs are, in one sense or another, unconscious.

An account of psychoanalytic dialogue as a "genuine conversation" should highlight how decisively such a hermeneutics differs from one that situates "interpretation as an exercise of suspicion" (Ricoeur, 1970). In Gadamer's conception, what safeguards such conversation from becoming mired in the projected "truth" of either partner's prejudices is its concern about arriving at the truth of what Gadamer calls a "subject-matter" (*die Sache*). It is to this "text" that our understanding is aimed, and not to the speaker's motives in producing it. As Gadamer writes: "It is part of any genuine conversation that one submits to the other, allows his viewpoint really to count and get inside the other far enough to understand not him, to be sure, as this individuality but rather what he says. That which has to be grasped is the substantive validity of his opinion so that we can be united with one another on the subject matter" (quoted in Warnke, 1987, p. 100). In the absence of such a commitment, one of the partners may respond, not to what the other is saying, but may rather reduce such views to their imputed conditions of genesis. Such a strategy, which, in other terms, describes the analysis of resistance in most psychoanalytic therapy, is antithetical to the atmosphere within which a dialogic "fusion of horizons" wherein new understanding for both partners can emerge. In committing ourselves to this perspective, we "anticipate the completeness" of the text, presuming its truth claims in order to be open to its truth. Gill's (1984) and Hoffman's (1983) assertions, a decade ago, that we must always grant the "plausibility" of the analysand's view of the transference situation took us a big step in this direction. As Ricoeur (1970) writes, in contrasting such a view to suspicion, we "believe in order to understand, understand in order to believe." Entering the psychoanalytic situation with such presuppositions fosters an atmosphere far removed from a hermeneutics aimed at "the reduction of the illusions and lies of consciousness" (p. 32).

The concept of a moral framework is similar to Gadamer's concept of "solidarity" (both are variations on Hegel's *Sittlichkeit*), which is constituted

---

Unlike validity claims to truth or normative rightness, which can be redeemed through the giving and accepting of reasons, truthfulness claims are only redeemed by consistency of behavior. For this purpose, it is unavailing to inquire, "Why do you believe that you believe that?" In the public realm, what matters is that the subject consistently acts as if he believes it. In psychoanalysis, on the other hand, this is precisely the question that interests us.

Cognitivist reconstructions are based in the trans-subjective nature of the give and take of *arguments* in which other types of validity claims can be challenged and redeemed. The redemption of truthfulness claims, on the other hand, is behavioral and rests upon a criterion of privileged subjective awareness adequate to the social coordination of action. Psychoanalytic theories provide heuristics for tracing the genesis and contours of our motivated lack of awareness bearing, not primarily on the question, "What should I do?" but rather, "Who should I be?" They attempt to explicate the basis of existential evaluation, not the coordination of action. They are ill suited as reconstructions of authentic self-presentations construed as a component of social interaction.

by the set of ethical norms that the dialogue participants recognize as valid and already hold in common. This is the "subject matter" that structures their dialogue and establishes its goals. It is this solidarity, not either of the individual participants, that provides criteria for deciding about valid norms (Kelly, 1990). In Gadamer's (1976) conception of dialogue, solidarity is open to modification through experience. "There is always a world already interpreted, already organized in its basic relations, into which experience steps as something new, upsetting what has led our expectations and undergoing reorganization itself in the upheaval" (p. 15). Solidarity both conditions the dialogue and keeps it open to modification because such openness to doubt is part of the ethical tradition itself. This keeps moral norms from being simply subjectivist.

Operating from the solidarity of an at least somewhat shared moral orientation to authenticity, psychoanalytic therapy in the social-constructivist model aims to problematize the "intuitive moral comportment" of the participants. What this involves is the creation of a "way of being" between the conversants, which might provoke a response somewhat analogous to the "involved deliberation of an intuitive expert facing a familiar but problematic situation" (Dreyfus and Dreyfus, 1990, p. 248). Pulled out of habitual (or, as our cognitivist cousins might say, schema-driven or "mindless") construals by discordant information, the intuitive expert may turn to a "deliberation about the appropriateness of her intuitions" (p. 248). These are not, in principle, inaccessible to reflection, but they may have been incapable of formulation within the purview of the initial "solidarity." The therapist's socially sanctioned freedom to ask "obvious," embarrassing, rude, and silly questions helps to evoke such deliberation, not only by drawing attention to the absences, gaps, and inconsistencies in the analysand's narrative as figure, but by creating the possibility for these to be seen by shifting the ground (D. B. Stern, 1992). This requires, not a stance of detached reflection or a theory-informed application of "general interpretations," but rather an appeal to thicken the analysand's phenomenological self-descriptions in order to call into question the categorization of situations otherwise understood according to preexisting schemas. If the analysand is making errors of motivated "mindlessness," the analytic situation should be set up, if possible, to provide both the additional information and the safety to construct more "data-driven" assessments.

Heidegger (Dreyfus and Dreyfus, 1990) termed a response to the unique rather than the general situation "authentic care." We seek to thicken the phenomenological description to help distinguish situations that have come to be taken as indistinguishable by the analysand, by us, or by both, so that we may become capable of expanding the provision of "authentic care" between us. In addition, we err if we assume that most of these intuitions have heretofore been unformulated, brought into being in the crucible of the analytic conversation. Many have been thought before and are closer in character to personal secrets. Their telling in the psychoanalytic dialogue does transform their significance for the analysand, but this bears less on the "discovery of insight" than on their relational impact within the dyad's unfolding "dialectic of authenticity."

THE COMPETENCE TO CONVERSE

D. B. Stern raises the possible objection that the analysand comes to analysis precisely because she cannot "converse"—she is constrained by her prejudices into certain transference patterns. The question here revolves around our understanding of what impedes her ability to do so. If we believe that the determinants of her inability are inaccessible to hermeneutic understanding because they form part of an object domain that cannot be explicated within the competence of native speakers, then the analyst may bring to bear knowledge from an appropriate theoretical discourse and "apply" it to the analysand's incapacity. This is Habermas's viewpoint in his debate with Gadamer, and is also the implication of Fourcher's disagreement with D. B. Stern, as I will elaborate. But if, on the other hand, we view the impediment to conversation—that is, "transference resistance," and by extension, "the unconscious"—as unformulated linguistic potentiality, all that we can say is that the analysand cannot *yet* genuinely converse. But then, at the beginning of the analysis, neither can the analyst. Both begin the conversation constrained by the application of their prejudgments. The question, to which no answer can be given prospectively, is whether, given what Stern (1991) calls the "minuscule subset of invisible prejudices that analyst and patient create between them" (p. 65), they can create a genuine conversation that can reach agreement about the meanings of those prejudices through sufficient openness to the truth of the other's speech.

If we assume that the constraints upon "genuine conversation" derive not from a dynamic or prelinguistic "absolute unconscious" (to adopt Fourcher's, 1992, useful term), and are, on principle, open to hermeneutic explication, it does not follow that everyone is equally prepared to engage in such a conversation. The capacity for "genuine conversation" is a maturational achievement. The psychoanalytic pursuit of authenticity presupposes not only the social and cultural attributes of modernity, but a level of maturational development of the individual within that culture. It entails a level of decentered perspective taking that allows the analysand to conceive of alternative ways of seeing himself. This is possible only when one develops the cognitive ability to decenter from one's immediate perspective and entertain another's "truth." It is thus that our competence as hermeneuts is based in our unfolding capacity to open ourselves to the prejudices of the other person as containing a possible truth for us.

But such an openness can only be part of the picture. Merely taking the other's prejudices as "truth" means compliantly abandoning one's own. Kegan (1982), Kohlberg (1981), and other neo-Piagetians have illustrated in various domains that just such a "conventional" outlook organizes children's understanding (at least in our culture) at a point in the potential development of their perspective taking abilities. Such abilities are constrained by the person's achieved cognitive organization. "Genuine conversation" is constituted in the tension between accepting the "truth" of the other's "text" and applying one's own situated prejudices to it. To competently engage in such a conversation, one must have already acquired the cognitive competence to see the claims of the other as separate from, but nonetheless making claims upon, oneself. Analogously, this is why the motivating power of authenticity and self-fulfillment make no sense to a child or anyone else at this level of cognitive organization. These presuppose a level of perspective taking that allows one to envision other ways to be. This is amusingly illustrated if you've ever tried explaining "how you help people with their problems" to a young child. It is less amusingly so, if you have tried to engage someone in psychoanalytic therapy who has not consolidated this capacity.

A number of years ago, I was working in therapy with a young woman who had come to see me in order to "make sure" she was doing everything she could for the benefit of her six-year-old daughter. She was a single parent, having managed to separate from a verbally and occasionally physically abusive husband because of her resolve that witnessing such scenes might psychologically harm her daughter. Raising her daughter, in my view, had not been easy. From infancy, the child had been exquisitely sensitive to all manner of stimuli. Only through the most patient process of trial and error could this mother find ways of negotiating the simplest interactions without eliciting agonized screams. Over the course of years, routines became established that protected the child from overstimulation while strengthening her anticipatory and coping skills. Now, at age six, she was a very bright and increasingly competent person.

At first being told this story, my reaction was immediate. What had this been like for her? She presented it in a manner that bespoke infinite selflessness, but at what psychic cost? When I commented on how difficult this must have been, she looked at me uncomprehendingly. This was her child, anyone would have done the same. Did she ever feel that possibilities in her own life had been affected in ways that felt disappointing? Again incomprehension; what did I mean by her "own life"? Never in any of this, or in our discussions over the following months, did I sense any defensiveness or "resistance" in her responses. The "selflessness" felt genuine. My other explanations feeling forced, I chalked it up to saintliness.

This still might be right, but the idea of "embeddedness" in a particular cognitive organization may provide a useful alternative. What Kegan (1982) and his colleagues call "embeddedness" can be seen as a cognitive-developmental fixedness within a horizon of meaning. In this instance, that horizon was constrained by a limitation in the extent of perspective-taking to what he terms the "Interpersonal stage." Perhaps my client could not comprehend my questions because they minimally presupposed a more decentered "culture of identity." Her assimilations of my inquiries to her conventional, other-centered framework produced what, at the time, felt to me like an emotionally endearing but cognitively perplexing set of responses. It became clear that the web of questions bearing upon her sense of authenticity as expressed in her relationship with her daughter were, quite literally, incomprehensible to her. This is not to imply that altruism, or even what we might think of as total self-sacrifice, is in any way at odds with an ideal of authenticity. Quite the contrary, I concur with Taylor (1991) that investment in what lies outside the self is integral to any moral ideal for a self constituted in and through dialogic relations with others. What I am suggesting is that at a certain level of cognitively dependent, interpersonal maturation, those raised within the cultural precincts of modernity understand such "other-directedness" through the lens of self-fulfillment and authenticity. The question, then, becomes: do I feel like I am being "truly me" when I devote myself totally to my daughter's needs? And of course, from the perspective I am advocating, it is an open and hermeneutically accessible question.

WHAT DOES AN ANALYST WANT?

The other restriction on the possibility of genuine conversation is a thoroughgoing incommensurability of moral frameworks. I will not deny in principle the possibility that we will encounter someone from a culture whose vision of the good is so fundamentally discontinuous with our own, both currently and historically, that our hermeneutic translation principles leave us nonetheless in a state of mutual incomprehension. It is a situation unlikely to arise, however, in such an extreme form in the context of psychotherapeutic practice. It is characteristic of our society that although no single moral framework holds sway, either for communities or as the basis of an individual's identity, few can live in the modern world without being profoundly affected by the frameworks that sustain Western individualism. While we encounter, and attempt to help explicate, the conflicts between these often unarticulated frameworks in the course of any psychoanalytic therapy, we see the particular ideal implicit in the psychoanalytic project most clearly when we encounter an explicitly articulated and conflicting perspective.

This became clearest to me in the course of "treating" a woman who had become a fundamentalist, "born-again" Christian. No experience has so brought home for me just how "shot through with suggestion" (to take a phrase from Gill, 1991) the therapist's "way of being" in the psychoanalytic situation really is. Twice a week she would bring her bible and insist upon reading me excerpts. Just as regularly, I would attempt to explore with her "what this meant." Whatever else emerged, the constant was that she was bringing me "the word of the lord, Jesus Christ" and she did this because she "loved me." Without going into more detail, what I want to highlight here is the shift in my understanding of "what was going on" in the broad sense. During the period in which we were meeting, it was clear to me that she was trying to convert (and perhaps seduce) me, and we spent many hours discussing various aspects of this dynamic. I was guided in this by my own beliefs (drawn from many sources) about the psychological needs that had led her to embrace her faith. I tried somehow to leave these in tension with the possibility that there is something about faith which is not reducible, which does indeed "passeth understanding." What only became clear to me later was that I had been trying to convert her. I say this not as an admission of countertransference or misplaced missionary therapeutic zeal. Rather, it became more "visible" in this case than in most that this is what we *do* in psychoanalytic therapy. We subtly (and sometimes not so subtly) advocate for a way of looking at oneself and one's relation to the world. We don't say, "being born again" is illegitimate, but instead, "let us understand what motivates you to try to 'find yourself' through 'finding God.' " And we believe that the latter doesn't presuppose and privilege any particular moral framework. But from within a moral framework that recognizes revelation, our pursuit of self-fulfillment would seem at best misguided, and at worst hell-bound. Ours is a tradition that teaches that tradition cannot provide us with canonical answers to our most basic moral questions, and that we must find our "own path." We try to make social constructivists of our analysands. We encourage them to appreciate the usefulness of identifying the constitutive role of their own activity in their "reality." We hope they become genuine conversants who are open to the accommodating experience of other perspectives. Certainly, this is not a morally neutral, meta-ethical stance in relation to the analysand's faith. In other words, we are advocates for a particular, modern, "autonomous," decentered, self-tolerant ideal of the self. What allowed this relationship to take on a psychoanalytic character at all was the fact that, unlike a member of a "traditional culture," this woman was a fundamentalist in the context of modernity, which inexorably shapes even the character of her faith. Additionally, and this, of course, was at the center of our dialogic journey, she had come to me, not a pastoral counselor, for help in making sense of some painful parts of her life. But even if she had come explicitly seeking "to find herself," the invisibility of our shared framework would in no way mitigate the particularity of the therapy's moral thrust.

The two features touched upon—cognitive-developmental limitations in perspective taking and cultural incommensurability—might provide a point of departure for a hermeneutic approach to the question of "analyzability."

"ABSOLUTE" AND "RELATIVE" UNCONSCIOUS: WHAT IS THERE TO TALK ABOUT?

The exchange between D. B. Stern and Fourcher has done a great service to psychoanalytic therapists and others concerned with the clinical ramifications of the epistemological and ontological turn we have been discussing. Fourcher (1992) has argued elegantly, from within the social-constructivist "camp," for maintaining the concept of an "absolute" unconscious that, because of its prelinguistic roots, maintains an effective presence as an absolute "otherness" to linguistic consciousness. Alongside Stern's vision of a "relative unconscious," which describes a potential not yet attended to or formulated, Fourcher claims that clinical experience forces us to recognize aspects of experience that are both prior to and other than their representation in reflective linguistic consciousness. Although we may speak of them, our speech cannot comprehend them; they maintain a quality of absolute unconsciousness. In this distinction, Fourcher makes reference to Ricoeur (1970), who approvingly characterized Freud's as a "mixed discourse" of force and meaning, and to Habermas (1971), who saw the unconscious as made up of "split-off symbols," which, removed from the public-language game, had to be regarded as quasi-causal. As we have noted, Habermas argued that they are an appropriate object of theoretical discourse, as the linguistic competence of native speakers is unable to explicate this "other" realm. With admirable metaphoric lucidity, Fourcher (1992) labels such interventions, which work upon the analysand qua object, as interpretation acting "like a shovel." Such interpretation is held to acknowledge people's dogged resistance to change in the face of dialogic explication and understanding. "Its value is to codify the formal otherness of human self-alienation" (p. 324). On the other hand, we have interpretation used "like a lens" for the explication of the focally unattended "relative unconscious."

How is the analyst to know, prospectively, in the midst of the dialogue, whether it is the "absolute" or the "relative" unconscious she is encountering? What set of theoretical rules allow her to distinguish? And what is the effect on the possibility of "genuine conversation" for the analysand when the analyst shifts to a mode of interaction wherein her speech is "unanswerable" and the analysand is its descriptive object? Because such interpretations are on a different "level" of discourse, they are not "open to discussion" in the hermeneutic sense. Psychoanalysis at one time was concerned about the effects of "inexact interpretation" (Glover, 1931). Now we must question the belief that there can or should be "exact interpretations," even in the limited sense that what is being elucidated preexists the social context in which it is being articulated. Any such attitude implies that the analyst knows that this is the analysand's "stuff" and not her own, or more properly and obscurely, the dyad's. Such a stance positions the analyst into the asocial "neutrality" we have sought to disavow.

In his reply to Stern's discussion, Fourcher (1992) raises the moral crux of his position: "If our analytic knowledge is limited to linguistic consciousness, whence comes the competence to recognize absences in our narratives? More important, if the unconscious aspect of experience is limited only to what can be explicated in linguistic consciousness, then how is it possible for any thing new to be thought?" He sums up stating, "I simply want to protect the important notions of social constructiveness and the social relativity of experience from being reduced to a linguistic subjectivism—a premise, I believe, upon which no liberating, no moral therapeutics can be founded" (p. 367).

The issue Fourcher raises, the concern that "mere" hermeneutic explication of linguistic consciousness leaves us trapped within the prejudiced confines of the "hermeneutic circle" with no theoretical vantage point to critique the conformity of our received traditions, goes directly back to the dispute we have glossed between Habermas and Gadamer. But it has a longer history as well. Stern points out its roots in Sartre's critique of Freud. It appears in a different form in Marcuse's (1955) championing of the instincts as a bastion of resistance against the "conformist culturalism" of his old colleague Fromm and the "interpersonalists." More recently, it is echoed in an exchange over Dreyfus and Wakefield's (1988) advocacy of a "breadth psychology" informed by Heideggarian phenomenology, wherein Kovel (1988) responds that in such an approach, "there is no theoretical basis for illusion, self-deception, repression, and the whole panoply of devices by means of which false consciousness is inwardly installed. In the practical setting, there is no way not to take the patient's communications as transparent" (p. 292). What is at stake is the very possibility of a "hermeneutics of suspicion" that can be socially situated but somehow can obtain a species-wide foothold from which to construct a vantage point to identify and explicate the "illusions" and "false consciousness" that wind through our traditions. It is the wish for a theory about how people understand their lives, which does not itself rest on a framework of what is held to be good in those lives. Although I don't believe that such a wish is sustainable, it rests upon an important moral impulse. I would like to see if we can elaborate a perspective from within our distinctively modern moral ideal that can address at least some of the uneasiness.

Fourcher's concern is, as it should be, for psychoanalysis to be able to serve as a moral therapeutics. We need a practice that assumes that we are able to become the kind of people we feel we should be. If this wish is no more than a circular "illusion," we lack the requisite epistemological wherewithal to prove it so. If it is crucial to our development of a sense of contingency and expanded self-acknowledgement and self-tolerance that we recognize areas of experience anterior and inaccessible to linguistic formulation, then indeed our narratives should portray these. But, and I believe this to be the case, if our lives are best described in the terms in which we already live them, then the "shovel" stance serves to limit the reach of the kind of explication that may lead to a greater sense of authenticity. To the degree that people in our culture have adopted Freudian metaphors as a way of explaining and describing their lives, only to that degree are those terms part of our best account of how those lives are actually lived.

The "subject matter" of the analytic dialogue is "always already" a negotiation over a moral framework, over the pair's "solidarity." No matter what "language" the analyst speaks, or whether she asks a question, fails to verbally respond to a statement, or makes a Kleinian mythopoetic interpretation about ingested part-objects, her attention in whatever form always raises the question for the analysand: "Who does she want me to be, now?" Whether we believe we are using interpretation like a "lens," like a "shovel," or like a backhoe, it still leaves the analysand with the inevitable interpretive task of trying to make sense of what the analyst "wants." And the situation of negotiating who one needs to be for the other, with its inseparable accompaniment of sorting out the extent of one's self, is the recapitulation of the constitutive "dialectic of authenticity" that is the centerpiece of psychoanalytic therapy.

CONVERSATION, MORAL NORMS, AND MODERNITY

Our commitment to "genuine conversation" is, of course, itself the product of a particular moral orientation. The norms of such conversation—the openness to the other's "truth," the focus on the "subject-matter" rather than strategic manipulation, the modification of preexisting "solidarity" through "experience"—are themselves contingent upon a moral framework that doesn't, on principle, call a halt to the conversation when it borders on apostasy. As Benhabib (1992) points out, Habermas's attempt to reconstruct an "ideal speech situation" as the universal presupposition of argumentative speech founders on precisely the inability to derive its conditions without the shared assumptions of universal respect and egalitarian reciprocity. Such assumptions cannot be independent of a historically rooted theory of the good. But this needn't deter us from pursuing a "historically self-conscious universalism" based upon a " 'thick description' of the moral presuppositions of the cultural horizon of modernity" (p. 30).

In arguing for a procedural model of moral conversation, Benhabib notes that "the standpoint of communicative ethics has been made possible by the culture of modernity in which the justification of norms and values and their reflective questioning have become a way of life" (p. 40). Within that horizon, she argues persuasively for a model of practical discourse that takes as "higher" and "better" a decentered, "post-conventional" stance, which calls upon each conversant to rehearse the other's perspective and to seek understanding and "reasonable agreement" in a conversation that is open-ended, with all norms open to discursive challenge.

Highlighting the value of expanded potential for reflexivity in modernity is partially a response to the potentially conservative implications of Gadamer's neo-Aristotelian, communitarian position. As we have seen, many share the suspicion that any such hermeneutics that dispenses with all systematic procedures may be incapable of steering us beyond a conventional moral attitude. In such an attitude, a "distinction between social acceptance and hypothetical validity has become articulable" (p. 42), but norms may still be justified by invoking the authority of tradition. A classical example is Aristotle's argument that it is wrong for Greeks to enslave one another, but not morally reprehensible to enslave the "barbarians." In response, Benhabib argues from within our modern moral framework that "only a moral point of view which can radically question all procedures of justification including its own, can create the conditions for a moral conversation which is open and rational enough to include other points of view, including those which will withdraw from conversation at some point. In this sense communicative ethics 'trumps' other less reflexive 'moral points of view' " (p. 43).

Nonetheless, as a specifically therapeutic endeavor, psychoanalytic therapy places limits upon the reciprocity of speech roles in the dialogue. A major factor distinguishing therapeutic "genuine conversation" from other forms of practical discourse is the "ritualized asymmetry" of the participants' roles (Hoffman, 1991). The therapist brings an expertise based upon experience in carrying on such conversation, but also a commitment to focus on subject matter rooted in the concerns that have brought the analysand to therapy. As Hoffman (1992) has noted, the authority that this socially institutionalized asymmetry grants the therapist may well be an ineluctable and irreplaceable component of therapeutic efficacy. Despite the reflexive exploration of the "solidarity" of the therapeutic relationship, there remains an element of such socially situated, "unanalyzable," influence. This is inevitable, given the cultural system that legitimates such conversation as therapeutic.

Whereas the increased social differentiation and resultant increase in role-distance and diversity of need-dispositions characteristic of modernity has created unprecedented opportunities for reflexivity, there can be no quasi-natural or transcendental guarantor of the possibilities for liberation. We must live without philosophical or theoretical assurances about our capacity to transform ourselves and the world.

For a hermeneutic construal to be persuasive, it need not argue that all experience is ultimately articulable in ordinary language. It just recognizes that this is all we have to talk with. As D. B. Stern (1992) writes, "We cannot meaningfully discuss what we have not yet been able to say" (p. 360). When Fourcher's analyst interprets that his analysand's mumbling is a resistance to the analyst's verbosity, the intervention necessitates an interpretation by the analysand of the analyst's moral insinuation. Even if the analysand "accepts" the interpretation with a seeming epiphany, such as "I never realized that before," there is little reason for us to theorize that "that" existed before to be "realized." It may well be that the contents of consciousness exist only in relation to the particular probes that occasion their articulation (Dennett, 1991). Or, perhaps, they constitute a knowledge that, like many of the "rules" we follow unreflectedly in daily life, is not represented, but rather is embodied in practices. Such bodily encoded practices form part of the background upon which explicit understanding must tacitly depend. We may be able to articulate reasons for such practices up to a point. But such a description is misleading if it is understood as representing an underlying structural cause rather than a somewhat reified attempt to capture a moment in an ongoing process of renegotiation, which such practices undergo in every dialogic encounter (Taylor, 1995).

But whether or not we believe that an "underlying experience" preexists its linguistic representation is not crucial to our immediate concern. Only if a theoretical formulation could "capture the reality" of that experience and act directly upon it would the situation call for a "shovel." Instead, any intervention is an attempt to persuade the analysand to try out a particular moral vocabulary. If that vocabulary happens to include stories of an "inexpressible otherness of experience," such tales can also be translated into, and become part of, the everyday language in which we live and explain our lives.

RORTY ON PSYCHOANALYSIS: AUTHENTICITY OR IRONY?

Richard Rorty's reading of Freud appears to provide a provocative challenge to the conception of psychoanalysis as rooted in a moral ideal of authenticity. His pragmatic disavowal that psychoanalytic theory should or could adequately describe some "underlying reality" situates his portrayal of the psychoanalytic situation as an attempt to persuade us of the appeal of a particular moral vision. To Rorty, for whom ontology and epistemology have outlived their usefulness, this makes psychoanalysis no different from physics and literature.

From the "positivist" perspective, only knowledge accrued through "objective" methods was seen as embodying valid truth claims. Phenomenological and hermeneutic philosophy argued a distinction in the characters of valid knowledge corresponding to irreducible differences in the nature of their objects. The situated, immanent relationship of investigators who were simultaneously actors in a meaningful social reality required disciplines that were unapologetically interpretive. Rorty's postmodern pragmatism turns the positivist claim on its head. Once again, only one sort of truth claim is taken as persuasive. Now, that is the claim of persuasiveness itself. What conditions "truth" in physics, no less than in astrology, is the preexisting language-game of the investigators. If there is sufficient agreement as to the applicability of the language-game and sufficient standardization as to its application, the discipline can produce useful, and hence "true," knowledge. Any attempt to explain is, in essence, an attempt to persuade. What counts as "good reasons" is dictated by the terms of the language-game or "vocabulary" we live with.

In his most extensive engagement with psychoanalysis, Rorty (1986) encourages us to abandon all our talk of "true" and "false" selves and work towards a "nominalistic and ironic" view instead. Actually, he claims that Freud so prompts us but, as others have pointed out, his reading of Freud takes substantial liberties in its selectiveness (King, 1986; Wallwork, 1991). No matter, since his is an exhortation, not an exegesis. What does matter is whether he provides a persuasive account of the phenomenology of psychoanalytic therapy.

In my view, analysands do not so much "find" their "true self" in psychoanalytic therapy as become able to risk exposure of parts of themselves that they have either kept secret or systematically left unattended. They do not so much discover a pre-given essence as accept and acknowledge the range of their experiences *as* themselves. And crucially, they do so in the context of a relationship with another person whose recognition they seek and feel they must maintain. Thus, the self does not come to be viewed as a random assortment of contingent needs, as Rorty suggests, so much as "oneself," with diverse and often conflictual manifestations, unified by the experience of recognition by the other. This is why the language of relational psychoanalytic developmental theories is replete with metaphors of recognition, which are central to the 'self's' fate in the process of self-acknowledgement (Benjamin, 1988). Such terms as "mirroring," "affect attunement," and "good-enough mothering" are all concerned with this dialectic of recognition.[5] This should be no surprise, as it is just such recognition, taken for granted in other times and places, whose achievement becomes problematized and thematized in modern life.

Much of therapy is a process of self-acceptance and self-acknowledgment. One becomes able to formulate aspects of experience and thereby to acknowledge them as being part of oneself.[6] By thickening one's phenomenological descriptions of self in a dialogical encounter, one recognizes oneself in the other's recognition of the agentic continuity of the constructed narratives. The central question is often: "If these wishes, thoughts, desires, and experiences are a part of me, of this first-person narrative I experience as myself, will I still be granted the recognition that I feel I must retain in order to continue to be me?"

Rorty (1986) suggests that psychoanalysis helps us to recognize the illusion of the "true self" as an essence and to see that "all parts of the soul" are equally plausible candidates for the "true self." He suggests that to say this is "to discredit the idea of a 'true self' and the idea of the true story about how things are." Further, "maturity will, according to this view consist . . . in an ability to seek out new redescriptions of one's own past—an ability to take a nominalistic, ironic view of oneself" (p. 9). For Rorty, Freud is an advocate for the aesthetic life of unending curiosity that "seeks to extend its own bounds rather than find its center" (p. 11). Psychoanalysis liberates us "by helping us see ourselves as centerless, as random assemblages of contingent and idiosyncratic needs rather than as more or less adequate exemplifications of a common human essence" (p. 12).

While Rorty no doubt finds this a congenial moral identity for the aesthetic life he joyfully advocates, I believe it fails as a commonly recognizable account of the experience of psychoanalytic therapy. While I agree that what we deem to be progress or "maturity" in the psychoanalytic situation is aptly described as seeking alternative ways to define one's past

---

[5]Benjamin argues that the process of recognition is caught in an irresolvable paradox between the needs for self-assertion and for attunement. In this view, autonomy and rationality are tied to separation and disidentification from the mother and are a hallmark of typical male development in cultures in which women are primary caretakers. The development of autonomy is thus premised on the denial of recognition of the (m)other.

Weir (1992, 1995) has argued that Benjamin derives her model of self-as-paradox by a conflation of self-assertion with separation and autonomy, and of recognition with relationship and immediate connection. Benjamin has made an important contribution in emphasizing the necessity of mutual recognition, and not merely subject-(self-)object attunement in the development of ideal selfhood. Weir's critique stresses that the route to such robust intersubjectivity runs, not in opposition to, but through the adoption of a third-person cognitive stance towards oneself and others in one's social group. Particular identifications alone leave too little basis for an openness to the multiplicity of identities and their interpretation available and, in fact, demanded at our stage of modernity.

[6]This constantly raises the question, who (or what) is responsible or, as the analysand more often experiences it, who is to blame? See Lear (1991) and Spezzano (1993, chapter 5).

using new "vocabularies," this does not imply adopting a "nominalistic" self-conception. Instead, by enriching the vocabularies available for self-description, we increase the sense of self-continuity, of identity, by bringing the previously contingent and idiosyncratic into the realm of the intersubjectively representable, the realm of speech. No "true self" pre-exists this, except as an experience of absence, of feeling fraudulent, in sum, of inauthenticity.

Maturing is not the recognition that what we feared we were missing or had to hide had never been more than an empty "name" all along. It is, instead, that all of it is oneself, no part any "truer" than any other, and that acknowledging this will not remove us from the circuits of human recognition.[7] It is here where Rorty's description falls shortest of clinical experience. Caught up in the exuberance of the self as playfully boundless and random, being "fed its best lines" by a witty unconscious, the account gives no real phenomenological weight to the impact of the other on the self, on the conditions of safety. It is not the "true self" we strive to find or create in psychoanalytic therapy, for this only "exists" in a binary opposition to a "false self"; it is a metaphor for what is missing. Our aim is the self-acknowledgement of "oneself" through speech and its recognition by the other. This interpersonal context, central to all dialogical theories of the self and the therapeutics they imply, is absent in any meaningful sense from Rorty's vision of psychoanalysis. Thus, his statement that "psychoanalysis differs from history, novels or treatises on moral philosophy only in being more painful, in being more likely to produce radical change, and in requiring a partner" (Rorty, 1986, p. 10) reflects a failure to grasp that its pain and its possibilities are a consequence of his final, interpersonal ingredient.

PSYCHOANALYSIS:
MODERN OR POSTMODERN?

Rorty's vision brings into sharp outline that the account I have been advocating of psychoanalytic therapy is of a modern, as opposed to postmodern, therapeutics. Authenticity is very much a modern ideal. Although it is premised in the increased possibilities for reflexivity and postconventional perspective taking in modern life, it also values a narrative centeredness that provides a sense of self-continuity and identity. By placing

---

[7]In some sense, then, psychoanalytic therapy attempts to uncouple the characteristic yoking of responsibility and blame in modern Western culture. As such, it may serve as an intervention into, and contestation of, the contemporary configuration of what Connolly (1991) terms "the paradox of ethics." That is, it shifts the received relations between identity and responsibility such that it calls the immutability and naturalness of the prevailing patterns into question while maintaining the necessity of a set of standards.

his portrayal of the "nominalist" self explicitly on the level of moral discourse, Rorty distinguishes himself from a range of postmodern positions inspired by the work of Lacan, Lyotard, and Derrida. The postmodern celebration of fragmentation and discontinuity seems to present itself as an alternative framework with which to structure our moral allegiances.

But it isn't up to the task. The postmodern disavowal and deconstruction of all frameworks leaves it to deliver its critique as the "news from nowhere." As has often been noted, the radically external, genealogizing stance that impugns the mundane self-understanding of social actors that is characteristic of postmodern approaches is self-undermining. It gets stuck in a "performative contradiction" (Habermas, 1986) whereby the arguments ineluctably make appeal to standards of argumentative reason that such critiques claim to deconstruct. While I do not wish to rehash this argument (see Connolly, 1991, and Whitebook, 1995, for divergent instructive responses), there is a particular feature of postmodern deconstructions of the "self" which is interesting in our present context: their implicit ideal. The multiple, fragmented selves who are merely the effects of the "chain of signifiers" in the "always already" preexisting structure of language—these selves who do not so much speak as are spoken through—find consolation and perhaps even a sense of superiority in the authenticity that the awareness of their decentered state grants them. Disclaiming any agentic standpoint whatsoever, they displace their truth-claims into the heroic authenticity of acknowledging the "truth" of their fragmentation and "inauthenticity."[8] Their moral framework is as parasitic on the modern ideal of authenticity as their demand to explore the farthest reaches of their multivariate selves is on the supposed illusion of rights secured by the liberal state. Ultimately, the allure of the postmodern vision of the self, as well as of Rorty's pragmatist version, rests to a significant degree on our search to find a self-conception into which we can fit the range of our experiences in order to provide the sense that we are being "true to ourselves."

An account of the psychoanalytic dialogue in the context of the moral ideal of authenticity that forms its horizon, which assimilates the psychoanalytic dialogue to a hermeneutic "genuine conversation" about the practical contours and constraints upon living a "good life" for the analysand, will provide our best account of both what should and "always already" does occur in psychoanalytic therapy. One major advantage of such a "moral account" is that it locates the subject matter of

---

[8]See, for example, Paul de Man's (1984) praise for the authenticity of the postmodern critic's attitude that recognizes its own inauthenticity (cited in Sass, 1992). For an account sympathetic to the postmodern critique of the "unitary" self, which also appreciates the terrifying experience common among those who fail to consolidate a "core" sense of self, see Flax (1990).

the dialogue in the context of the shared tradition that sanctions the legitimacy of such conversation as a therapeutics. It is through a process of interrogating the practical applications of moral thought and explicating its previously unformulated prejudgments that psychoanalysis seeks to bring about a particular variety of "moral education."

REFERENCES

Aron, L. (1992), Interpretations as expressions of the analyst's subjectivity. *Psychoanal. Dial.*, 2:475–507.

Bellah, R. N., Madsen, R., Sullivan, W. M., Swidler, A. & Tipton, S. M. (1985), *Habits of the Heart*. Berkeley, CA: University of California Press.

Benhabib, S. (1992), *Situating the Self*. New York: Routledge.

Benjamin, J. (1988), *The Bonds of Love*. New York: Pantheon.

Bloom, H. (1973), *The Anxiety of Influence*. New York: Oxford University Press.

Connolly, W. E. (1991), *Identity/Difference*. Ithaca, NY: Cornell University Press.

Cooke, M. (1994), *Language and Reason*. Cambridge, MA: MIT Press.

Cushman, P. (1991), Ideology obscured: Political uses of the self in Daniel Stern's infant. *Amer. Psychol.*, 46:206–219.

de Man, P. (1984), *Blindness and Insight*. Minneapolis, MN: University of Minnesota Press.

Dennett, D. (1991), *Consciousness Explained*. Boston, MA: Little, Brown.

Dreyfus, H. L. & Dreyfus, S. E. (1990), What is morality?: A phenomenological account of the development of ethical expertise. In: *Universalism vs. Communitarianism*, ed. D. Rasmussen. Cambridge, MA: MIT Press, pp. 237–264.

———— & Wakefield, J. (1988), From depth psychology to breadth psychology: A phenomenological approach to psychopathology. In: *Hermeneutics and Psychological Theory*, ed. S. B. Messer, L. Sass & R. L. Woolfolk. New Brunswick, NJ: Rutgers University Press, pp. 272–288.

Dunne, J. (1993), *Back to the Rough Ground*. Notre Dame, IN: University of Notre Dame Press.

Eagle, M. (1984), *Recent Developments in Psychoanalysis*. Cambridge, MA: Harvard University Press.

Fairbairn, W. R. D. (1952), *An Object Relations Theory of the Personality*. New York: Basic Books.

Flanagan, O. (1991), *Varieties of Moral Personality*. Cambridge, MA: Harvard University Press.

Flax, J. (1990), *Thinking Fragments*. Berkeley, CA: University of California Press.

Foucault, M. (1978), *The History of Sexuality, Vol. 1*. New York: Pantheon.

Fourcher, L. (1992), Interpreting the relative and absolute unconscious. *Psychoanal. Dial.*, 2:317–329.

Freud, S. (1933), New introductory lectures on psychoanalysis. *Standard Edition*, 22:5–182. London: Hogarth Press, 1964.

Gadamer, H. G. (1976), *Philosophical Hermeneutics*. Berkeley, CA: University of California Press.

Gill, M. M. (1982), *Analysis of Transference*. New York: International Universities Press.

———— (1983), The interpersonal paradigm and the degree of the therapist's involvement. *Contemp. Psychoanal.*, 19:200–237.

———— (1984), Psychoanalysis and psychotherapy: A revision. *Internat. Rev. Psycho-Anal.*, 11:161–179.

———— (1991), Indirect suggestion: A response to Oremland's *Interpretation and Interaction*. In: *Interpretation and Interaction*, J. D. Oremland. Hillsdale, NJ: The Analytic Press, pp. 137–162.

Glover, E. (1931), The therapeutic effect of inexact interpretation. *Internat. J. Psycho-Anal.*, 12:397–411.

Greenberg, J. (1991), *Oedipus and Beyond*. Cambridge, MA: Harvard University Press.

Grunbaum, A. (1984), *The Foundations of Psychoanalysis*. Berkeley, CA: University of California Press.

Habermas, J. (1971), *Knowledge and Human Interests*. Boston, MA: Beacon Press.

———— (1979), *Communication and the Evolution of Society*. Boston, MA: Beacon Press.

———— (1986), *The Philosophical Discourse of Modernity*. Cambridge, MA: MIT Press.

———— (1990), *Moral Consciousness and Communicative Action*. Cambridge, MA: MIT Press.

Hacking, I. (1995), *Rewriting the Soul*. Princeton, NJ: Princeton University Press.

Hoffman, I. Z. (1983), The patient as interpreter of the analyst's experience. *Contemp. Psychoanal.*, 19:389–422.

———— (1991), Discussion: Toward a social-constructivist view of the psychoanalytic situation. *Psychoanal. Dial.*, 1:74–105.

———— (1992), Some practical implications of a social-constructivist view of the psychoanalytic situation. *Psychoanal. Dial.*, 2:287–304.

Kegan, R. (1982), *The Evolving Self*. Cambridge, MA: Harvard University Press.

Kelly, M. (1990), The Gadamer/Habermas debate revisited: The question of ethics. In: *Universalism vs. Communitarianism*, ed. D. Rasmussen. Cambridge, MA: MIT Press, pp. 139–159.

King, R. H. (1986), Self-realization and solidarity: Rorty and the judging self. In: *Pragmatism's Freud*, ed. J. H. Smith & W. Kerrigan. Baltimore, MD: Johns Hopkins University Press, pp. 28–51.

Kohlberg, L. (1981), *Essays on Moral Development*. New York: Harper & Row.

Kohut, H. (1977), *The Restoration of the Self*. New York: International Universities Press.

Kovel, J. (1988), Freud's ontology, agency and desire: Commentary on Hubert L. Dreyfus and Jerome Wakefield. In: *Hermeneutics and Psychological Theory*, ed. S. B. Messer, L. Sass & R. L. Woolfolk. New Brunswick, NJ: Rutgers University Press, pp. 289–294.

Layton, L. (1990), A deconstruction of Kohut's concept of the self. *Contemp. Psychoanal.*, 26:420–429.

Lear, J. (1991), *Love and Its Place in Nature*. New York: Farrar, Straus & Giroux.

MacIntyre, A. (1981), *After Virtue: A Study in Moral Theory*. Notre Dame, IN: University of Notre Dame Press.

Mahler, M. S., Pine, F. & Bergman, A. (1975), *The Psychological Birth of the Human Infant*. New York: Basic Books.

Marcuse, H. (1955), *Eros and Civilization*. Boston, MA: Beacon Press.

McCarthy, T. (1982), *The Critical Theory of Jurgen Habermas*. Cambridge, MA: MIT Press.

Mitchell, S. (1992), Introduction. *Psychoanal. Dial.*, 2:279–285.

Ricoeur, P. (1970), *Freud and Philosophy*. New Haven, CT: Yale University Press.

Rorty, R. (1986), Freud and moral reflection. In: *Pragmatism's Freud*, ed. J. H. Smith & W. Kerrigan. Baltimore, MD: Johns Hopkins University Press, pp. 1–27.

Sass, L. (1992), *Madness and Modernism*. New York: Basic Books.

Smith, J. H. (1986), Primitive guilt. In: *Pragmatism's Freud*, ed. J. H. Smith & W. Kerrigan. Baltimore, MD: Johns Hopkins University Press, pp. 52–78.

Spezzano, C. (1993), *Affect in Psychoanalysis*. Hillsdale, NJ: The Analytic Press.

Stern, D. B. (1983), Unformulated experience. *Contemp. Psychoanal.*, 19:71–99.

——— (1985), Unformulated experience and transference. *Contemp. Psychoanal.*, 23:484–491.

——— (1989), The analyst's unformulated experience of the patient. *Contemp. Psychoanal.*, 25:1–33.

——— (1991), A philosophy for the embedded analyst: Gadamer's hermeneutics and the social paradigm of psychoanalysis. *Contemp. Psychoanal.*, 27:51–80.

——— (1992), Commentary on constructivism in clinical psychoanalysis. *Psychoanal. Dial.*, 2:331–363.

Stern, D. N. (1985), *The Interpersonal World of the Infant*. New York: Basic Books.

Taylor, C. (1988), The moral topography of the self. In: *Hermeneutics and Psychological Theory*, ed. S. Messer, L. Sass & R. L. Woolfolk. New Brunswick, NJ: Rutgers University Press, pp. 298–320.

——— (1989), *Sources of the Self*. Cambridge, MA: Harvard University Press.

——— (1991), *The Ethics of Authenticity*. Cambridge, MA: Harvard University Press.

——— (1995), *Philosophical Arguments*. Cambridge, MA: Harvard University Press.

Wallwork, E. (1991), *Psychoanalysis and Ethics*. New Haven, CT: Yale University Press.

Warnke, G. (1987), *Gadamer*. Oxford: Polity Press.

Weir, A. (1992), The paradox of the self: Jessica Benjamin's intersubjective theory. *Thesis Eleven*, 32:141–153.

——— (1995), Toward a model of self-identity: Habermas and Kristeva. In: *Feminists Read Habermas*, ed. J. Meehan. New York: Routledge.

Whitebook, J. (1995), *Perversion and Utopia*. Cambridge, MA: MIT Press.

Winnicott, D. W. (1965), *The Maturational Processes and the Facilitating Environment*. New York: International Universities Press.

Afterword

Singing the Songs of Creation: A Brief Postscript

CHARLES SPEZZANO

For the moment, and perhaps only for the moment, we find *ourselves* at the center of all cosmologies, not because the species is more intelligent or more powerful or more significant than any other but because we alone are capable of giving voice to the cosmos; it is our immense good fortune and grave responsibility to sing the songs of creation [Dobbs, 1995, p. 41; italics added].

In 1894 John Dewey wrote an essay entitled "Christianity and Democracy" in which he wrote:

The revelation of truth must continue as long as life has new meanings to unfold, new action to propose. An organization may loudly proclaim its loyalty to Christianity and to Christ; but if, in laying down what is this truth, it assumes a certain guardianship of Christian truth, a certain prerogative in laying down what is this truth . . . if in short the organization attempts to preach a fixity in a moving world and to claim a monopoly in a common world—all this is a sign that the real Christianity is now working outside of and beyond the organization, that the revelation is going on in wider and freer channels [p. 5].

In the same way that Dewey argued for Christianity to understand that its own spiritual health requires "the continuously unfolding, never ceasing discovery of the meaning of life" (p. 4), the chapters of this book have argued for religious, psychoanalytic, and spiritual traditions to continue to unfold by opening themselves up to each other's capacity to illuminate meaning and possibility.

Psychoanalysis, for example, usually asserts that religious and spiritual traditions have tried in vain to transcend the emphasis the mind must put, in creating meaning, on its embodiedness. Religious and spiritual critics of psychoanalysis, in turn, have asserted that psychoanalysis sells short the

231

human ability to transcend individual embodiedness in the creation of meaning. In the preceding chapters, by contrast, one can find not only the continuation of this tension but also glimpses of a willingness to hold in dialectic tension the interplay of embodied and transcendent meanings that may be emerging into human consciousness all the time.

Similarly, there was once a seemingly unbridgeable gap between psychoanalysis viewed as a valueless encounter (or an encounter that strove to transcend valuing for straight knowing) and religious/spiritual emphases on the necessity, if not the inevitability, of shared values. Here again in this volume the gap was repeatedly bridged as the authors steadily evolved a sense that the act of valuing stands beside Freud's loving and working as an essential human activity. The beliefs of the analyst and analysand are no longer beside the point, and neither are they ever entirely free from personal history and human biology. That the analyst is attempting to substitute one set of beliefs for another seems almost self-evident—even if we go no further than to recognize that the analyst constantly communicates a belief in the omnipresence of the unconscious in all human experience. When the patient has religious and spiritual beliefs, however, these, as several of our authors have made clear, cannot simply be categorized as pathological. In fact, they are, for many people, primary ways of becoming clear about the nature of one's affective experiences.

That the psychoanalytic and spiritual traditions should be coming together seems a sign of the times. Physicists, long envied by those in the "softer" sciences as holders of the heavyweight title in matters of truth and knowledge, have recently developed a cosmological tilt. Stephen Hawking's bestselling *A Brief History of Time* ends with the proclamation that when scientists explain why the universe began they are approximating knowledge about the mind of God. Going Hawking one better, Tulane University physicist Frank Tipler, in his *The Physics of Immortality*, attempts to demonstrate scientifically the existence of God.

So, the intersection of psychoanalysis and religion can be found in the same neighborhood as the corner of physics and transcendence. We keep returning to that neighborhood, to the matters addressed in this volume, because they are part of us. We find ideas about spirit emerging into consciousness alongside ideas about the cosmos and about life. We find them continuing to emerge into consciousness unabated even after centuries of immersion in logic, reason, and experiment. We also find feelings of awe and transcendence emerging with them. As Dobbs (1995) has written: "Precisely when we grasp the vastness of the universe we also glimpse an equally vast interior, the enormous geography of the soul" (p. 40). Psychoanalysis, too, we might add, when it grasps the vastness of the affect, desire, conflict, and defense, also glimpses the vast interior of the soul. "Words may fail us," as Dobbs went on to say, "forcing us to rely on hackneyed descriptions ... but what we actually sense, if only for an instant, is largeness of spirit" (p. 40).

This largeness of spirit is what every author in this volume seemed both to possess and to write with and about. As we have accepted the dialectic tension between logical empiricism and hermeneutics in psychoanalysis, we have begun, to paraphrase Dobbs, valuing the amplitude and not simply the verisimilitude of mind, measuring human thought by how widely it ranges as well as how closely it appears to us to approximate the truth. Spirituality and religion, both Eastern and Western and both the discourses and the feelings, have not simply become objects of study for psychoanalysis. They have begun, in the minds of authors such as those in this volume, to interact and to generate, through this interaction, a new discourse and a heightened and expanded sense of our shared humanity.

REFERENCES

Dewey, J. (1894), Christianity and democracy. In: *John Dewey, the Early Works, Vol. 4.* Carbondale, IL: Southern Illinois University Press, 1971, pp. 3–10.
Dobbs, E. (1995), Without earth there is no heaven. *Harper's*, February, pp. 33–41.

Index